ZAGATSURVEY®

2003

WASHINGTON, DC BALTIMORE RESTAURANTS

**Local Editors and Coordinators:
Olga Boikess and Marty Katz**

Editor: Sinting Lai

**Published and distributed by
ZAGAT SURVEY, LLC
4 Columbus Circle
New York, New York 10019
Tel: 212 977 6000
E-mail: washbalt@zagat.com
Web site: www.zagat.com**

Acknowledgments

We are grateful to Charles Adler, Chuck Alexander, Bernice August, Alicia Ault, Richard K. Bank, Gloria Berthold, Greg Bland, Mary Ann Brownlow, Tom Bryant, Karen Cathey, Lisa Cherkasky, Jean and Gary Cohen, Kerry Craven, Tony Curtis, Fred Deutsch, Lori Edwards, Elaine Eff, Lorraine and Megan Fitzsimmons, Gail Forman, Mary Frank, the Justin Franks, Eliza Gonzalez, Alexandra Greeley, Linda Gregory, Judy Harris, Kelly Hereth, Bonnie Hockstein, Colin Hood, Hoppy Hopkins, Michele E. Jacobs, Barbara Johnson, Michael Karlin, Danny Katz, Bill Kopit, Dennis Kurgansky, Judy Levenson, Sue Ellen Malone, Jim Marley, Angie Miller, Lynda Mulhauser, Jack Nargil, Jo-Ann Neuhaus, Kendi O'Neill, Nancy Pollard, Megan Ryan, Alan Schlaifer, Susan K. Shuman, Robert Singleton, Sol Snyder, Ken Tomashiro and Juliet Zucker for their support. Our special thanks go to Sawanee and Pete Nivasabutr and Pamela Horvath for their assistance.

This guide would not have been possible without the hard work of our staff, especially Reni Chin, Shelley Gallagher, Jessica Gonzalez, Diane Karlin, Natalie Lebert, Mike Liao, Dave Makulec, Rob Poole, Robert Seixas, Christy Stabin and Sharon Yates.

Contents

What's New

The restaurant industry in the Washington, DC/Baltimore area has responded, admirably, to the September 11 attacks on America. With Reagan National Airport closed for several weeks, and tourism at a halt, it instituted value-minded promotions such as DC's first-ever restaurant week last November to reconnect with its local customers.

Rising Young Stars: The meteoric rise of rookies Colvin Run Tavern and Maestro in Tysons Corner, as well as Downtown's Tosca, amply demonstrates the DC region's commitment to its dining-out scene. Also evidence of widespread confidence in this area's growth is the opening of a flock of high-end establishments, notably Downtown's Cafe 15 and jordans, Mon Ami Gabi in Bethesda, Signatures in the Penn Quarter and Georgetown's Washington Harbour Club.

Little Bites/Less Bucks: Catering to the public's desire for a relaxing experience, worthy additions are offering interesting wines and small plates to sample and share. Among them: Cleveland Park's Bardeo Wine Bar, Bar Rouge near Scott Circle and Topaz Bar off Dupont Circle, along with an opulent branch of Lebanese Taverna on thriving new Pentagon Row, near the rebuilt Pentagon.

Toque Talents in the Neighborhood: With many people now staying closer to home, ambitious young Americans such as Boulevard Woodgrill, Portabellos, Rays The Steaks, all in Arlington, as well as Franklins in Hyattsville, are allowing more and more patrons to eat and drink well in their own suburban backyards.

Hello and Farewell: As we look forward to greeting even more fresh faces in the upcoming months – especially Drew Nieporent's 15 ria bistro, the brasserie Poste and Zola at the soon-to-open International Spy Museum – we mourn the passing of chef and mentor Jean-Louis Palladin.

Homegrown Dreams Realized: Meanwhile, the scene in Baltimore has also rebounded strongly, with business especially steady at neighborhood places. Combalou Cafe's cheese-centric world goes the fashionable carts one better, serving sampler platters in a cave-themed room. Soigné proves that old Bawlmer isn't too stodgy for edgy Pacific Rim fusion cuisine. Cerando's Kitchen & Bistro illustrates that fine New American dining can appeal to strip-mall shoppers. In Columbia, the instant popularity of Cafe de Paris serves as a reminder that if they build it, we will come – even to an office building lobby – if the food is good.

Money Matters: For all the diversity and quality offered, dining in Washington, DC and Baltimore is fairly reasonable, with an average tab of $31.86 and $30.08, respectively.

Washington, DC
Baltimore, MD
July 30, 2002

Olga Boikess
Marty Katz

About This Survey

For 24 years, Zagat Survey has reported on the shared experiences of diners like you. Here are the results of our *Washington, DC/Baltimore Restaurant Survey*, covering some 775 restaurants. This marks the 17th year we have covered restaurants in the Washington, DC area.

By regularly surveying large numbers of avid local restaurant-goers about their collective dining experiences, we hope to have achieved a uniquely current and reliable guide. For this book, more than 4,300 people participated. Since the participants dined out an average of 2.6 times per week, this *Survey* is based on roughly 586,000 meals annually.

Of our surveyors, 53% are women, 47% men; the breakdown by age is 15% in their 20s, 23% in their 30s, 19% in their 40s, 25% in their 50s and 18% in their 60s or above. In producing the reviews contained in this guide, our editors have synopsized our surveyors' opinions, with their exact comments shown in quotation marks.

Of course, we are especially grateful to our editors, Olga Boikess, a Washington lawyer and avid restaurant-goer who has edited this *Survey* since it was first published in 1987, and Marty Katz, a Baltimore writer and photographer.

To help guide our readers to Washington, DC/Baltimore's best meals and best buys, we have prepared a number of lists. See Washington, DC's Most Popular (page 9), Top Ratings (pages 10–15) and Best Buys (page 16), and Baltimore's Most Popular (page 155), Top Ratings (pages 156–160) and Best Buys (page 161). To assist the user in finding just the right restaurant for any occasion, without wasting time, we have also provided many handy indexes.

As companions to this guide, we also publish *America's Top Restaurants* and *Top U.S. Hotels, Resorts & Spas,* as well as *Zagat Surveys* and Maps to more than 70 other markets around the world. Most of these guides are also available on mobile devices and at **www.zagat.com,** where you can also vote and shop.

To join our next *Washington, DC/Baltimore Survey* or any of our other upcoming *Surveys,* all you need to do is register at zagat.com and select the *Survey* in which you'd like to participate. Each participant will receive a free copy of the resulting guide when it is published.

Your comments, suggestions and even criticisms of this guide are also solicited. There is always room for improvement with your help. You can contact us at washbalt@zagat.com or by mail at Zagat Survey, 4 Columbus Circle, New York, NY 10019. We look forward to hearing from you.

New York, NY
July 30, 2002

Nina and Tim Zagat

Key to Ratings/Symbols

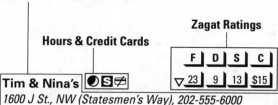

Name, Address & Phone Number

Hours & Credit Cards

Zagat Ratings

	F	D	S	C
Tim & Nina's 🌙 [S] ⊘	▽23	9	13	$15

1600 J St., NW (Statesmen's Way), 202-555-6000

◪ All "mahogany and marble", this "meat-and-greet mecca" (dubbed Prime Stakes) Downtown boasts the ultimate "see-or-be-seen dining" experience, featuring reversible one-way glass booths ("look out or let others look in") and "direct hot lines to the White House"; "pick your own salad" from the hydroponic planters and follow with "big beef", while cameo appearances from investors – including all living past presidents and the *West Wing* cast – give new meaning to "stargazing potential."

Review, with surveyors' comments in quotes

Restaurants with the highest overall ratings and greatest popularity and importance are printed in CAPITAL LETTERS.

Before each review a symbol indicates whether responses were uniform ■ or mixed ◪.

Hours: 🌙 serves after 11 PM
[S] open on Sunday

Credit Cards: ⊘ no credit cards accepted

Ratings: Food, Decor and Service are rated on a scale of **0** to **30.** The Cost (C) column reflects our surveyors' estimate of the price of dinner including one drink and tip.

F Food	**D** Decor	**S** Service	**C** Cost
23	9	13	$15

0–9 poor to fair
10–15 fair to good
16–19 good to very good
20–25 very good to excellent
26–30 extraordinary to perfection
▽ low response/less reliable

For places listed without ratings or a cost estimate, such as an important **newcomer** or a popular **write-in,** the cost is indicated by the following symbols.

I $15 and below
M $16 to $30
E $31 to $50
VE $51 or more

Washington, DC's Most Popular

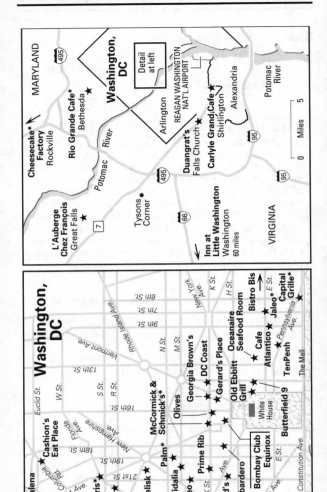

MARYLAND

495

Washington, DC

Detail at left

REAGAN WASHINGTON NAT'L AIRPORT

Arlington

Alexandria

Shirlington

Carlyle Grand Cafe

Duangrat's Falls Church

Potomac River

495

95

95

Tysons Corner

66

7

L'Auberge Chez François Great Falls

VIRGINIA

Inn at Little Washington Washington 60 miles

Cheesecake Factory Rockville

Rio Grande Cafe Bethesda

Potomac River

Miles 0 5

Washington, DC

New York Ave.

6th St. 7th St. 9th St.

K St. H St.

Bistro Bis

Capital Grille*

Jaleo* Pennsylvania Ave.

Oceanaire Seafood Room

Cafe Atlantico

TenPenh The Mall

N St. M St.

Rhode Island Ave.

Vermont Ave.

Georgia Brown's

DC Coast

Gerard's Place

Old Ebbitt Grill

Euclid St. W St. 13th St.

S St. R St.

McCormick & Schmick's*

Olives

16th St.

Florida Ave.

New Hampshire Ave.

Cashion's Eat Place

Palm*

Prime Rib

White House

Butterfield 9

Bombay Club

Equinox E St.

Constitution Ave.

Palena

18th St. 19th St. 21st St.

Obelisk

Vidalia

Galileo

Kinkead's

K St.

Virginia Ave.

Taberna del Alabardero

Columbia Rd.

Lebanese Taverna*

Calvert St.

Connecticut Ave.

Ruth's Chris*

Nora

Massachusetts Ave.

Citronelle

Marcel's

Pennsylvania Ave.

Theodore Roosevelt Island

Q St.

Morton's of Chicago*

Bistrot Lepic

N St. M St.

Georgetown

Prospect St.

Clyde's*

Makoto

1789

Wisconsin Ave. R St. 35th St.

Potomac River

66

Mile 0 1/2

* Check for other locations

---

8   www.zagat.com

Washington, DC's Most Popular

Each of our reviewers has been asked to name his or her five favorite Washington, DC area restaurants. The places most frequently named, in order of their popularity, are:

1. Kinkead's
2. L'Auberge Chez François
3. Inn at Little Washington
4. Citronelle
5. Galileo
6. Jaleo
7. DC Coast
8. Carlyle Grand Cafe
9. TenPenh
10. Vidalia
11. Obelisk
12. 1789
13. Nora
14. Cashion's Eat Place
15. Ruth's Chris
16. Gerard's Place
17. Prime Rib
18. Cheesecake Factory
19. Clyde's
20. Equinox
21. Marcel's
22. McCormick & Schmick's
23. Cafe Atlantico
24. Lebanese Taverna
25. Palm*
26. Bistrot Lepic
27. Oceanaire Seafood Room
28. Morton's of Chicago
29. Capital Grille
30. Butterfield 9
31. Old Ebbitt Grill
32. Georgia Brown's
33. Bistro Bis
34. Makoto
35. Taberna del Alabardero
36. Palena
37. Bombay Club
38. Duangrat's
39. Olives*
40. Rio Grande Cafe*

It's obvious that many of the restaurants on the above list are among the Washington, DC area's most expensive, but if popularity were calibrated to price, we suspect that a number of other restaurants would join the above ranks. Given the fact that both our surveyors and readers love to discover dining bargains, we have added a list of 80 Best Buys on page 16. These are restaurants that give real quality at extremely reasonable prices.

---

* Tied with restaurant directly above it

Top Ratings

Top lists exclude restaurants with low voting.

Top 40 Food Rankings

29 Inn at Little Washington	Seasons
28 L'Auberge Chez François	Duangrat's
27 Makoto	Colvin Run Tavern
Kinkead's	La Bergerie
Maestro	Palena
Gerard's Place	Persimmon
Citronelle	DC Coast
Prime Rib	TenPenh
Obelisk	Ashby Inn
26 Marcel's	Equinox
Galileo	i Ricchi
Melrose	Hollywood East Cafe
Vidalia	Cashion's Eat Place
Four & Twenty Blackbirds	Jerry's Seafood
1789	Le Relais
Tosca	Pizzeria Paradiso
25 Taberna del Alabardero	Peking Gourmet Inn
Nora	Tachibana
L'Auberge Provençale	Heritage India
Bistrot Lepic	Rabieng

Top Food by Cuisine

American (New)
27 Kinkead's
26 Melrose
    Vidalia
25 Nora
    Seasons

Chinese
25 Hollywood East Cafe
    Peking Gourmet Inn
23 Mr. K's
    Full Kee
22 New Fortune

French
28 L'Auberge Chez François
25 La Bergerie
24 La Chaumiere
23 La Miche
    Le Gaulois

French (Bistro)
25 Bistrot Lepic
24 Bistro Bis
23 Montmartre
21 Lavandou
    Petits Plats

French (New)
27 Gerard's Place
    Citronelle
26 Marcel's
25 Le Relais
24 Willard Room

Hamburgers
24 Five Guys
    Carlyle Grand Cafe
23 Addie's
22 Occidental
18 Clyde's

Indian
25 Heritage India
    Bombay Club
24 Connaught Place
    Haandi
23 Bombay Bistro

Italian
27 Maestro
    Obelisk
26 Galileo
    Tosca
25 i Ricchi

Japanese

27 Makoto
25 Tachibana
   Sushi-Ko
24 Sushi Taro
   Kaz Sushi Bistro

Latin/South American

23 Cafe Atlantico
21 Lauriol Plaza
20 Grill from Ipanema
19 Green Field
   Andale

Louisiana

23 RT's
22 Black's Bar
20 Louisiana Express
19 219
   Warehouse B&G

Mediterranean

23 Mediterranee
   Olives
   Le Tarbouche
22 Kazan
   Neyla

Mexican/Tex-Mex

21 Rio Grande Cafe
   Lauriol Plaza
19 Guajillo
   Mi Rancho
   Cactus Cantina

Middle Eastern

23 Lebanese Taverna
   Le Tarbouche
22 Bacchus
21 Faryab
20 Skewers/Cafe Luna

Pan-Asian

25 TenPenh
24 Yanÿu
   Asia Nora
21 Cafe Asia
20 Spices

Pizza

25 Pizzeria Paradiso
24 Pasta Plus
23 Dolce Vita
22 2 Amys
20 Faccia Luna

Seafood

27 Kinkead's
25 DC Coast
   Jerry's Seafood
24 Pesce
23 Blue Point Grill

Southern

26 Vidalia
23 Majestic Cafe
22 Georgia Brown's
20 Florida Ave. Grill
   B. Smith's

Spanish

25 Taberna del Alabardero
23 Jaleo
21 Mar de Plata
   Lauriol Plaza
20 Andalucia

Steakhouses

27 Prime Rib
24 Ruth's Chris
   Sam & Harry's
   Morton's of Chicago
   Palm

Thai

25 Duangrat's
   Rabieng
23 T.H.A.I.
   Sweet Basil
22 Neisha Thai

Vietnamese

24 Huong Que
   Taste of Saigon
22 Pho 75
   Nam Viet
   Saigonnais

Top Food by Special Feature

Breakfast*

23 Bread Line
22 La Colline
20 Old Ebbitt Grill
   Louisiana Express
   Ben's Chili Bowl

Brunch

27 Maestro
26 Melrose
   Four & Twenty Blackbirds
25 Seasons
   Cashion's Eat Place

Chef's Table

27 Citronelle
26 Marcel's
   Galileo
   Tosca
20 Matisse

Dining Alone

27 Kinkead's
26 Marcel's
25 DC Coast
24 Kaz Sushi Bistro
23 Johnny's Half Shell

Family Dining

23 Lebanese Taverna
22 Matuba
   2 Amys
21 Tara Thai
   Rio Grande Cafe

Hotel Dining

27 Maestro
   Ritz-Carlton Tysons Corner
   Citronelle
   Latham Hotel
26 Melrose
   Park Hyatt Washington
25 Seasons
   Four Seasons Hotel
24 Bistro Bis
   Hotel George

Newcomers/Rated

25 Colvin Run Tavern
23 Montmartre
22 Spezie
   2 Amys
   Bardeo Wine Bar & Cafe

Newcomers/Unrated

Cafe 15
Grille 88
jordans
Mon Ami Gabi
Restaurant 7

Worth a Trip

29 Inn at Little Washington
   Washington, VA
26 Four & Twenty Blackbirds
   Flint Hill, VA
25 L'Auberge Provençale
   Boyce, VA
   Ashby Inn
   Paris, VA
21 Rail Stop
   The Plains, VA

---

* Other than hotels

Top Food by Location

**Adams Morgan/
Dupont Circle East**

25 Cashion's Eat Place
24 Sushi Taro
   Pasta Mia
22 Saigonnais
21 Lauriol Plaza

Capitol Hill

24 Bistro Bis
23 Montmartre
22 La Colline
21 Barolo
   La Brasserie

Dupont Circle

27 Obelisk
25 Nora
   Pizzeria Paradiso
24 Pesce
23 Johnny's Half Shell

Georgetown/Glover Park

27 Citronelle
26 1789
25 Bistrot Lepic
   Seasons
   Heritage India

Golden Triangle/Downtown

25 Equinox
   Bombay Club
23 Olives
   Bread Line
22 Oval Room

**Penn Quarter/MCI Center/
Chinatown**

23 Capitol Grille
   Cafe Atlantico
   701
   Jaleo
   Full Kee

**Woodley Park/
Cleveland Park**

25 Palena
24 New Heights
   Yanÿu
23 Lebanese Taverna
22 Nam Viet

Bethesda

25 Persimmon
24 Ruth's Chris
   Haandi
23 Jaleo
   Cafe Bethesda

Old Town, Alexandria

25 La Bergerie
24 Five Guys
23 Blue Point Grill
   Le Gaulois
   Majestic Cafe

Tysons Corner

27 Maestro
25 Colvin Run Tavern
24 Sam & Harry's
   Morton's of Chicago
   Palm

West End

26 Marcel's
   Melrose
24 Asia Nora
20 Ritz, Grill (Wash. DC)
17 Blackie's

Top 40 Decor Rankings

28 Inn at Little Washington
Maestro
27 L'Auberge Chez François
Willard Room
26 Seasons
Lightfoot
Taberna del Alabardero
Citronelle
Bombay Club
Prime Rib
L'Auberge Provençale
25 1789
Colvin Run Tavern
Teatro Goldoni
TenPenh
Marcel's
Ashby Inn
Ritz, Grill (Pent. City)
Ritz, Grill (Wash. DC)
24 Le Tarbouche

Melrose
Bistro Bis
Morrison-Clark Inn
Old Angler's Inn
La Ferme
Sequoia
DC Coast
Butterfield 9
Neyla
Caucus Room
Kinkead's
Tosca
Yanÿu
Makoto
23 Two Quail
Palena
Tabard Inn
Nora
Oceanaire Seafood Room
Asia Nora

Outdoors

Cafe Milano
Gerard's Place
L'Auberge Chez François
Lauriol Plaza
Old Angler's Inn

Perry's
Sea Catch
Sequoia
701
Tahoga

Romance

Asia Nora
La Bergerie
Le Tarbouche
Nora

Palena
Tabard Inn
Two Quail
Yanÿu

Rooms

Citronelle
DC Coast
Galileo
Lafayette
Maestro
Melrose

Red Sage
Restaurant 7
Taberna del Alabardero
TenPenh
Topaz Bar
Willard Room

Views

Le Rivage
New Heights
Perry's
Rico y Rico

Roof Terrace/Kennedy Ctr.
Ruth's Chris
Sequoia
701

Top 40 Service Rankings

29 Inn at Little Washington
28 Maestro
   L'Auberge Chez François
26 Obelisk
   Prime Rib
   Seasons
25 Citronelle
   Makoto
   Kinkead's
   L'Auberge Provençale
   Melrose
   Bombay Club
   Taberna del Alabardero
   Willard Room
   1789
   Marcel's
24 Gerard's Place
   Colvin Run Tavern
   Ashby Inn
   Ritz, Grill (Pent. City)

   La Bergerie
   Vidalia
   Sam & Harry's
   Galileo
   Mr. K's
   Nora
23 Ruth's Chris
   Connaught Place
   Four & Twenty Blackbirds*
   Morrison-Clark Inn
   Palm
   i Ricchi
   701
   Morton's of Chicago
   La Chaumiere
   Caucus Room
   Capital Grille
   Oval Room
   TenPenh
   Tosca

---

* Tied with restaurant directly above it

Best Buys

Top 40 Bangs for the Buck

List derived by dividing the cost of a meal into its ratings.

1. Five Guys
2. Ben's Chili Bowl
3. California Tortilla
4. Firehook Bakery
5. Burro
6. El Pollo Rico
7. Bob & Edith's Diner
8. Burrito Brothers
9. Bread Line
10. Cafe Midi
11. Florida Ave. Grill
12. A&J
13. Pho 75
14. Crisp & Juicy
15. C.F. Folks
16. Tryst
17. Hard Times Cafe
18. Moby Dick
19. Teaism
20. Diner
21. Visions
22. Hope Key
23. Rocklands
24. Udupi Palace
25. Generous George's
26. Vegetable Garden
27. Delhi Dhaba
28. Parkway Deli
29. Haad Thai
30. Dean & DeLuca
31. Faccia Luna
32. Chi-Cha Lounge
33. Hollywood East Cafe
34. Havana Breeze
35. Pizzeria Paradiso
36. La Madeleine
37. T.H.A.I.
38. Oodles Noodles
39. Benjarong
40. Joe's Noodle House

Other Good Values

Afghan
Amma Vegetarian
Ben's Whole Hog
Bombay Club
Cactus Cantina
Cafe Asia
Cafe Divan
Café Olé
Caribbean Feast
Carlyle Grand Cafe
Ching Ching Cha
Colorado Kitchen
Connaught Place
Cubano's
Duken
Eat First
Franklins
Full Key
Huong Que
Islander Caribbean
Johnny's Half Shell
Kuna
Lauriol Plaza
Lebanese Taverna
Little Saigon
Mark's Kitchen
Meze
Myanmar
Nam's of Bethesda
Negril
Pasta Mia
Ray's The Steaks
Samadi Sweets
Skewers/Cafe Luna
Taqueria Poblano
Taste of Morroco
Temel
Thanh Thanh
Washington Cafe
Wok & Roll

Washington, DC
Restaurant Directory

Washington, DC

F	D	S	C

A&J [S] ≠ 21 | 8 | 16 | $13

Woodmont Ctr., 1319C Rockville Pike (bet. Talbott St. & Templeton Pl.), Rockville, MD, 301-251-7878
Little River Ctr., 4316B Markham St. (Little River Tpke.), Annandale, VA, 703-813-8181
◪ Discover Beijing in your own "backyard" at these "bare-bones" suburban quick stops in Rockville and Annandale, where the "buzz of Chinese speakers vouches for their dim sum", noodle soups and "street-food" dishes; adventurous types who "line up for the food, not the ambiance" or the service ("courteous", if often uninformative), are always eager to "try new things" at "unbeatable" prices; N.B. no reservations, no booze, no plastic.

Acropolis ◐ – | – | – | M

1337 Connecticut Ave., NW (bet. Dupont Circle & N St.), 202-496-5480
Trendy to the nth degree, this festive new late-night scene just below Dupont Circle features flashy decor (envision classic Greek motifs, deep blue velvet, a faux fountain) and an endless bar (measuring 65 feet, it's reputed to be the longest in DC); the menu spotlights Greek specialties, along with sushi, plus there's live jazz on Tuesdays and dancing on weekends.

Addie's [S] 23 | 15 | 20 | $35

11120 Rockville Pike (Edson Ln.), Rockville, MD, 301-881-0081
◪ Legions laud the "creative comfort food" and "civility" that mark this "vibrant" New American set on strip mall–lined Rockville Pike; while its cheery "dollhouse funk" decor suits its unique bungalow setting, some complain of "tight quarters" and wish its "homey" looks were as "sophisticated" as its cooking, though in nice weather the patio is a "particular delight."

Afghan [S] – | – | – | M

2700 Jefferson Davis Hwy. (Raymond Ave.), Alexandria, VA, 703-548-0022
"It's not that the menu is extraordinary", it's how carefully the kitchen prepares its "authentic" "Afghan comfort foods" that sets apart this "friendly", "family-owned" standby in Alexandria; it draws customers from around the Beltway with its "amazing appetizers (the best part of the dining experience)", "really tasty" kebabs and weekday lunch buffet (an especially "good value"); the consensus: it's a "solid" bet.

Al Tiramisu [S]   22 | 18 | 21 | $39

2014 P St., NW (bet. 20th & 21st Sts.), 202-467-4466

◪ "Charming and intimate", this Dupont Circle trattoria "takes you to Italy" with its "glorious, fresh" fare, "superior" regional wines, "hideaway" feel and "warm" service; the "ebullient" chef-owner describes his nightly specials in an irresistible way, but cynics warn "watch out for the [off-menu] prices" because his "magic with truffle oil and pasta" comes with an "ouch factor."

Amma Vegetarian Kitchen [S]   ▽ 20 | 10 | 17 | $13

3291 M St., NW (bet. Potomac & 33rd Sts.), 202-625-6625
344A Maple Ave. E. (bet. Beulah Rd. & Park St.), Vienna, VA, 703-938-5328

◪ Herbivores "have to have the dosas and the coconut chutney" at this "dependable" Southern Indian kitchen in Georgetown (where the upstairs table dining is spare but "sunny") and its "simply" appointed, self-serve Vienna sibling; despite a few gripes about the "boring" menu (basically, "variations on a few basic dishes"), they provide a "fast, cheap" veggie option."

Andale   19 | 20 | 19 | $33

401 Seventh St., NW (D St.), 202-783-3133

◪ "Alison Swope's love affair with contemporary Mexico" is clearly evident at her "lively" new Penn Quarter bistro that's staffed by "attentive" people who "get you out in time" for an event at the nearby Shakespeare Theatre or MCI Center; a few "kinks" notwithstanding, the "upscale" menu is "promising", featuring "imaginative" "nuevo" "twists" on the classics, all "artfully presented"; P.S. "don't miss the churros" with hot chocolate for dessert.

Andalucia [S]   20 | 16 | 20 | $34

4931 Elm St. (bet. Arlington Rd. & Woodmont Ave.), Bethesda, MD, 301-907-0052
12300 Wilkins Ave. (Parklawn Dr.), Rockville, MD, 301-770-1880

■ Separately owned, these "old-world" Iberians are known for their "way with fish" (many imported from Europe), "great" paella and other "tasty", "authentic" Andalusian dishes; the Bethesda branch boasts "nicer", more modern Mediterranean decor and a "delightful" owner-host, while the Rockville venue features a "family"-friendly atmosphere and flamenco entertainment (on weekends), but both "always welcome" with "friendly yet professional" service and they're "not impossible" to get into.

Andaman [S]   17 | 17 | 19 | $24

4828 Cordell Ave. (Woodmont Ave.), Bethesda, MD, 301-654-4676

◪ "Thai meets nouveau cuisine" in an "open", "fashionably" modern (read: "bare") setting at the edge of Bethesda's restaurant zone; the seafood-centered menu highlights lots of little plates, which admirers tout as a "great concept" that fosters "social dining", but doubters say these "pricey" tapas amount to the "wrong tastes at the right time."

Angelo & Maxie's Steakhouse S 18 | 19 | 18 | $42
901 F St., NW (9th St.), 202-639-9330
Reston Town Ctr., 11901 Democracy Dr. (bet. Library St. & Reston Pkwy.), Reston, VA, 703-787-7766
◪ "Trying hard to skew young", this pair of "red-meat havens" near the MCI Center and in Reston features white-chocolate martinis ("a must"), bargain happy-hour deals, "blaring" pop sounds, even a cigar store on-site; it earns points for its "dark", retro ambiance and "delicious" steaks, but connoisseurs sniff that it exhibits "no real sophistication" and beef too about "slow", "uneven" service.

Arbor S ▽ 16 | 17 | 16 | $28
2400 18th St., NW (Belmont Rd.), 202-667-1200
■ "Hip but accessible", this "casual, good-looking" New American's "cheerful" demeanor, updated comfort food (generally "well done") and interesting wines appeal when you're looking "for something between a diner and finer dining" in Adams Morgan; even its critics concede that it boasts one of the city's "best" people-watching patios, making it a "lovely" spot for weekend brunch.

Ardeo S 21 | 21 | 20 | $40
3311 Connecticut Ave., NW (Macomb St.), 202-244-6750
◪ "Classy" and "customer-conscious", this Cleveland Park spot cossets clients in "posh yet comfortable" postmodern surroundings that showcase "tasteful" New American dishes that are "art nouveau on a plate"; celebrity-spotting ("pundits and Bushies" alike) gives it an edge, even if a few doubters drub it "overpriced and overhyped."

Argia's S 18 | 17 | 17 | $29
124 N. Washington St. (bet. Broad St. & Park Ave.), Falls Church, VA, 703-534-1033
◪ Loyalists who maintain "high hopes" for this modern Italian bistro in Falls Church "arrive early" for "homemade" pastas and "hearty" entrees (available in both individual and sharing portions) delivered in an "attractive", mural-dominated space; detractors, however, complain about food that "doesn't always measure up" ("bland" flavors), "excessive noise" and "slow" service.

Artie's S 21 | 18 | 21 | $27
3260 Old Lee Hwy. (south of Fairfax Circle), Fairfax, VA, 703-273-7600
■ "Deservedly popular", this Fairfax "standby" earns praise for "consistently good American food at reasonable prices", served by a "well-trained" staff in a room "redesigned" with a New England boathouse motif; note that it doesn't accept reservations (though you can call ahead to put your

name on a list), so it can be "tough to get in on weekends", when the crowds descend for its "outstanding" "blackened prime rib special" (available Fridays and Saturdays only), but regulars agree it's "worth the wait."

Arucola S   17 | 14 | 17 | $29
5534 Connecticut Ave., NW (Morrison St.), 202-244-1555
◪ Surveyors are decidedly divided about this Upper NW Italian osteria – proponents tout it as a "delightful meeting place" that offers rustic dishes like "scrumptious" roast chicken and homemade pastas (plus, the kids are sure to be "happy with the pizzas" from the wood-burning oven), but opponents nix "hit-or-miss" cooking served in "cramped" quarters by "arrogant" "Fabio look-alikes"; the "great summer deck dining", however, gets everyone's blessing.

Ashby Inn S   25 | 25 | 24 | $50
692 Federal St. (Rte. 17), Paris, VA, 540-592-3900
■ "Love is in the air" at this "delightfully" "romantic" 1829 inn set in the tiny village of Paris in Virginia's hunt country, and it's only enhanced by the "marvelous" vista of the Blue Ridge Mountains ("look for stars"); the smitten swoon over the "first-rate" daily New American menu and weekly changing global wine list and recommend that you pair a leisurely meal with "a tour of the local wineries"; N.B. dinner Wednesday–Saturday and Sunday brunch only.

Asia Nora   24 | 23 | 23 | $45
2213 M St., NW (bet. 22nd & 23rd Sts.), 202-797-4860
◪ "Elegant", "imaginative" Pan-Asian fusion cuisine "beautifully" presented by a "quietly attentive" staff in "relaxing Zen"-like environs draws an "interesting" clientele to this West End boîte for a "romantic night out" or an "urbane" business dinner; enamored epicures celebrate an "exquisite" organic menu filled with "bites of joy", but big appetites balk at the inverse relationship between portions ("small") and tabs ("pricey").

Austin Grill S   16 | 15 | 16 | $21
750 E St., NW (bet. 7th & 8th Sts.), 202-393-3776
2404 Wisconsin Ave., NW (bet. Calvert St. & Observatory Ln.), 202-337-8080
7278 Woodmont Ave. (Elm St.), Bethesda, MD, 301-656-1366
8430A Old Keene Mill Rd. (Rolling Rd.), Springfield, VA, 703-644-3111
South Austin Grill S
801 King St. (Columbus St.), Alexandria, VA, 703-684-8969
◪ Brace yourself for a cattle call at this "affordable" chain of Tex-Mex cantinas, which ropes in plenty of revelers with its "bustling" under-30 bar scene that's fueled by "high-octane" swirlies; heavy traffic notwithstanding, purists gripe about "greasy" "gringo" grub, dismissing it as an "insult to Dubya's Administration."

Bacchus   22 | 17 | 20 | $29

1827 Jefferson Pl., NW (bet. 18th & 19th Sts.), 202-785-0734
7945 Norfolk Ave. (Del Rey Ave.), Bethesda, MD,
301-657-1722 S

◪ "A grazer's delight", this "long-running" pair of Middle
Eastern meccas below Dupont Circle and in Bethesda
pleases palates with a wide "variety" of "authentic" meze
that taste "like grandma's (if you happen to be Lebanese)";
the waiters "love to give advice" about the "alluring" menu,
so come prepared "to share" and "make a meal of the
appetizers"; despite somewhat "dated" decor, it's "always
a good bet" for an "enjoyable" meal; P.S. the Maryland
branch features "scenic courtyard" dining.

Bailiwick Inn S   ▽ 22 | 23 | 23 | $52

4023 Chain Bridge Rd. (Main St.), Fairfax, VA, 703-691-2266

◪ "For a special occasion with special people", consider
this "refined" Fairfax retreat set in an 1800s Federal-style
inn (on the National List of Historic Places), whose "erudite
hosts" and "attentive" servers present five-course dinners
that start with "drinks and hors d'oeuvres in the parlor"
before moving on to the "civilized, cozy dining room"; the
Continental-American fare is "well prepared", if "not
terribly innovative", leading a few wallet-watchers to carp
"for the price, there are more exciting options."

Banana Café ◑ S   – | – | – | M

500 Eighth St., NE (E St.), 202-543-5906

"Arty" and "funky" yet "unpretentious", this "popular"
"tropical" "jewel" on Capitol Hill is a "great" place to "try
new and wonderful things"; the Latin menu features Cuban
and Puerto Rican specialties that are "nothing fancy but
just plain good" (especially anything with pork) and it's
"reasonably priced", while the "atmospheric" "piano bar
upstairs" is a "hoot", but "plan to spend a lot of time" here,
as the staff is on "slow" island time.

Bangkok Blues S   – | – | – | M

926 W. Broad St. (West St.), Falls Church, VA, 703-534-0095

Cool jazz and hot Thai food are both cooking at this Falls
Church storefront where music memorabilia and videos
set the scene for a broad menu that plays Siamese riffs
on American favorites (like water buffalo wings with a
vermouth-chile glaze and Bangkok broil with a brandy
sauce), as well as offering traditional curries and such,
leading fans to applaud that it's hitting all the right notes.

Bardeo Wine Bar & Cafe S   22 | 21 | 20 | $29

3309 Connecticut Ave., NW (bet. Macomb & Porter Sts.),
202-244-6550

■ "Hats off" to this "chic" new "hot spot" that's "turning
Cleveland Park into NYC's SoHo"; "a hip singles' scene
and a good date place", it's where oenophiles gather for a

"night's worth" of sipping "excellent wines" and nibbling "imaginative" New American tapas; it has "everything you love about Ardeo" (its next-door sibling), "only it's smaller and cheaper" (and "younger and noisier").

Barolo   21 20 19 $40
223 Pennsylvania Ave., SE (bet. 2nd & 3rd Sts.), 202-547-5011
☑ "Talented" chef-owner Enzo Fargione's "interesting" Piedmontese dishes (always "good, sometimes great") and all-Italian wine list draw a diverse clientele of "politicians", dating duos and food-and-wine mavens to this "quaint" Capitol Hill townhouse "near the Folger Theatre"; though a few detractors detect "aloof" service, most regard it as a "charming" "treasure – if you can stand all the lobbyists."

Bar Rouge S   – – – M
Hotel Rouge, 1315 16th St., NW (bet. Massachusetts Ave. & O St.), 202-232-8000
"Would it were a restaurant, not really just a bar" sigh trend-conscious gourmands of this svelte new Scott Circle lounge concept whose low-key milieu sets the stage for sophisticated sipping and small-plate sharing; while subtle tones define the decor, the International menu is tinted crimson (as in tuna wrapped in smoked salmon with a carrot-tequila emulsion), as is the naughty house drink, "Sin on the Rocks."

BeDuCi S   19 18 19 $36
2100 P St., NW (21st St.), 202-223-3824
☑ Partisans of this Dupont Circle Mediterranean plug its "diverse menu" (including what some consider the "best couscous in town"), "admirable wine list" ("masterfully" described by an "incredibly friendly" proprietor) and "enticing" all-weather sidewalk veranda; a vocal minority, however, dismisses "overpriced" food that "fails to inspire", "hit-or-miss" service and the "touristy" vibe.

Benjarong S   22 20 20 $23
Wintergreen Plaza, 885 Rockville Pike (Edmonston Dr.), Rockville, MD, 301-424-5533
■ The ambiance is "calm" and "relaxing", but the "delicious traditional" Thai food (its "outstanding" fried mussels are "a must") at this Rockville "favorite" is a real "eye-opener", packing "lots of flavor, not just heat"; combined with "warm" service and a "tasteful" setting that belies its strip-mall surroundings, it adds up to a "good value", though the price of "popularity" is a "long wait" on weekends.

Ben's Chili Bowl ●S≠   20 11 16 $9
1213 U St., NW (bet. 12th & 13th Sts.), 202-667-0909
■ Though the U Street corridor may be "changing", not so this "legendary" "late-night" American diner, which since 1958 has been satisfying people from all walks of life with its

"sinful" half-smokes (a grilled dog split and smothered with chili and onions and served on a bun), "real-deal cheese fries" and "fabulous shakes"; it's an "extraordinary melting pot" with "interesting" people-watching, a "charged and chaotic" atmosphere and the "best juke in the 202", so "cholesterol, schlomesterol" be damned.

Ben's Whole Hog Barbecue S   ▽ 23 | 9 | 16 | $14

7422 Old Centreville Rd. (Yorkshire Ln.), Manassas, VA, 703-331-5980

■ Out in the countryside of Manassas, "very friendly" chef-owner Ben Morris cooks his "terrific BBQ" the time-honored way – slowly, over a hickory wood fire; this is "the real thing for 'cue lovers", who just "crave" his pork ribs, beef brisket and "tasty" sauces (when it's available, don't say no to the "out-of-this-world" pork chili); the heaping plates are served by "pleasant, helpful" folks in an ultra-casual log-cabin setting so "funky" that "you'll always be overdressed."

Big Bowl S   18 | 19 | 16 | $21

2800 Clarendon Blvd. (Fillmore St.), Arlington, VA, 703-875-8925
Reston Town Ctr., 11915 Democracy Dr. (bet. Library St. & Reston Pkwy.), Reston, VA, 703-787-8852

☑ "Finally, some pizzazz in Reston" cheers the contingent that "mobs" this "glitzy" Asian-style dining complex for its "diverse menu", "wonderful stir-fry bar" and "fun", "kid-friendly" atmosphere (and prices); the ingredients are always "fresh" and some of the dishes are "interesting", but "don't expect authentic cooking at this Americanized chain"; outright opponents who dub it "Big Noise, Big Disappointment", though, warn "all flash and no substance"; N.B. at press time, a branch was set to open in Arlington.

Bistro Bis S   24 | 24 | 22 | $45

Hotel George, 15 E St., NW (bet. Capitol St. & New Jersey Ave.), 202-661-2700

■ Just "steps from the Capitol", this "sophisticated" French bistro housed in the Hotel George cossets with a "film noir elegance" and "polished" but "not intimidating" manners; the kitchen's "clever" takes on Gallic classics and the cellar's *très* "fine" collection of regional wines make it a "great place for celebrating an event", while the "who's who" scene around the "fabulous" zinc-topped bar earns it the sobriquet "Manhattan in DC."

Bistro Bistro S   15 | 17 | 16 | $28

4021 28th St. S. (Quincy St.), Arlington, VA, 703-379-0300

☑ "Casually upscale" with a "welcoming" atmosphere, this mural-lined "neighborhood bistro" in Shirlington satisfies supporters with a "reliable" ("competent", if "nothing special") New American–Mediterranean menu, convivial bar and "nice" outdoor tables; doubters, however, who deem it entirely "average", point to "lackluster" fare and "spotty" service; still, it'll do "in a pinch."

Bistro Français ◐ [S] 20 18 19 $32
3128 M St., NW (bet. 31st St. & Wisconsin Ave.), 202-338-3830
■ "If you can't make the evening flight to Paris", this "veritable" French bistro in Georgetown will transport you there with its "honest" bourgeois fare (the early-bird deal is a "brilliant" bargain) and "charming" environs, all "warm woods" and brass; it gets even "better" in the "wee hours" (open till 3 AM weeknights, 4 AM weekends), when off-work chefs and club-goers alike pile in for a "serious" meal, or just the "best" eggs Benedict around.

Bistro 123 20 16 20 $38
246 Maple Ave. E. (bet. Glyndon & Park Sts.), Vienna, VA, 703-938-4379
◪ "Don't judge a book by its cover" urge Francophiles who hail this "cozy, personal" (despite its "strip-mall" ambiance) Vienna bistro for its "fine treatment of classic dishes", "quiet" room and "solid" service; devotees say dining is "especially enjoyable out on the patio", but the less impressed complain about food that "comes up flat" and a "stuffy" staff.

Bistrot Belgique Gourmande [S] ▽ 22 14 21 $28
302 Poplar Ln. (Union St.), Occoquan, VA, 703-494-1180
■ Visit once and you'll feel like part of the "friendly", "close-knit" family that runs this "quirky" (to put it mildly) Occoquan outpost where "hearty", "authentic" Belgian bistro classics (including "incredible" *pommes frites* and for dessert, "fabulous waffles") and a "huge selection" of "wonderful", "unusual beers" ("fun to explore") make dinner well "worth the drive"; N.B. note that the hours are "irregular" and there's only one seating per night, Thursday–Sunday.

Bistrot du Coin [S] 18 19 13 $30
1738 Connecticut Ave., NW (bet. R & S Sts.), 202-234-6969
◪ Wildly popular, this "Parisian food hall" re-creation above Dupont Circle provides a "raucous", "fun escape" to Montmartre thanks to its "smoky" zinc bar, "lively" vibe and "delicious" "tried-and-true" bistro "staples" ("great steak frites" and "remarkable mussels"); critics, though, gripe that the food, "dripping in duck fat", is delivered with Gallic "disdain", confirming their "negative stereotype" of the French as "rude and difficult" people, and warn too of "deafening noise."

BISTROT LEPIC [S] 25 20 22 $42
1736 Wisconsin Ave., NW (S St.), 202-333-0111
◪ Chef-owner Bruno Fortin's "adorable little French place" in Upper Georgetown turns out "top-notch" bistro dishes with "panache" (his signature veal cheeks are the "best"

in the city, and he does "wonders with fish"); the cooking
is such a "wonderful treat" that his many admirers readily
forgive minor flaws, namely the "tight" spacing, the "noise"
and the "Franco-efficient (read: chilly)" service.

Blackie's S   17 | 17 | 18 | $39

1217 22nd St., NW (bet. M & N Sts.), 202-333-1100

☑ Veterans of this vintage West End steakhouse are pleased
that its "expensive renovation" didn't alter its "cool old DC"
appeal; the French-style grillwork remains, as does the
"plush bar", but the surroundings have been made to feel
more "inviting", while the same "classics" emerge from
the kitchen; dissenters, however, nix the merely "decent"
menu, "'50s" feel and "inconsistent" service.

Black's Bar & Kitchen S   22 | 17 | 19 | $36

*7750 Woodmont Ave. (bet. Cheltenham Dr. &
Old Georgetown Rd.), Bethesda, MD, 301-652-6278*

☑ A "good-looking crowd "packs" this "easygoing" New
American "hangout" in Bethesda for "absolutely delicious"
seafood, notably "creative", "piquant" Gulf Coast–inspired
preparations and a "great oyster selection"; the patio and
rooftop deck are such "delights" that boosters can overlook
the "sketchy" service, but dissenters feel the "noise" from
the bar gets so loud "it makes eating here a chore."

Blue Iguana S   18 | 16 | 18 | $25

12727 Shoppes Ln. (Fair Lakes Pkwy.), Fairfax, VA, 703-502-8108

☑ "Tucked away in a tacky" Fairfax shopping strip, this
"funky little oasis" with a "Jimmy Buffett atmosphere",
a DJ-spiked bar scene and a New American menu with a
"tantalizing" twist is a "find" for local techies and shoppers
at the nearby "big-box stores"; faultfinders, however,
observe that the "innovative offerings often leave something
to be desired", as does the service.

Blue Point Grill S   23 | 19 | 21 | $37

600 Franklin St. (Washington St.), Alexandria, VA, 703-739-0404

☑ "Heavenly" seafood courtesy of the "Sutton Place
Gourmet next door" (they share owners) is the star at this
tony Alexandria "jewel" where the "beautiful" piscine
specimens are "cooked just right" (it's also "the place for
oysters"); though a few find it "snobby" and "overpriced",
well-heeled fin fanciers who think that its "intimate" interior,
"classy" bar and "relaxing" patio make it a "perfect
rendezvous" retort just "point me the way to that fresh fish."

Bob & Edith's Diner S   16 | 11 | 17 | $11

2310 Columbia Pike (Wayne St.), Arlington, VA, 703-920-6103 ◑
*4707 Columbia Pike (Four Mile Run Dr.), Arlington, VA,
703-920-4700*

■ "On weekend mornings, the line always stretches out the
door" at this 24/7 Arlington "dive" (and its newer nearby

clone), which satisfies the hankering for "artery-clogging", "dirt-cheap" all-American diner eats slung by wisecracking servers who "don't take any lip"; its "small-town feel" draws everyone from "young musicians and Congressmen" to "Harley moms and families" to "yuppies and folks with lavender hair", so even at "3 AM", you "can't beat" the "roaring" "drama" here.

Bobby Van's Steakhouse 21 | 20 | 21 | $48
809 15th St., NW (bet. H & I Sts.), 202-589-0060
☑ "Big steaks" and dry martinis are the order of the day at this masculine "power place" Downtown, a "lobbyist's" haven that prides itself on its "porterhouse for two" and "attentive" treatment (albeit "not guaranteed" for "non-star eaters"); still, critical carnivores are convinced that "you can do better elsewhere for the same price."

Bombay Bistro S 23 | 15 | 20 | $22
Bell's Corner, 98 W. Montgomery Ave. (Adams St.), Rockville, MD, 301-762-8798
3570 Chain Bridge Rd. (bet. I-66 & Lee Hwy.), Fairfax, VA, 703-359-5810
■ The "fabulous" lunch buffet "bargain" and "informative" service featured at this pair of "cheerful" Indian bistros in Rockville and Fairfax provide a "great" introduction to one of the ancient cuisines of the Subcontinent; the dishes on the "varied" dinner menu are just as "consistently well prepared", making it a "wonderful", "casual" option.

BOMBAY CLUB S 25 | 26 | 25 | $40
815 Connecticut Ave., NW (bet. H & I Sts.), 202-659-3727
■ Only steps from the White House, this "lovely" Indian "oasis" distinguished by "refined elegance" transports visitors "back to the days of the Raj" with "gracious", "unobtrusive" pampering that makes even bureaucrats "feel like viceroys"; as "first-class" as the service is the "superb" fare, "subtly spiced" yet "bursting with flavor", making this "special-occasion" destination one of the "best dining experiences in DC."

Bombay Palace S 22 | 20 | 21 | $33
2020 K St., NW (bet. 20th & 21st Sts.), 202-331-4200
■ "Generously spiced" "traditional" Northern Indian dishes marked by "complex flavors" are the focus at this K Street "standby"; with its "reliably excellent" menu, "fairly formal" surroundings and "polished" service, it's "a real deal" that's definitely "a cut above the usual."

Bombay Tandoor S ▽ 19 | 17 | 20 | $23
8603 Westwood Center Dr. (Leesburg Pike), Tysons Corner, VA, 703-734-2202
☑ Situated in a "boring" Tysons Corner business district with "sparse" dining options, this "commendable" Indian

"find" is a "success" thanks to its "solid cooking" (especially the "outstanding appetizers and great breads") and "warm" environs; even if "there's better" in the region, its "weekday lunch buffet" (frequented by lots of dot-commers) is regarded as "one of the best in Northern Virginia."

Boulevard Woodgrill **S** – – – M
2901 Wilson Blvd. (Fillmore St.), Arlington, VA, 703-875-9663
Overlooking the bustling Clarendon corridor, this casual American is centered around a wood-fired grill replete with a rotisserie that cooks anything that swims, flies or grazes; grown-ups can gather at the handsome, well-stocked bar or settle into a comfortable, roomy booth, while grape nuts will appreciate the fact that the wine-loving owner sells Cabernets and Chardonnays at a fraction of what they'd cost at a Downtown restaurant.

Brasserie at the Watergate 18 20 18 $44
(fka Dominique's)
Watergate South, 600 New Hampshire Ave., NW (Virginia Ave.), 202-337-5890
☑ Located opposite the Kennedy Center, this "attractive" French-American brasserie is "handy" for both pre-theater dining and "mixing with the cast" after the show; yet, while one faction regards it as a "fine", "accommodating" "boon" for arts patrons, another pans it as a "disappointingly pale comparison to the original" Dominique's and cautions about "slow" service, especially irksome "when you need to get to the opera on time."

Brasserie Monte Carlo **S** – – – E
7929 Norfolk Ave. (Cordell Ave.), Bethesda, MD, 301-656-9225
"One of Bethesda's nicer additions", this "petite" New French–Mediterranean brasserie evokes the "Côte d'Azur with its colorful mural" and "lively" vibe; it's a "real find" for "simple" but "delicious" "favorites" "beautifully prepared" and delivered by a "friendly, competent" crew in "pleasant" ("charming", even) surroundings at prices that aren't out of line.

Bread Line 23 11 14 $12
1751 Pennsylvania Ave., NW (bet. 17th & 18th Sts.), 202-822-8900
☑ "Elevating fast food" to high art, Mark Furstenberg's International bakery/cafe on Pennsylvania Avenue has made many an addict out of the employees at the White House and World Bank, who can't get enough of his "fantastic" artisanal breads, "clever" sandwiches or "divine" desserts; "first-timers shouldn't be thrown off by the noise", the "spartan" decor or the "confusing lines", because this place is really an "amazingly" "well-oiled machine" and it may be the "best cheap lunch ever."

Broad Street Grill **S** | 14 | 13 | 16 | $22

132 W. Broad St. (Lee Hwy.), Falls Church, VA, 703-533-1303

◪ A "nice family place in a Falls Church neighborhood desperately in need of one", this American grill "fills a void" with its "upscale bar food" and "kid-friendly" ways (every Wednesday night, Silly Lily the Clown entertains), while the "bustling bar" pulls in lots of sports fans; more serious eaters, however, complain that it "can't seem to get the dishes quite right" and warn too about "slow" service.

B. Smith's **S** | 20 | 22 | 19 | $36

Union Station, 50 Massachusetts Ave., NE (Columbus Circle), 202-289-6188

◪ Both "delicious and inexplicable", the Swamp Thing (the signature dish of mixed seafood in a mustard-based sauce over greens) exemplifies the contrast between this soulful restaurant's "down-home" Southern (and Cajun-Creole) cooking and its "spectacular" "landmark" Union Station setting; while it functions as a "classy" site for a Capitol Hill business lunch, granola types gripe that it can be "hard to eat healthy" here and add that the food is as "uneven" as the service.

Buca di Beppo **S** | 15 | 19 | 18 | $23

1825 Connecticut Ave., NW (Florida Ave.), 202-232-8466
122 Kentlands Blvd. (Great Seneca Hwy.), Gaithersburg, MD, 301-947-7346

◪ "Over the top", this ultra-"kitschy", "family-style" chain is about "as Italian as Iceland", yet few seem to care because everyone's too busy stuffing themselves from the "heaping platters" of "garlicky" red-sauce crowd-pleasers while "looking at the campy masterpieces" ("love the Pope's head lazy Susan!"); egged on by the "energetic" servers, most have a "rowdy" "good time" (it's "so tacky it's fun"), but gourmands who find the whole concept "bizarre" warn that it's "all about quantity, not quality."

Burma **S** | 21 | 9 | 16 | $18

740 Sixth St., NW (bet. G & H Sts.), 202-638-1280

◪ "Worth the hunt" (it's hidden away on the second floor), this "offbeat" Burmese "alternative" in Chinatown with "very plain" "Soviet-era" decor and a "sleepy" atmosphere tantalizes curious palates with "unusual spicing" that's "quite distinct" from other Southeast Asian cuisines; with its "excellent variety of unique dishes" ("try the green tea leaf salad"), it's "a great representation of a rarely found" style of cooking and a "real bargain" to boot.

Burrito Brothers | 15 | 9 | 13 | $9

1718 Connecticut Ave., NW (Florida Ave.), 202-332-2308 **S**
2418 18th St., NW (bet. Belmont & Columbia Rds.), 202-265-4048 **S** ⇔

(continued)

(continued)
Burrito Brothers
1825 I St., NW (bet. 18th & 19th Sts.), 202-887-8266 ⊟
1815 M St., NW (bet. 18th & 19th Sts.), 202-785-3309
205 Pennsylvania Ave., SE (2nd St.), 202-543-6835 ⊟
*Union Station, 50 Massachusetts Ave., NE (Columbus Circle),
202-289-3652* S
*7505 Leesburg Pike (Pimmit Dr.), Falls Church, VA,
703-356-8226* S

☑ "Cheap, fresh and fast", these Mexican franchises sustain Gen Y with "filling" burritos that are like a "three-course meal" wrapped in a soft tortilla (they're "so big" they're a "major cause of afternoon naps"); though the digs are "utilitarian" (to say the least), the eats provide a "healthier" alternative to typical "fast food", but critics feel they're getting "outclassed" by "better" (less "bland") versions from the "national chains."

Burro S
16 | 10 | 13 | $9
2000 Pennsylvania Ave., NW (20th St.), 202-293-9449
☑ "Extra spice" and a "healthy" orientation set apart this Golden Triangle Tex-Mex that's known for its "yummy burritos", "tasty" fish tacos and "rocking salsa"; "like its namesake, it's a steady" performer (aficionados insist its "quality and value" always "kick butt"), though opponents dismiss the "basic" eats ("decent" but "nothing special") and "fight-for-a-seat" atmosphere.

Busara S
21 | 20 | 19 | $25
2340 Wisconsin Ave., NW (Calvert St.), 202-337-2340
*8142 Watson St. (International Dr.), Tysons Corner, VA,
703-356-2288*
■ "Chic and trendy", with a crowd to match, these "upscale" Siamese twins "satisfy" with "fresh and zingy flavors" that'll "delight your palate"; "throngs of power-lunchers" take "clients" to the Tysons Corner branch for "something different" (such as the 'shrimp bikini' dressed in a spring roll wrapper and "spicy Bangkok-style bouillabaisse") turned out in "sexy" blue neon–lit surroundings, while the Glover Park site's "lovely courtyard" nearly rivals its sea bass as the "star attraction."

BUTTERFIELD 9 S
23 | 24 | 22 | $46
600 14th St., NW (bet. F & G Sts.), 202-289-8810
☑ "All the senses are pleased" at this "swank" Downtown New American "darling" ("as cool and self-assured as *The Thin Man*" that inspired it), which "beautifully presents" "innovative" dishes and "impressive wines"; as "elegant" as the "sophisticated" setting is the "smooth" service, but some detractors feel like they've dialed the "wrong number", adding that the "erratic" menu ("sometimes wonderful, sometimes simply ok") should be better at these "upper-tier" prices.

Cactus Cantina [S] 19 | 17 | 17 | $21

3300 Wisconsin Ave., NW (Macomb St.), 202-686-7222

◪ It's "a little too loud and a little too rowdy", but that's "what makes" this "festive" Cleveland Park cantina such a "crowd" "favorite", not to mention the "great margaritas"; the "endless chips, freshest salsa" and "large portions" of "yummy burritos, enchiladas and other" affordable Mexican/Tex-Mex "standards" guarantee that "you won't go home hungry" or broke, but be ready for a "too-long" wait and "inexperienced" servers.

Cafe Asia [S] 21 | 18 | 17 | $21

1134 19th St., NW (bet. L & M Sts.), 202-659-2696
1550 Wilson Blvd. (Pierce St.), Arlington, VA, 703-741-0870

◪ The "$1 apiece sushi may be the best happy-hour deal around" cheer boosters of these "happening" Pan-Asian cafes in the Golden Triangle and Arlington, where "sharply dressed go-getters" congregate; the "diverse" Far Eastern menu "covers all the bases", and it's presented by "drop-dead" gorgeous waitresses in a "stylish", "sprawling" space that quickly gets "packed", engendering a "love-the-food, hate-the-wait" mantra.

CAFE ATLANTICO [S] 23 | 22 | 21 | $37

405 Eighth St., NW (bet. D & E Sts.), 202-393-0812

■ Young chef Christy Velie is "doing great things" at this "sexy", "multilevel" Penn Quarter Nuevo Latino, which will "spice up your evening" with "innovative" dishes such as "outstanding" guacamole ("made at the table"), "not-to-be-missed" quesadilla de huitlacoche, "fantastic desserts" and "dangerous" cocktails; not only is it "chaotic fun" and a "unique" "adventure", but it offers a "fabulous" Saturday dim sum–style brunch.

Cafe Bethesda [S] 23 | 19 | 21 | $40

5027 Wilson Ln. (Cordell Ave.), Bethesda, MD, 301-657-3383

◪ "Treasured" for a "special night out" "off-the-beaten-path" in Bethesda, this "pretty" New American "find" is a "personalized" place in which to enjoy "creative" French-influenced cooking that remains "reliably good" (chef changes notwithstanding); though wallet-watchers deem it "pricey", devotees appreciate its "intimate" scale and "warm", "unpretentious" ambiance.

Cafe Deluxe [S] 18 | 17 | 18 | $26

3228 Wisconsin Ave., NW (Macomb St.), 202-686-2233
4910 Elm St. (bet. Arlington Rd. & Woodmont Ave.), Bethesda, MD, 301-656-3131
1800 International Dr. (Leesburg Pike), Tysons Corner, VA, 703-761-0600

◪ "Always worthwhile", with "lots of action" going on at the "handsome" bar, this strategically located trio of bistro-style "favorites" is a "good all-purpose restaurant" with "something for everyone" on the "snazzy", "affordable" American "comfort-food" menu, including "fantastic meatloaf (nothing like mom's)"; you get "honest eats at honest prices" and the "friendly" crew is "kind to kids", but there's a drawback: "everybody likes it", so it's "perpetually" "too crowded" ("wish they took reservations") and "noisy."

Cafe Divan S   – | – | – | M
1834 Wisconsin Ave., NW (34th St.), 202-338-1747
Cleverly designed with wraparound windows, warm cherry wood and distinctive cinnamon-and-copper-colored tiles, this eye-catching new Upper Georgetown bistro provides a stylish backdrop for chef Yucel Atalay's (ex Nizam's) Ottoman cooking – meze, brick-oven *pides* (Turkish-style pizzas), grilled shrimp, doner kebab and *pastirma* (spicy sun-dried beef); it's all visually appealing, agreeably priced and available for takeout too.

Cafe 15 S   – | – | – | VE
Sofitel Lafayette Square, 806 15th St., NW (bet. H & I Sts.), 202-737-8800
Contemporary French luxe is the lure at the White House precinct's latest lobbying lair, a petite place with a seasonal menu overseen by three-star Michelin chef Antoine Westermann that's well-suited to the dignified, deco-feeling hotel dining room; Le Bar, its jewel-toned lounge with plush armchairs and couches arranged for informal meetings, offers more casual dining options; be forewarned, though, that the lofty prices are as Parisian as the fare.

Cafe Japoné ◐ S   18 | 15 | 16 | $26
2032 P St., NW (21st St.), 202-223-1573
◪ Stark contrasts mark this "lively" Dupont Circle boîte: in the "smoky", noirish karaoke lounge upstairs, a crowd of twentysomethings meets till "late at night" for sake, "decent" sushi and "nonstop entertainment" (a "cheesy" "blast"), while downstairs in the all-white dining room, a more mature clientele settles in for Japanese "fusion" fare; purists who "give it a miss", though, say it "pales in comparison with other places" and warn "don't come looking for a quiet dining experience."

Cafe Midi S   17 | 16 | 16 | $14
1635 Connecticut Ave., NW (R St.), 202-234-3090
◪ Dupont Circle denizens help themselves to "sprightly" French-accented Mediterranean dishes at this "cafeteria-style" cafe that features a variety of "choices" from the "wholesome" salad bar along with "a few hot dishes"; get your goodies to go or, better yet, repair to the "sunny" second-floor dining room, a "perfect" spot to "linger" while you "chat, read or work on your computer"; foes, though, feel it's "a bit pricey, considering that it's a mostly self-serve" operation.

Cafe Milano S　　　　21　20　18　$45
3251 Prospect St., NW (Wisconsin Ave.), 202-333-6183

■ "VIP worlds collide" at this Georgetown Italian "scene" where "*Sopranos* sorts meet *Sex and the City*" wanna-bes; the "young and famous" are fawned over (and seated in the coveted downstairs room) by the "showy" staff, while mere mortals are shuttled to the "quiet" alcove upstairs, but wherever your table, you'll dine on "surprisingly good" food; even if detractors are "annoyed" by the "attitude", voyeurs "love the excitement and energy."

Café Mileto S　　　　21　16　20　$24
Cloppers Mill Village Ctr., 18056 Mateny Rd. (Great Seneca Hwy.), Germantown, MD, 301-515-9370

■ "Large parties" of "young families" "stampede" to this "neighborhood" Southern Italian in Germantown to dig into its "well-stocked" lunch buffet, "unusually good" pasta-night special (a "Monday tradition"), "wonderful wood-oven pizzas" and other "homey" fare; though it's stuck in a "shopping center" and the service can be "rushed", the "friendly" faces and "bargain" prices matter more to regulars, making it an "oasis in bland suburbia."

Café Olé S　　　　20　15　17　$22
4000 Wisconsin Ave., NW (Upton St.), 202-244-1330

■ Handy "before or after" a movie, this teeny Tenleytown "treasure" fills the bill with a "delicious" "variety" of meze, "small plates" bursting with "great Mediterranean flavors" ("order lots" and share, easy to do when the prices are such "a wonder"); at lunchtime (self-service only), "daily customers" line up for "terrific" soups, sandwiches and salads, then vie for a table out on the "thoroughly pleasant" patio (the "clincher").

Cafe Promenade S　　　▽　20　23　20　$38
Renaissance Mayflower Hotel, 1127 Connecticut Ave., NW (bet. L & M Sts.), 202-347-2233

■ "DC's elite" can always be spotted at this "ultimate power-breakfast" haunt set in the lobby of the Mayflower hotel; it's the place to "close a deal" over lunch too while dining on "consistently" "good" Mediterranean fare in "elegant" environs "enhanced by a skylight", and it's a "Washington tradition" for an "excellent Sunday brunch" or "dainty" afternoon tea; N.B. it features an all-you-can-eat seafood buffet on Friday nights.

Cafe Taj S　　　　20　16　17　$25
1379 Beverly Rd. (Old Dominion Dr.), McLean, VA, 703-827-0444

■ McLean's own "jewel" of India, this "cozy" fixture is "dependable" for its "especially good" lunch buffet (a true "value"), which stars "excellent butter chicken" "so creamy we could eat the sauce as soup"; service can be "perfunctory" during the day, but the dinner experience is "more refined", "attractively" presenting "well-executed" tandoori dishes and "lovely" vegetarian choices such as saag paneer in a "peaceful" atmosphere at "fair prices."

California Tortilla [S] 20 13 19 $10

4862 Cordell Ave. (bet. Norfolk & Woodmont Aves.), Bethesda, MD, 301-654-8226
Cabin John Shopping Ctr., 7727 Tuckerman Ln. (Seven Locks Rd.), Potomac, MD, 301-765-3600
Rockville Town Ctr., 199E E. Montgomery Ave. (Maryland Ave.), Rockville, MD, 301-610-6500

■ "Witty" and "spunky", this Cal-Mex burrito team turns fast food into an "easy", "wholesome" "adventure" with its "interesting" selection of "huge", "high-quality and healthy" wraps doused with your choice of "awesome" hot sauces; the counter-people "customize" each order with a "smile", making it easy to overlook the "decor shortcomings."

CAPITAL GRILLE [S] 23 23 23 $47

601 Pennsylvania Ave., NW (6th St.), 202-737-6200
1861 International Dr. (Leesburg Pike), Tysons Corner, VA, 703-448-3900

◪ "Seeking out your Congressman?" – try the bar at this "manly" "political mecca" within sight of the Capitol, or "rub elbows with Beltway bandits" at the "elegant" Tysons Corner power hub; both "delight" conservative carnivores with "dry-aged" porterhouse steaks, a "classic" "boys' club feel" and "polished", "knowledgeable" service, but "prepare to wait" if you're not "connected" to a party "bigwig" or "celebrity."

Caribbean Feast ▽ 22 10 15 $12

823 Hungerford Dr. (bet. Mannakee & Washington Sts.), Rockville, MD, 301-315-2668

◪ "Don't let the nondescript exterior fool you" because inside this Rockville storefront awaits the "best jerk chicken" in town; "add some plantains, rice and beans and cornbread, listen to the reggae in the background and for just a moment you're in Jamaica"; a "cafeteria-style" "dive" it may be, but the "healthy portions" of "good, cheap eats" "make it worth it", and it's the "closest you'll get to the Caribbean" while still in Maryland.

CARLYLE GRAND CAFE [S] 24 21 22 $31

4000 S. 28th St. (Quincy St.), Shirlington, VA, 703-931-0777

◪ One of Shirlington's "all-around favorites", this "lively" "pleaser" "gives the public what it wants" – an "eclectic", "stupendous" New American menu that "accommodates any dining need", "arty", "contemporary" surroundings, "attentive" service and a "fair quality-price ratio"; patrons would give it "extra points" if the "acoustics problem was addressed" and if they could "make reservations" "instead of calling ahead" to put their names on a "long" waiting list.

CASHION'S EAT PLACE [S] 25 | 21 | 21 | $39

1819 Columbia Rd., NW (bet. Biltmore St. & Mintwood Pl.), 202-797-1819

■ A "great meal is guaranteed" at this Adams Morgan New American "star" where Ann Cashion, a "dream of a chef", crafts "amazing" "seasonal" dishes that are "original without going too far"; inside, it's "romantic in a modern, edgy way", with "no pretensions", while the "neat" patio outside is a prime perch for "people-watching"; P.S. it's a "real treat" that's "not to be missed, so if it proves too "hard to get a table" try to snag a seat at the "inviting" bar.

Caucus Room 22 | 24 | 23 | $49

401 Ninth St., NW (D St.), 202-393-1300

◪ Just a stone's throw from Capitol Hill, this "state-of-the-art lobbyist's hangout" with an "imposing gentlemen's club" atmosphere is a "very Washingtonian" political hub; whether you opt for a "leather booth" or a "private" room, you can expect "very good" steaks ("so big it should be called the Carcass Room") and New American fare served by, "seemingly, one waiter per chair", though the powerful tabs lead pundits to quip "with these prices, [co-investors] Tom Boggs and Haley Barbour can leave their day jobs."

Centro Italian Grill [S] 18 | 19 | 17 | $37

4838 Bethesda Ave. (bet. Arlington Rd. & Woodmont Ave.), Bethesda, MD, 301-951-1988

◪ Set on a major Bethesda thoroughfare, this "sleek" and "airy" Northern Italian appeals with "flavorful" grilled fish and "modern" decor; critics (and there are more than a few), though, who cite "undistinguished" cooking, "deafening noise" and "spotty" service, dismiss it as a "triumph of style over substance", but that surely hasn't halted the traffic flow.

Cesco [S] 22 | 18 | 19 | $42

4871 Cordell Ave. (Norfolk Ave.), Bethesda, MD, 301-654-8333

◪ "Authentic" Tuscan cuisine (including the "best osso buco ever") matched by "super" regional wines brings the "pleasures" of Northern Italy to this Bethesda enclave; insiders try to go when chef-owner Francesco Ricchi is present (he splits his time with his DC venue Etrusco), because it can otherwise be "disappointing", but those who deem it "decent but way overpriced" and "overrated" "won't be back."

C.F. Folks ⊅ 23 | 10 | 18 | $15

1225 19th St., NW (bet. M & N Sts.), 202-293-0162

◪ Granted, this "hole-in-the-wall" International lunch counter below Dupont Circle is "dingy" and "cramped" and the service "can be pushy" (if not downright "surly"), but it has its "priorities" straight – "it's all about food" here, and it's "shockingly good"; those in-the-know advise "don't bother with the menu, just stick to the daily specials" and then "sit elbow-to-elbow with Washington bigwigs" while listening to "opera in the background."

CHEESECAKE FACTORY ◐S   19 17 17 $23

Chevy Chase Pavilion, 5345 Wisconsin Ave., NW (bet. Jenifer St. & Western Ave.), 202-364-0500
White Flint Mall, 11301 Rockville Pike (Nicholson Ln.), Rockville, MD, 301-770-0999

◪ "Eat dessert first" is clearly the strategy at this "horribly" "popular" chain, because given the "mammoth" size of its "solid" American dishes (from an equally "mind-boggling" menu) you risk not having precious room for its "better-than-sex" namesake cheesecakes (which, of course, is the "reason to go"); yes, the "wait" is "a killer" and the quarters a "madhouse", but few can resist its "are you tough enough to overstuff" challenge; P.S. try to "snag a table in the bar" area to avoid the no-reserving hassle.

Chef Geoff's S   – – – M

3201 New Mexico Ave., NW (Nebraska Ave.), 202-237-7800
In the "tony" Foxhall neighborhood of the Upper NW, this "simpatico" New American bistro is a "welcoming", "casual" option for "pleasing", "creative" fare paired with affordable wines by the glass; the "young, energetic" team is still "finding its footing", but when the chef "does it right, he shines", and everyone's "excellent attitude" lends it such a "unique charm" that "you want them to succeed"; P.S. though the interior is "comfortable", the "beautiful" terrace allows for "relaxing" alfresco dining under the stars.

Chez Marc   ▽ 23 19 21 $40

7607 Centreville Rd. (bet. Leland & Rugby Rds.), Manassas, VA, 703-369-6526
◪ Treasured as "a well-kept secret" by food lovers, this "one-of-a-kind" Classic French cafe set in an "unlikely" Manassas location specializes in "authentic" dishes running the gamut from "excellent" pâté de foie gras and lobster with saffron beurre blanc to "wonderful" Grand Marnier soufflé; it's very much the domain of chef-owner Marc Fusilier, who exudes pride in his Gallic gastronomic honors and quirky sense of decor, but detractors conclude it has "potential, but didn't deliver."

Chi-Cha Lounge ◐S   16 22 15 $19

1624 U St., NW (16th St.), 202-234-8400
◪ Twentysomethings "chill" at this "cool" New U lounge by sipping a signature Chi-Cha cocktail, smoking a hookah filled with flavored tobacco and listening to varied live music in a "sultry", "dim" "Andean village" setting; though "food isn't the main draw" here, the Latin American tapas are "perfect for sharing" while nestled into one of the "mismatched" velvet couches; P.S. you may want to "bring a flashlight" and perhaps an "iron lung."

China Star S　　　　–　–　–　I

Montgomery Village Shopping Ctr., 18204 Contour Rd.
(Lost Knife Rd.), Gaithersburg, MD, 301-947-0104
Interesting dishes from the Shanxi province in northern
China set apart this Gaithersburg fixture – many kinds of
dumplings, little savory buns (try the soup-filled ones) and
hand-pulled noodles, as well as multiregional entrees like
crispy beef; the prices are inexpensive at any time, but the
lunchtime buffet is a true bargain.

Ching Ching Cha S　　　▽ 20　25　22　$18

1063 Wisconsin Ave., NW (bet. K & M Sts.), 202-333-8288
■ "Welcoming sunlight" pours though the atrium of this
"beautiful", "civilized" teahouse set "among the fray of
Georgetown", making it a "peaceful oasis" in which to
enjoy a "wonderful", formal Asian tea; the "amiable" staff is
"knowledgeable about the large variety of brews available"
and serious about authenticity ("don't even think of asking
for sugar"), and the menu offers "tasty" "snacks" and "light
and satisfying" bento boxes, but best of all is the "total
relaxation for your mind."

Chutzpah S　　　　18　10　14　$16

12214 Fairfax Towne Ctr. (Monument Dr.), Fairfax, VA,
703-385-8883
◪ Mavens award this busy Fairfax deli's "overstuffed"
pastrami and corned beef sandwiches, "very decent
chopped liver", "excellent half-sour pickles" and other
"fresh quality" items the highest accolade – "just like
NYC" – even though the joint is too "sterile"-looking and
the help "more incompetent than rude"; sticklers, however,
retort it "takes chutzpah" indeed to pass this "sandwich
shop" off as a "real deli" ("who are they trying to kid?").

Cities S　　　　20　22　17　$39

2424 18th St., NW (bet. Belmont & Columbia Rds.), 202-328-7194
◪ "It's all about atmosphere and attitude" at this eclectic
Adams Morgan fashion plate where every year a different
city is featured (currently it's Tokyo), with the theme carried
out in the "high-style" designer backdrop and menu; the
"*très* cosmopolitan" bar scene is its chief attraction, but
those who settle in for a "leisurely" meal praise the kitchen's
"originality and flair", adding that the "people-watching
makes up for the spotty service."

CITRONELLE S　　　27　26　25　$66

(aka Michel Richard's Citronelle)
Latham Hotel, 3000 M St., NW (30th St.), 202-625-2150
■ Revel in a "gastronomic tour de force" at this "national
destination" in Georgetown, the "unforgettable" brainchild
of "jovial" chef-owner Michel Richard; from the show
kitchen emerge "intricate", "inventive" New French
dishes, "accompanied by "superb" wines and "expertly

served" in an "attractive" California-"chic" interior with a color-shifting mood wall; "from start to finish", "it doesn't get much better than this", but for an even more "extraordinary" evening, book the private chef's table.

City Lights of China [S] 21 12 17 $21

1731 Connecticut Ave., NW (bet. R & S Sts.), 202-265-6688

◪ Dupont Circle's shining source for a "Chinese-food fix", this "hole-in-the-wall" has cultivated a loyal following with its broad menu of "reliably" "above-average" "standards"; given its "cheesy" basement digs and the staff's "brusque" behavior, many prefer to take out (the "fast delivery" makes it a speed-dialer's dream), but critics feel that Meiweh (run by the former owner) "puts its lights out."

CLYDE'S [S] 18 20 19 $27

Georgetown Park Mall, 3236 M St., NW (Wisconsin Ave.), 202-333-9180

70 Wisconsin Circle (Western Ave.), Chevy Chase, MD, 301-951-9600 ◐

1700 N. Beauregard St. (Seminary Rd.), Alexandria, VA, 703-820-8300

Reston Town Ctr., 11905 Market St. (Reston Pkwy.), Reston, VA, 703-787-6601 ◐

8332 Leesburg Pike (Chain Bridge), Vienna, VA, 703-734-1901 ◐

■ "Dependable and affordable", these "Washington institutions" are "inviting" places for "all-purpose" dining, drawing in everyone from age "3 to 83"; appointed with lots of "glass and brass" to give them "class", they feature "middle-of-the-road" American saloon eats enlivened by "good-deal" seasonal specials; considering that they're franchises, customers are glad to report "few failings."

Coco Loco 16 17 14 $29

810 Seventh St., NW (bet. H & I Sts.), 202-289-2626

◪ Chinatown's Brazilian pioneer still satisfies bottomless appetites with its "decent" churrascaria, an all-you-can-eat "meat lover's" "orgy" (there's an antipasti bar too, though that may be beside the point); pickier palates proclaim it's "losing steam" ("less interesting each time"), but those who "just want to shake their booties" ask "who cares" about the food when we can "drink and dance" instead ("after hours", it turns into a "sizzling" salsa club)?

Coeur de Lion [S] ▽ 23 24 24 $50

Henley Park Hotel, 926 Massachusetts Ave., NW (10th St.), 202-414-0500

■ One of Downtown's "most charming brunch" sites, this "romantic" rendezvous features a series of dining rooms made "cozy" by old brick, stained-glass details and a pair of fireplaces; exuding "quiet class", it's a pleasant place for "fine" New American fare that may be "better than you'd expect" from a hotel.

Colorado Kitchen ⬛

▽ 24 | 20 | 20 | $20

5515 Colorado Ave., NW (Kennedy St.), 202-545-8280

◪ Hats off to Gillian Clark for bringing her "super" American cooking, both "homey" and "inventive", to an iffy Northeast "neighborhood that needs good restaurants" like her "cute" bistro; fans appreciate the small- and large-plate options on the menu and find the atmosphere "so relaxing and lighthearted" that minor service slips are easily forgiven; besides, the "staff warms up with regulars", and once you sample her "homemade doughnuts", you'll be one too.

COLVIN RUN TAVERN ⬛

25 | 25 | 24 | $56

Fairfax Sq., 8045 Leesburg Pike (Gallows Rd.), Tysons Corner, VA, 703-356-9500

◪ An "upbeat" haven of "city sophistication among the glut of Tysons Corner steakhouses", this "exciting" "addition" courtesy of Bob Kinkead looks nothing like a tavern; it's a "warm", "comfortable" "class act" with an "outstanding" New American menu that specializes in "exceptional" roasted meats "carved at the table" by "polished" servers; though a few faultfinders quibble that it "needs to smooth out some edges", groupies already consider it "easily one of the best in Northern Virginia."

Connaught Place ⬛

24 | 19 | 23 | $24

10425 North St. (bet. Chain Bridge Rd. & University Dr.), Fairfax, VA, 703-352-5959

■ Rivaling the "big name" Indian establishments in DC, this Fairfax "gem" has "outstanding everything" – "authentic", "perfectly seasoned" dishes, a "calm" atmosphere ("never a rushed feeling") and "attentive" service; it's also "one of the best values around", offering a "bargain" lunch buffet as well as a "wonderful" pre-theater menu; whether you come "in jeans or dress up for a night out", the "gracious" staff will "make you feel grand"; N.B. there's live sitar music on weekends.

Coppi's ⬛

19 | 17 | 17 | $24

1414 U St., NW (bet. 14th & 15th Sts.), 202-319-7773

◪ "Bicycling fanatics" brake for the "eclectic" pizzas topped with "unusual combinations" at this "funky", "cycle-themed" U Street Italian; though the wood-burning oven also turns out some "unique" dishes from Liguria, regulars "crowd" in for the "good" "designer" pies and "divine" Nutella dessert calzones, even if hard-to-please types give it "two thumbs-down."

Corduroy ⬛

23 | 17 | 21 | $42

Sheraton Four Points Downtown, 1201 K St., NW (12th St.), 202-589-0699

■ "Hidden" "out of the way" on the second floor of the Four Points hotel is this "wonderful", "roomy" New American "surprise", whose unobtrusive location may explain why it lacks the "wider audience" that those who've "discovered" it say it "deserves"; it's worth checking out because "impressive" chef-owner Tom Power executes "simple" yet "gourmet" dishes based on the seasons (always on the menu, though, is his "spectacular" roasted chicken, which "puts mom's to shame").

Crisp & Juicy [S] 21 | 5 | 12 | $11

Sunshine Sq., 1331G Rockville Pike (Congressional Ln.), Rockville, MD, 301-251-8833
Leisure World Plaza, 3800 International Dr. (Georgia Ave.), Silver Spring, MD, 301-598-3333
4540 Lee Hwy. (Glebe Rd.), Arlington, VA, 703-243-4222 ⇍
913 W. Broad St. (bet. Oak & Spring Sts.), Falls Church, VA, 703-241-9091

◪ Most aptly named, this Peruvian chain is a "once-a-week" staple for scores of Beltway-area families who "couldn't live without" its "deliciously" "crisp and juicy" spit-roasted chicken; teamed with "tasty" yuca fries, black beans and rice and "divine" hot sauces, it adds up to a "very cheap", "sooo good" meal, though the exceedingly "plain" setting and "hard chairs" lead many to "take out."

Crystal Thai [S] – | – | – | M

Arlington Forest Shopping Ctr., 4819 Arlington Blvd. (Park Dr.), Arlington, VA, 703-522-1311

Best known for its seasonal soft-shell crab specialties, this "authentic" Arlington Thai earns customer loyalty with its other "consistently delicious" dishes too ("try the yummy Panang chicken" or the crispy whole fish); not only are the prices "reasonable", but after a recent redo, the chandelier-lit digs are even somewhat "elegant" (albeit the tables are still "a bit scrunchy").

Cubano's [S] ▽ 18 | 16 | 17 | $23

1201 Fidler Ln. (Georgia Ave.), Silver Spring, MD, 301-563-4020

◪ "Cheerful" and "festive", this "much needed" Cuban "addition" "brightens" the Silver Spring dining scene with "zesty", "authentic" (if "a little heavy") cooking; a "mix of neighborhood families and young professionals" digs into Cuban sandwiches (available till midday only – "a real shame"), "fabulous fried yuca", "excellent *ropa vieja*" and other nicely "spiced" "comfort foods", all "reasonably priced"; it may be "uneven" so far (though "when it's on, it's great"), but it's "rapidly improving."

Da Domenico 21 | 17 | 21 | $36

1992 Chain Bridge Rd. (Leesburg Pike), Tysons Corner, VA, 703-790-9000

◪ Regulars at this Tysons Corner "power lunch" haunt "don't even bother to open" the Northern Italian menu; they know to order the "awesome" marinated veal chop, then sit back and be well taken care of by the "accommodating" staff and the "hospitable", "opera-singing" owner, who's an attraction in himself ("we love Dom!"); it may get "a bit crowded", but "you'll always feel at home" in this "quaint" room, even if a few find it merely "so-so."

Daily Grill S   17 17 18 $27

1200 18th St., NW (M St.), 202-822-5282
Georgetown Inn, 1310 Wisconsin Ave., NW (N St.), 202-337-4900
Tysons Galleria, 2001 International Dr. (Chain Bridge Rd.), Tysons Corner, VA, 703-288-5100

◪ "Lots of business gets done" at these "mainstream" American "hangouts" where "classy happy-hour crowds" gather amid "clubby" surroundings for "good comfort food" including "hearty" chicken pot pie and a "killer" Cobb salad; while they're undeniably "popular", critics dismiss the "ordinary" fare and "haphazard" service and add that it's "a little expensive for a daily encounter."

DC COAST   25 24 23 $45

Tower Bldg., 1401 K St., NW (14th St.), 202-216-5988

◪ "Electricity is in the air" at this "young power brokers'" pacesetter Downtown that boasts a "gorgeous" deco-style two-tiered space and a "fabulous" New American seafood-slanted menu "inspired by three coasts"; despite "unacceptable" noise (sit upstairs if you can), a "velvet-rope" vibe and tabs in the "luxury" stratosphere, followers promise that you'll have a "memorable" meal, because, after all, "food is the real star here."

Dean & DeLuca   19 13 13 $16

3276 M St., NW (33rd St.), 202-342-2500 S
1299 Pennsylvania Ave., NW (13th St.), 202-628-8155

◪ At Georgetown's "gourmet express" – a "lively" cafe that owes its "exceptional variety" of "imaginative" New American "light fare" to its "DeLuxe" market annex – you'll spot "genteel" locals ("and their dogs") sunning on the "charming" piazza while enjoying a "delicious" bite; during the summertime, weekend brunch comes with live jazz, but note that the "indifferent" counter service and "Paris"-league prices are in effect year-round; N.B. there's a smaller branch Downtown.

Delhi Dhaba S   19 11 16 $16

4455 Connecticut Ave., NW (Yuma St.), 202-537-1008
7236 Woodmont Ave. (bet. Bethesda Ave. & Elm St.), Bethesda, MD, 301-718-0008
2424 Wilson Blvd. (Barton St.), Arlington, VA, 703-524-0008
K-Mart Shopping Ctr., 454 Elden St. (Grant St.), Herndon, VA, 703-467-8484

◪ What started out as a "good, cheap", cafeteria-style curry-in-a-hurry parlor (whose decor amounted to the endlessly playing Bollywood videos) near the Arlington Courthouse has branched out into "more restaurantry" offshoots in Upper NW and Bethesda (the Herndon outlet is mostly carryout); stalwarts say all of them offer "authentic food at great prices", but skeptics who find them "mediocre" to begin with think that quality varies with the location.

Diner ●⬤S   16 | 17 | 16 | $16

2453 18th St., NW (bet. Belmont & Columbia Rds.), 202-232-8800
☑ Filling a "major need" in Adams Morgan, this 24-hour "instant classic" with a "cool" retro style pulls in hordes of hungry, young hipsters round-the-clock; it's a "required stop" for post-clubbers, refueling them with all-American comfort eats like breakfast favorites, the "best" gravy fries and "world-class" shakes; the servers are "hardworking" but overburdened, leading wags to quip "good late-night food, but by the time you get it, it's morning."

District ChopHouse & Brewery ⬤S   19 | 20 | 18 | $32

509 Seventh St., NW (bet. E & F Sts.), 202-347-3434
☑ Just a toss away from the MCI Center, this "popular" "meat 'n' potatoes" palace set in a former bank really "hops" on game nights; fans hail it for its "blue-collar" American lineup of "big" beef, "onion rings stacked high" and "great handcrafted beers", delivered in a "lively" atmosphere (read: "unbearable din") at "cost-conscious" prices, but opponents rank it at the "lower end of chain steakhouses."

Dolce Vita ⬤S   23 | 16 | 21 | $26

10824 Lee Hwy. (Main St.), Fairfax, VA, 703-385-1530
☑ How sweet life would be if there were more "great neighborhood" "finds" like this "cozy" Fairfax Italian, embraced for turning out "wonderful, smoky pizzas" and "lovely" pastas amid "clever" decorations and "romantic" serenades; then, maybe this "tight" room wouldn't be "packed shoulder-to-shoulder" at prime time, frustrating even the faithful with "forever" waits.

DUANGRAT'S ⬤S   25 | 21 | 22 | $28

5878 Leesburg Pike (Glen Forest Dr.), Falls Church, VA, 703-820-5775
☑ "Classic" Thai food enhanced by "classy" touches – white tablecloths, "beautiful" flowers, chandeliers and "pleasing" waitresses in "colorful" native attire – continues to earn this "exotic" Falls Church "treasure" lavish praise; the menu offers "many wonderful", "fragrant" choices, most of them "heavenly", virtually guaranteeing that even "first-timers" will "love" this "visual and gustatory treat"; the only downside: it's "always crowded", despite its "out-of-the-way" location.

Duken ●⬤S   – | – | – | I

1116 U St., NW (12th St.), 202-667-8735
Abuzz with a lively cross section of DC's large Ethiopian community, this New U gathering place provides a good

introduction to that country's interestingly spiced stews,
scooped up with spongy injera bread and eaten with
the hands; it functions even more as a social center on
weekends, when there's live entertainment, while on
Sunday afternoons, it puts on a native coffee ceremony.

Eat First ● S | 21 | 8 | 16 | $18 |

609 H St., NW (6th St.), 202-289-1703

◪ Sinophiles "eat often" at this "plain" but "friendly"
Chinese that relocated to another site in Chinatown last
year, because it continues to deliver ("fast") a "fantastic
selection of authentic" fare at "absurdly cheap" prices;
there's still "no ambiance", but that hardly matters when
the food is "as tasty as ever"; even if a few feel that some
of the "magic" has been lost in the move, diehards who
"welcome it back" urge it's "worth another try."

eCiti Cafe & Bar | 18 | 16 | 17 | $34 |

8300 Tyco Rd. (Leesburg Pike), Tysons Corner, VA, 703-760-9000

◪ Word is that this once hyper-"trendy" mingle-dine-and-
dance scene in Tysons Corner is feeling the "high-tech bust";
while there is "less buzz" and more "pink slip" parties
going on, a "smaller" crowd of followers still appreciates
its "adventurous" New American menu and "renovated"
warehouse digs; bears may dub it a "dot-bomb", but bulls
retort at least there's "less pretense" in the house nowadays.

El Mariachi S | – | – | – | I |

765C Rockville Pike (Wootton Pkwy.), Rockville, MD, 301-738-7177

"Visited regularly by sweaty runners", soccer moms with
hungry players and lots of families, this "friendly", "tolerant"
"neighborhood gem" on Rockville Pike is "always packed"
with aficionados of "simple but sumptuous" Mexican and
Salvadoran cooking; those who "return" often swear that
"everything is authentic", "robust" and "inexpensive",
making it a "real" "pleasure to eat here."

El Pollo Rico S⊟ | 25 | 5 | 15 | $11 |

2541 Ennalls Ave. (Veirs Mill Rd.), Wheaton, MD, 301-942-4419
2917 Washington Blvd. (Fillmore St.), Arlington, VA, 703-522-3220

◪ "Finger-licking", "irresistible" "spit-roasted" chirpers sold
at "prices so cheap you feel guilty" lure "Washingtonians
of every stripe" to these Peruvian "queen of chicken" dives
in Wheaton and Arlington; "nothing else can challenge"
these "addictive" birds, but since "there's always a line
and no good place to sit" (no booze, no frills and no plastic
either), most opt for the "terrific takeout."

Elysium S | ▽ 23 | 26 | 23 | $55 |

*Morrison House, 116 S. Alfred St. (bet. King & Prince Sts.),
Alexandria, VA, 703-838-8000*

■ When you sup amid the "old-money" appointments of
this posh hotel dining room in Old Town, you're treated to

a 'chef of your own' who comes to your table for a tête-à-tête before custom-designing your New American dinner courses based on seasonal, organic ingredients; whether or not you opt for the "perfectly matched" wine pairings, every "wonderful" morsel is presented with "exemplary care", making this "fabulous" "experience" one of a kind.

EQUINOX S   25 21 23 $49
818 Connecticut Ave., NW (I St.), 202-331-8118

◪ Owners Todd and Ellen Gray and their "warmhearted" staff obviously "really like what they're doing" at this "superb" New American "centrally located" near the White House, and they lend it "genuine" appeal; a recent James Beard award nominee, "talented" chef Todd showcases his "original", "sumptuous" seasonal dishes in a "tasteful", "comfortable" room, eliciting "huzzahs" from admirers, even if a minority "expects more from such hype."

Etrusco S   22 22 20 $43
1606 20th St., NW (bet. Q & R Sts.), 202-667-0047

◪ "Emulate the life of the pleasure-loving Etruscans" at this "buzzy", "beautiful" Dupont Circle "favorite" where chef-owner Francesco Ricchi does "marvelous things to ordinary ingredients", conjuring up the "earthy" "tastes of Italy" (with a focus on Tuscany) in such dishes as his "splendid" osso buco; though the kitchen can be "erratic" and the service likewise "dicey", partisans insist it's "worth the effort to try to hit it on the right night."

Evening Star Cafe S   22 18 19 $29
2000 Mount Vernon Ave. (Howell Ave.), Alexandria, VA, 703-549-5051

◪ "Personality" plus a "folksy, small-town" atmosphere sets the stage for a "grown-up" but "not too fancy" New American dining experience at this Del Ray "hangout"; it's a "neighborhood treasure", despite "spotty" service, attracting a loyal following that can choose seating in the "funky" (though "cramped") dining room, the "colorful" wine bar upstairs or out on the patio, a "welcoming" place to "watch the world go by."

Faccia Luna Trattoria S   20 15 17 $19
2400 Wisconsin Ave., NW (bet. Calvert St. & Observatory Ln.), 202-337-3132
823 S. Washington St. (bet. Green & Jefferson Sts.), Alexandria, VA, 703-838-5998
2909 Wilson Blvd. (Fillmore St.), Arlington, VA, 703-276-3099

◪ Hearth-baked "pizzas with pizzazz" and "good, cheap Chianti make up a great Saturday night" at these "reliable" Italian sources for "family-friendly", "cost-effective" dining; they're "not so fancy" inside, but the outdoor seating areas enhance their "breezy" ambiance, while the "harried" waiters display a "high tolerance for screaming children";

purists, however, who find it "not too exciting", "don't see what all the fuss is about."

Fadó Irish Pub S   15 | 20 | 16 | $20

808 Seventh St., NW (bet. H & I Sts.), 202-789-0066

◪ Handy to the MCI Center, this "Disneyfied version" of a "dark, smoky" Dublin pub is "always packed" before and after a game; it's "beer first and everything else second" here, though its "hearty", "cardiac-arresting" Irish food does have its homesick fans; P.S. its "Monday-night trivia quiz is a cool way to be a nerd."

Fairfax Room ◑ S   – | – | – | E

Westin Embassy Row, 2100 Massachusetts Ave., NW (21st St.), 202-293-2100

Once the site of the legendary Jockey Club (DC's version of NYC's '21' Club), this Embassy Row hotel venue now features a high-end New American menu of trendily packaged crowd-pleasers like seafood martinis and lobster risotto; the minimalist dining room, though, still retains a West Coast feel, while the wood-paneled lounge continues to be an inviting place for a drink and a bite by the fireplace.

Faryab S   21 | 16 | 20 | $25

4917 Cordell Ave. (bet. Norfolk Ave. & Old Georgetown Rd.), Bethesda, MD, 301-951-3484

■ As world events focus attention on its native land, this Bethesda Afghan remains a "pleasant", "friendly" refuge brightened with homeland photos, artifacts and tapestries; it's a "warm" backdrop for a "delectable", "authentic" menu that makes it "easy to order something new" or stick with "delightfully spiced" favorites like its "world-class" lamb kebabs and "must-have pumpkin stew"; as if that weren't enough, it's also a "good value."

Felix S   20 | 21 | 18 | $32

2406 18th St., NW (bet. Belmont & Columbia Rds.), 202-483-3549

◪ "Hip", young things "slide into a martini and enjoy the upscale", "eclectic" New American menu and "campy James Bond" vibe at this slice of "SoHo" in Adams Morgan that's also known for its "excellent" kosher-style dinner every Friday (don't ask); many guests start or end their evening in the "chic" Spy Lounge next door (featuring "tasty tunes"), making this "swinging singles'" scene "the place for a total evening's" worth of "fun."

Filomena Ristorante S   20 | 20 | 19 | $35

1063 Wisconsin Ave., NW (bet. K & M Sts.), 202-338-8800

◪ The "pasta mamas" making "great ravioli" in the window of this Georgetown Italian set the stage for the "fun", "loud" "grandma's basement" scene in the dining room below, where every day a "generous", "too tempting" lunch buffet is offered at a bargain price; aside from the "homey" food, its "fantastic", over-the-top holiday decorations make it beloved by "kids" of all ages ("Washington personalities" too); P.S. the recent arrival of chef Enzo Febbaro (ex Centro) "could make it overcome its touristy" image.

Finemondo   – – – E
1319 F St., NW (bet. 13th & 14th Sts.), 202-737-3100
Rustic Italian chic defines this comfortable new Downtown venue whose offerings run the gamut from happy-hour bruschetta to four-course tasting menus; the kitchen specializes in spit-roasted meats, along with uncommon dishes (like codfish cooked in a clay pot with potatoes and black olives, and sea bass in a hay-and-salt crust), while a private dining room reminiscent of a wine cellar completes the appealing package.

Firehook Bakery & Coffeehouse   21 14 15 $11
3411 Connecticut Ave., NW (bet. Macomb & Newark Sts.), 202-362-2253 S
3241 M St., NW (bet. Potomac St. & Wisconsin Ave.), 202-625-6247 S
215 Pennsylvania Ave., NW (2nd St.), 202-277-1333 S
1909 Q St., NW (19th St.), 202-588-9296 S
912 17th St., NW (bet. I & K Sts.), 202-429-2253
214 N. Fayette St. (bet. Cameron & Queen Sts.), Alexandria, VA, 703-519-8020 S
105 S. Union St. (King St.), Alexandria, VA, 703-519-8021 S
◪ Neighborhood-oriented and locally owned, this "friendly", "casual" chain of American bakery/coffeehouses "keeps Starbucks from taking over the world" with its "excellent selection" of "crusty" breads and "tempting" baked goods, along with its "gourmet" sandwiches, soups and salads; critics, though, note that expansion has its price – what was an "original" concept now has a "cookie-cutter" feel.

Five Guys S⌿   24 8 15 $9
4626 King St. (Beauregard St.), Alexandria, VA, 703-671-1606
107 N. Fayette St. (King St.), Alexandria, VA, 703-549-7991
7622 Richmond Hwy. (Fordson Rd.), Alexandria, VA, 703-717-0090
6541 Backlick Rd. (Old Keene Mill Rd.), Springfield, VA, 703-913-1337
14001 Jefferson Davis Hwy. (Longview Dr.), Woodbridge, VA, 703-349-2888
◪ "Grease city" it may be, but "there are no better" burgers than the ones prepared at this "beyond-basic" Northern Virginia chain where the "big, sloppy" patties come "dripping with toppings" (don't forget the "awesome" made-from-scratch fries); it's a "total dive" and you should "feel lucky if you find a place to sit", but "what a treat when all you want is a great" meal on a bun; P.S. it's such a "bargain" that it was voted the No. 1 Bang for the Buck in the Washington area.

Fleming's S 23 23 22 $49

1960A Chain Bridge Rd. (International Dr.), Tysons Corner, VA, 703-442-8384

◪ An "outstanding selection of wines by the glass" (more than 100) distinguishes this "contemporary" steakhouse chain with "good buzz"; it aims to entice with an "attractive" open layout, less masculine decor and a "non-smoking" policy, but the menu is quite traditional, highlighting "excellent" aged cuts like its signature porterhouse; faultfinders say it's "not quite Ruth's Chris or Morton's", but for that exact reason boosters appreciate it as a "refreshing change" of pace.

Florida Ave. Grill 20 13 18 $14

1100 Florida Ave., NW (11th St.), 202-265-1586

◪ "Everything is fried, unapologetically fattening and good"-tasting at "DC's most famous diner", a Northwest Soul Food "institution" where folks from every walk of life have been coming in for years for "grits, biscuits, country ham and friendly AM life"; redolent with the "smell of old grease" and filled with Southern memorabilia, it's "a tradition worth preserving" proclaim the legions of loyalists that'd be "devastated" if it ever closed its doors.

Fontina Grille S ▽ 19 20 19 $28

King Farm Village Ctr., 801 Pleasant Dr. (bet. King Farm & Redland Blvds.), Rockville, MD, 301-947-5400

■ "Lively" and airy, this smart-looking Southern Italian newcomer is "off to a good start" say settlers in the Montgomery County enclave of Rockville; the "cooking is adept" – from the crisp-crust wood-fired pizzas and "fine" pastas to the "best" eggplant dishes and "interesting", updated specials – providing ample reasons for locals to dine near their new houses and office complexes.

Fortune S 21 12 15 $21

North Point Village Ctr., 1428 Reston Pkwy. (bet. Baron Cameron Ave. & Leesburg Pike), Reston, VA, 703-318-8898
6249 Arlington Blvd. (Patrick Henry Dr.), Seven Corners, VA, 703-538-3333

◪ On weekends, the "chaotic parade of pushcarts" whizzing around an "amazing array" ("we always get too full before we've tried everything of interest") of "delicious dim sum" can be either an "overwhelming" sight or "such a blast", but appetites will be rewarded nonetheless at this pair of "hangar"-size Chinese emporiums in Northern Virginia; "come with a large group to share" the small plates, or visit later in the day for Hong Kong–style seafood specialties.

FOUR & TWENTY BLACKBIRDS S 26 21 23 $44

650 Zachary Taylor Hwy. (Rte. 647), Flint Hill, VA, 540-675-1111

■ Nestled in the "scenic" Virginia foothills, this "delightful" New American "destination" is a "welcoming" "country gem" "in the middle of nowhere", making it a "perfect getaway from DC"; though the "imaginative" gourmet menu changes every three weeks, you "can't go wrong" with any selection because everything is homemade, "very fresh" and "exceptional"; it's "well worth the drive", so "if you haven't taken the time to dine here, you need to reevaluate your priorities."

Franklins 🖪   _ _ _ I

5123 Baltimore Ave. (Gallatin St.), Hyattsville, MD, 301-927-2740
Big and high-spirited, this newcomer brings solid, largely American food – BBQ, salads and sandwiches, as well as pizzas and pastas – to a mostly barren stretch of Hyattsville; the whimsical touches in the multipurpose room reflect the sensibilities of owner (and former toy seller) Mike Franklin (don't miss browsing in his General Store next door).

Full Kee ●🖪   23 7 14 $16

509 H St., NW (bet. 5th & 6th Sts.), 202-371-2233 ⊟
5830 Columbia Pike (Leesburg Pike), Falls Church, VA,
703-575-8232
🗹 Novices should be "careful" – the food is very "authentic" at this "spartan" Chinatown "mainstay" whose philosophy must be "if anybody will eat it, we'll cook it"; even if you're not so adventurous, you'll be more than satisfied with the "addictive shrimp dumpling soup" and other "astonishingly good" Cantonese choices, and if you go late (it's open till 1 AM on weeknights, 3 AM on weekends) you can catch local off-duty chefs dining and unwinding; N.B. there's a shiny outpost in Falls Church.

Full Key ●🖪   ▽ 21 7 14 $16

Wheaton Manor Shopping Ctr., 2227 University Blvd. W.
(Georgia Ave.), Wheaton, MD, 301-933-8388
🗹 A Chinese "soul food favorite", this "standby" is the "place to go" in Wheaton for the "best" Hong Kong–style noodle soups, fresh-made won tons "loaded with shrimp", "delicious" clams in black bean sauce and some "unusual" house specials, all priced "cheap"; the decor ("don't let it scare you") and "fast" food–like service may "scream carryout", but loyal customers don't much care because they "come here only for the food."

Gabriel 🖪   _ _ _ E

Radisson Barcelo Hotel, 2121 P St., NW (21st St.),
202-956-6690
We didn't survey this Spanish near Dupont Circle as it had planned to close temporarily for a major redo, but it changed its plans and continues to host an appreciative audience); still an "event" is its "amazing", "lavish" Sunday brunch (centered around a whole "roast pig that's on the menu in heaven"), presented in a "cozy, tasteful" setting; it's "quieter on weeknights" and also worth a visit for its

"flavorful" tapas, "innovative" Nuevo Latino dishes and "flights" of sherries.

GALILEO S 26 23 24 $58
1110 21st St., NW (bet. L & M Sts.), 202-293-7191
LABORATORIO DEL GALILEO ●
1110 21st St., NW (bet. L & M Sts.), 202-331-0880
■ Esteemed as the "Prada of Italian cuisine", this "rarified" "epicurean must" in the Golden Triangle is where DC players take their "best clients" for an "unmatched" "experience" orchestrated by Roberto Donna; for the "ultimate insider's dinner", book a table in the Laboratorio adjacent to the main room at Galileo, a private dining space with a state-of-the-art showcase kitchen, from which emerges a "spectacular", custom-designed series of 10–12 "complex" tasting courses "perfectly matched" with wines from the "divine" cellar.

Generous George's S 17 15 16 $16
3006 Duke St. (Cambridge Rd.), Alexandria, VA, 703-370-4303
☑ "Pandemonium" reigns at this "manic" Alexandria Italian parlor, a cavernous joint that caters to kids and "carb fiends" with its "kooky" decorations (think pink flamingos) and over-the-top menu of "big, yummy pizzas and pastas, or both together" in one dish; you better believe it's a total "assault on the senses", but if you're looking for somewhere to host a "birthday party for 10-year-olds, this is the place."

Georgia Brown's S 22 22 22 $38
950 15th St., NW (bet. I & K Sts.), 202-393-4499
■ "Check your heart at the door" at this "classy" Downtown "scene" with a clientele that epitomizes "chic" cultural diversity and then dig into "an embarrassingly large amount" of "delicious", "clever" ("and rich") Low Country cooking "not like grandma used to make" ("give in to temptation and get those fried chicken livers"); when it gets "jammed", the service inevitably "slows" down, but there's "no other place like it"; P.S. the Sunday jazz brunch is "awesome."

Geranio S 22 19 20 $37
722 King St. (bet. Columbus & Washington Sts.), Alexandria, VA, 703-548-0088
■ "Cozy", "dark" and "romantic", this "well-established" "charmer" set in a "quaint townhouse" in Old Town is a "real treat" for Italian food so "tasty" it'll "make you crave more" (the "osso buco is tops"); supporters swear that "everything" on the "rotating" menu is "excellent" and the "professional" staff always "unobtrusive", making it a "delightful" place to take "that special someone."

GERARD'S PLACE 27 22 24 $63
915 15th St., NW (bet. I & K Sts.), 202-737-4445
■ "Tasteful and restrained", Downtown's most "Parisian" of places "wows" devotees with "fabulous", "imaginative"

New French interpretations prepared with "finesse" (don't miss the "outstanding lobster" or "indescribable" chocolate soup); it's "always among the best" destinations in DC thanks to chef-owner Gerard Pangaud's "exquisite" touch, "elegant" surroundings and "precise" (if "arrogant") service; it's "in a class by itself – too bad the prices are as well", but "on Mondays, you can bring your own wine."

Good Fortune ◐ S | 21 | 13 | 16 | $19

2646 University Blvd. W. (bet. Georgia Ave. & Veirs Mill Rd.), Wheaton, MD, 301-929-8818

◪ The rolling dim sum carts on weekends make it way "too easy to order everything" in sight wail those addicted to this Wheaton Chinese's array of "expertly" made morsels (the lines form before noon, so better "go early"); considered one of the neighborhood's "best" Cantonese picks, it proves that "crowded", "dumpy" digs matter little when you "know how to cook a duck" like it does, though detractors feel it "waxes and wanes" too much.

Grapeseed S | 21 | 18 | 19 | $38

4865 Cordell Ave. (Norfolk Ave.), Bethesda, MD, 301-986-9592

◪ "What fun!" cheer boosters of this "urbane", "intimate" Bethesda bistro that "creatively pairs" "interesting" New American "mini-dishes" with a "treasure trove" of wines by the glass in a "welcoming" atmosphere that "encourages a long, leisurely" stay; oenophiles "can't say enough good things" about this "great date spot", but faultfinders deem it "uneven" and caution that the "cost adds up" quickly.

Green Field Churrascaria S | 19 | 16 | 18 | $29

1801 Rockville Pike (Randolph Rd.), Rockville, MD, 301-881-3397

◪ "Get really ready to eat" before going to this "sizzling" "*casa de carne*" in Rockville, where the set-price Brazilian barbecue deal begins with a trip to the extensive salad bar and hot food station (a "huge meal" right there), followed by an "endless" procession of servers who keep bringing skewers of "every kind of fire-roasted meat" to your table until you "roll yourself" out the door; skeptics, though, sniff "lots of food" but "mediocre quality."

Green Papaya S | 21 | 22 | 20 | $28

4922 Elm St. (Arlington Rd.), Bethesda, MD, 301-654-8986

◪ Offering a "beautiful introduction to refined Vietnamese cuisine", this "tranquil" tropical fantasy in Bethesda gives traditional fare an "original" appeal ("love" the 'golden pancake' and "fantastic" sugarcane shrimp); the kitchen's "emphasis on fresh ingredients" allows the dishes' "true flavors to shine through", but nitpickers feel that "as it's becoming more popular", it's becoming more "so-so."

Greenwood S　　　　19 19 15 $44

5031 Connecticut Ave., NW (Nebraska Ave.), 202-364-4444

▧ Few local chefs seem to spark as much controversy as Carol Greenwood – her considerable "cult following" adores the artistic Upper NW venue where she puts together an "always surprising" New American bill of fare "based on what's seasonal", though they admit that enough "time can lapse between courses to take a nap"; foes, meanwhile, find her so "intolerant of any menu substitutions" ("the customer is never right" here) that they "wouldn't go back on a bet."

Grille 88 S　　　　– – – E

1910 18th St., NW (bet. Florida Ave. & T St.), 202-588-5288

At Adams Morgan's newest locale for relaxed fine dining, cool blue tones and crisp white tablecloths provide the backdrop for a menu full of retro-inspired New American fare; look for classics such as clams casino, along with modish riffs like 'nachos' (ginger-smoked salmon, crème fraîche and wasabi flying-fish roe on crispy won ton skins) and chile-rubbed angus rib-eye steak, plus there's a piano bar for sophisticated sing-alongs and weekend cabaret.

Grillfish S　　　　19 17 17 $30

1200 New Hampshire Ave., NW (M St.), 202-331-7310

Ocean Grill S

4866 Cordell Ave. (bet. Norfolk & Woodmont Aves.), Bethesda, MD, 301-941-9058

▧ "Delish" and "easy", this separately owned pair of "eccentric" seafood "concepts" in the Golden Triangle and Bethesda "hits" the mark with "fresh" fish "simply" grilled (or, if you must, sautéed); neither the "wonderfully weird" "*Twilight Zone*" decor, "blaring music" or "too enthusiastic" servers discourage youthful fin fanciers, but the "older" demographic finds it all just "bizarre", starting with the erotic floor-to-ceiling mural behind the ornate stone bar.

Grill from Ipanema S　　　　20 18 18 $29

1858 Columbia Rd., NW (Belmont Rd.), 202-986-0757

■ "*Obrigado*" (thank you) "for the best local taste of Brazil" in Adams Morgan say admirers of this "buzzing" spot that mixes "killer caipirinhas" "worthy of Rio"; not only is a "great" "party" always going on, but it's the "place to go" for "authentic", "stick-to-your-ribs" food including "tasty" seafood stews and "interesting" dishes like "fried alligator."

Guajillo S　　　　19 13 15 $20

1727 Wilson Blvd. (bet. Quinn & Rhodes Sts.), Arlington, VA, 703-807-0840

▧ Nothing "run-of-the-mill" about this small, "noisy" Mexican newcomer near Rosslyn – not its "unconventional bar specials" nor its "unusual" salsas, "incredible" seviche, "excellent" chicken mole and other "authentic" items ("definitely a cut above the standard"); service is "pleasant", if somewhat "unrefined", while a "playful" color palette perks up the simple decor.

Gua-Rapo ●S   ▽ 17 20 16 $25

2039 Wilson Blvd. (Courthouse Rd.), Arlington, VA, 703-528-6500

◪ For "something different" in Arlington's Courthouse area, the "chic crowd" saunters over to this "swanky" new "see-and-be-seen" lounge with a blue-glass bar and "low", "comfy sofas", orders "good specialty drinks" and nibbles on mix-and-match items from the Nuevo Latino menu; detractors, however, report that it's "still working out the kinks" while "trying desperately to be as trendy as Chi-Cha Lounge" in DC (run by the same owner).

Haad Thai S   22 17 19 $20

1100 New York Ave., NW (11th St.), 202-682-1111
1472 Beauregard St. (Reading Ave.), Alexandria, VA, 703-575-1999

■ "The little Thai that could" aptly describes these lunchtime staples "convenient" to the DC Convention Center and the Mark Center in Alexandria, which "try hard and succeed" at satisfying surveyors with "wonderful", "authentically spiced" specialties; "lovely presentations", "fantastic" murals of faraway places, "prompt" service and "reasonable prices" only enhance the story; they're "always packed" during the day, but it's "easy to get a table at night."

Haandi S   24 17 21 $25

4904 Fairmont Ave. (Old Georgetown Rd.), Bethesda, MD, 301-718-0121
Falls Plaza Shopping Ctr., 1222 W. Broad St. (Leesburg Pike), Falls Church, VA, 703-533-3501

◪ Setting the Indian "standard" for many connoisseurs in the suburbs of Bethesda and Falls Church, this "terrific" traditional twosome with a "pretty-in-pink" color scheme "never lets you down" with its "tantalizing", "well-spiced" dishes (believe them when they tell you the lamb "vindaloo is hot") that "consistently" satisfy the "craving"; the less impressed, however, find the menu "unimaginative" and add that despite the staff's "genteel" manners, it can "feel like you're speed dining" here.

Hakuba S   ▽ 21 18 15 $26

Kentlands Market Sq., 706 Center Point Way (Great Seneca Hwy.), Gaithersburg, MD, 301-947-1283

■ Though not many respondents seem to know about this "tasteful", tranquil suburban sushi bar (which suits its tony Kentlands neighbors just fine), those who have visited it marvel that the fish is "so fresh we can't believe it's in Gaithersburg"; not only does it offer "some of the most original items in the DC area", but it also features a selection of "interesting" cooked dishes, as well as sake served (as it should be) in "your own cedar box."

Hama Sushi S   ▽ 21 14 20 $24

2415 Centreville Rd. (Fox Mill Rd.), Herndon, VA, 703-713-0088
◪ Most Herndon regulars "check out the daily specials board for the freshest selections" at their local Japanese sushi spot, which offers "good quality and value for the money" in a "bright", if "uninspired", setting; a familiar "variety" of traditional cooked dishes is available too, presented with the same "warm" service, making this standby an easy pick for "day-to-day dining."

Hard Times Cafe S   18 14 16 $15

4920 Del Ray Ave. (Old Georgetown Rd.), Bethesda, MD, 301-951-3300
4738 Cherry Hill Rd. (Baltimore Ave.), College Park, MD, 301-474-8880
1021 Washington Blvd. S. (Montrose Ave.), Laurel, MD, 301-604-7400
Woodley Gardens, 1117 Nelson St. (Montgomery Ave.), Rockville, MD, 301-294-9720
1404 King St. (West St.), Alexandria, VA, 703-837-0050
3028 Wilson Blvd. (Highland St.), Arlington, VA, 703-528-2233
K-Mart Shopping Ctr., 428 Elden St. (bet. Herndon Pkwy. & Van Buren St.), Herndon, VA, 703-318-8941 ◗
Springfield Plaza, 6362 Springfield Plaza (Commerce St.), Springfield, VA, 703-913-5600 ◗
14389 Potomac Mills Rd. (Gideon Dr.), Woodbridge, VA, 703-492-2950 ◗
◪ Sometimes the "proven pleasure" of a bowl of "great", "greasy" chili with a side of fried onion rings and a "cold beer" is worth the "serious heartburn risk", especially if downed in a joint with "character" like these American parlors with the "best" C&W jukeboxes around; skeptics, though, who sniff merely "serviceable", quip "one time was hard enough."

Havana Breeze   18 9 14 $15

1401 K St., NW (14th St.), 202-789-1470
◪ Providing a "refreshing" change from the nearby power haunts and generic carry-out dives, this "no-frills" Downtown "cafeteria" pleases the "office lunch" crowd with "real" Cuban sandwiches and other "down-home" fare that could rival its Miami counterparts; though the place is a "dump" and "service isn't a priority", the eats "deliciously" explain "why Hemingway loved Cuba" so much.

Hee Been S   22 14 19 $23

6231 Little River Tpke. (Beauregard St.), Annandale, VA, 703-941-3737
◪ A home away from home for "Korean families and military veterans homesick for the food of Seoul", this

Annandale refuge promises a "fantastic experience" for novices too; though a "bilingual dictionary would be useful" for exploring the menu, you can't go wrong with the "terrific barbeque grilled to order at your table"; despite its "unattractive" surroundings, addicts are more than happy to sing "we been, we been and we won't stop"; N.B. sushi is available too.

Heritage India S　　　25 23 21 $33
2400 Wisconsin Ave., NW (Calvert St.), 202-333-3120
4931 Cordell Ave. (Old Georgetown Rd.), Bethesda, MD, 301-656-3373
◪ "Lovely screens", historical photographs and native handicrafts evoke the "refined" atmosphere of a "wealthy Indian's private home" at this culinary ambassador in Georgetown, which "impeccably presents" "complex", "flavorful" fare that includes some "exquisite" dishes "not found" elsewhere; the cognoscenti regard it as a "wonderfully authentic" "jewel" but warn "watch out" for the "pushy" servers who are "intent on hiking up the tab"; P.S. "we're excited about the new Bethesda branch."

Hinode S　　　20 16 19 $25
4914 Hampden Ln. (Arlington Rd.), Bethesda, MD, 301-654-0908
134 Congressional Ln. (bet. Jefferson St. & Rockville Pike), Rockville, MD, 301-816-2190
◪ Utility players in the Montgomery County sushi league, these "reliable" Japanese fallbacks are valued by fans for their "bust-a-gut" lunch buffets and "fresh" fish ("nice 'cooked' sushi options" too), served in "family"-friendly environs that keep children happy with their colorful tanks; critics, however, who cite "plain", "uninspired" offerings and "distracted" service conclude they're "no bargains."

Hollywood East Cafe ◑S　　　25 10 19 $19
2312 Price Ave. (Elkin St.), Wheaton, MD, 301-942-8282
◪ Get your taste buds ready for a real "adventure" at this Wheaton Chinese where visitors can find "authentic" renditions of their "favorite childhood dishes" or choose from among a "long, exotic" menu of "intriguing" Cantonese "delights"; given the "miles" of posted specials too, the options may seem overwhelming, but don't worry because the "helpful (if a bit gruff) staff will translate" for you; the digs are "gritty", but it's an "excellent value" for such "complex, sophisticated Hong Kong–style" cooking.

Hope Key ◑S　　　20 8 16 $15
3131 Wilson Blvd. (Highland Ave.), Arlington, VA, 703-243-8388
◪ "The later the hour, the better the food" at this low-rent Arlington Chinese with "zero" ambiance, whose "authentic" chow (notably "perfect shrimp, chicken and eggplant in a hot pot") is a "real belly-filler"; doubters may deem it "so-

so", but at least you get a "ton of food for less $ than [the loose change] under your couch"; N.B. open till 1 AM on weeknights, 2:30 on weekends.

Hunan Lion [S] | 19 | 20 | 19 | $26 |

2070 Chain Bridge Rd. (Old Courthouse Rd.), Tysons Corner, VA, 703-734-9828

◪ "Consistently a cut above many other local Chinese restaurants", this Tysons Corner veteran is a "solid" place to "promptly" "satisfy your beef with broccoli craving" or enjoy other "well-prepared" standards from the extensive menu; while there may be "no surprises" here, regulars swear you "can't go wrong" with any of the dishes, which explains why it's about to "celebrate its 20th anniversary."

Hunan Palace [S] ▽ | 19 | 12 | 15 | $20 |

Shady Grove Shopping Ctr., 9011 Gaither Rd. (Shady Grove Rd.), Gaithersburg, MD, 301-977-8600

◪ "Plain" looking though it may be, this Gaithersburg Chinese is where "native Taiwanese go for their fix" (it's "one of the few places around that offer the true flavors" of that cuisine); though it features a broad, multiregional bill of fare, the best items are off the menu (including "great, fresh lobster and crab dishes"), which might clarify why those who don't persevere in ordering the most "authentic" selections judge the food "just fair."

Huong Que [S] | 24 | 15 | 22 | $22 |

(aka Four Sisters)

Eden Ctr., 6769 Wilson Blvd. (Roosevelt Blvd.), Falls Church, VA, 703-538-6717

■ "If you don't fall in love with the food (which you should)" at this "stellar" Falls Church Vietnamese, "you'll swoon over the service from the beautiful sisters" (for whom it's nicknamed); they're "sweet" "ambassadors of their native cuisine and culture", and they'll "patiently" guide you through the "dauntingly long menu"; "fortunately, just about everything" is "sublime" (particularly the clay pot specialties), thus "it's hard not to want to work your way through it all", especially when the tabs are so moderate.

Ichiro Hibachi
Steak House & Sushi Bar [S] | – | – | – | M |

11575 Old Georgetown Rd. (Executive Blvd.), Rockville, MD, 301-881-7822

Well equipped to handle a range of mealtime needs, this handsome new Japanese dining complex in Rockville features a sushi bar, twin tatami rooms and 10 communal hibachi tables where the entertaining chefs cook your meal right before your eyes; from the kitchen comes an assortment of bento boxes and traditional cooked dishes, but if you're looking for something different, check out the appetizer list.

Il Borgo S   21 | 20 | 22 | $38 |

1381A Beverly Rd. (bet. Elm St. & Old Dominion Dr.),
McLean, VA, 703-893-1400

⊠ Colorful banners welcome guests to this "festive"
McLean Italian; though ebullient Vittorio Testa has
departed, the same kitchen crew continues to turn out
"rich" pastas and "gourmet" dishes served by familiar,
"knowledgeable" waiters; it remains to be seen, however,
whether this old-timer can maintain its solid standards
and even win over the minority that has relegated its
"overdone" fare and "noisier-than-comfortable" room to
the "Lawrence Welk crowd."

Il Cigno   ▽ 19 | 18 | 18 | $34 |

Lake Anne Plaza, 1617 Washington Plaza N. (Shore Dr.),
Reston, VA, 703-471-0121

⊠ At its best for "alfresco dining" while "enjoying the view"
of the jet fountain on Lake Anne, this "reliable" Reston
Italian is also a "frequent stop" among the business
crowd, which congregates over "solid, if unexciting", fare;
the interior still has a modish Mediterranean feel to it, but the
"lovely" terrace now sports a "huge" (and "controversial")
tent, which "spoils" the outdoor experience for some.

Il Pizzico   23 | 17 | 21 | $29 |

Suburban Park, 15209 Frederick Rd. (Gude Dr.), Rockville, MD,
301-309-0610

⊠ "From the greeting" to the "fresh herbs growing on the
table" to the "high-quality" Italian cooking, "this place has
style", in sharp contrast to its Rockville "strip-mall" exterior;
headlining the menu are "simple", "wonderful" "homemade
pastas", while the specials are always "inspired", delivered
by "caring" waiters at a "more than fair price"; the only
drawback: trying to nab a table in the "intimate" room.

Il Radicchio S   17 | 14 | 15 | $22 |

223 Pennsylvania Ave., SE (C St.), 202-547-5114
1801 Clarendon Blvd. (Rhodes St.), Arlington, VA,
703-276-2627

⊠ "Good for a filling meal for not too much money", this
"no-nonsense" pair of Italian spaghetterias on Capitol Hill
and in Arlington serves its purpose with "all-you-can-eat
pasta" tossed with a "wide choice of sauces", "yummy,
wood-fired pizzas" and "tasty salads"; though it's "not
a place to take someone you want to impress" and the
service can be, shall we say, "lazy", it works for many as
an "informal" "standby."

I Matti S   20 | 17 | 18 | $32 |

2436 18th St., NW (bet. Belmont & Columbia Rds.),
202-462-8844

⊠ Habitués relish the "perfect mix of people-watching and
pasta" at this open-to-the-street Adams Morgan trattoria

"with buzz", which turns out "flavorful", "stylish" Northern Italian fare in "lively" surroundings; foes, however, complain about a "completely unremarkable experience", noting that "Galileo's Roberto Donna is no longer involved."

Inn at Glen Echo S   18 | 19 | 19 | $35

6119 Tulane Ave. (MacArthur Blvd.), Glen Echo, MD, 301-229-2280

◪ Overlooking Glen Echo Park, this "rustic" country "roadhouse" "feels like it's 100 miles" away from DC, making a meal out on the "pretty" deck a "treat" for a diverse clientele of families, business types and bikers; the Eclectic menu "features seasonal vegetables and appealing choices of meat, poultry and fish", while the bar (with live jazz on Sunday nights) reminds some of "*Cheers*", but critics feel the food's "a mixed bag."

INN AT LITTLE WASHINGTON S   29 | 28 | 29 | VE

Main & Middle Sts., Washington, VA, 540-675-3800

◪ "Two perfectionists" – Patrick O'Connell and Reinhardt Lynch – treat "dining as an art form" at their "exquisite" Virginia country inn, and it shows, as this "unequalled star" has again been voted No. 1 for Food, Decor and Service in the Washington area; the owners have long made it their mission to ensure that "each guest enjoys the whole evening", from the moment they step into the "over-the-top" "fantasy" setting through every bite of the "magical" New American courses served by an "exceptional" staff; "could any meal be worth this much money?" – this one is.

i Ricchi   25 | 23 | 23 | $49

1220 19th St., NW (bet. M & N Sts.), 202-835-0459

◪ "Recreating Tuscany" in the Golden Triangle, this "classy" country villa is a "premier" "fine-dining establishment" showcasing "outstanding" Northern Italian fare – from the "obscenely good breads" to the "rich risotto" and "luscious" pastas to the wood-fired *bistecca alla Fiorentina* and "super" regional wines – in "fancy" environs tended to by "knowledgeable", if "stuffy", servers; those who "love" it "wish they could eat here every day", but dissenters who find it "overrated" concede that its occasional "slips" would likely be noticed less if the tabs "weren't so pricey."

Islander Caribbean S   ▽ 18 | 13 | 18 | $22

1201 U St., NW (12th St.), 202-234-4971

◪ Trinidadian Addie Green, a "DC institution", presides over this "fun", festive Caribbean enclave on U Street, a bastion of "sophisticated island cooking"; order a "colorful, tropical drink" "with an umbrella", then sample an array of "tasty", "homemade" appetizers and entrees (including the "best plantains around" and "fabulous fish and stewed meats"), but better "get there an hour before you're hungry", as the joint operates in a decidedly leisurely manner.

Jaipur S
　　　　　　　　　　　　　　　　　　– – – M
9401 Lee Hwy. (Circle Woods Dr.), Fairfax, VA, 703-766-1111
As colorful as the Pink City for which it's named, this upscale
new Fairfax Indian reflects the noted culture and traditions
of the capital of the northern state of Rajasthan with its
brightly hued furnishings and rich cooking; inspired by the
cuisine reserved for the ruling Moghuls (exemplified by
such flavorful dishes as Jaipuri lamb), the varied menu
also includes many other regional specialties.

JALEO S
　　　　　　　　　　　　　　　　23 21 19 $29
480 Seventh St., NW (E St.), 202-628-7949
7271 Woodmont Ave. (Elm St.), Bethesda, MD,
301-913-0003
◪ What gives these "cool" "crowd-pleasers" in the Penn
Quarter and Bethesda their "amazing staying power"? –
more than 1,500 surveyors say it's their "upbeat" energy,
"delectable" Spanish tapas that are "fun-to-share" ("every
pick is better than the last", so have a "little of everything")
and "superb" Iberian wines; of course, the "downside" of
their raging success is the "frustrating" mob scene ("wish
they took reservations"), though the "best" sangria going
makes "waiting" in the "jam-packed bar" more bearable.

Jean-Michel S
　　　　　　　　　　　　　　　　22 19 22 $43
Wildwood Shopping Ctr., 10223 Old Georgetown Rd.
(Democracy Blvd.), Bethesda, MD, 301-564-4910
◪ Jean-Michel Farret's Bethesda namesake is like that
"slightly formal but congenial uncle, the one who taught you
the proper way to hold a wineglass", the one who would
know that these "traditional French dishes are done just
right"; the "older" clientele appreciates the "reliable, high-
quality" classics prepared here and feels right at home in the
"genteel" quarters, so even if some fuss about "snippy"
treatment, few can forgo that "unforgettable" soufflé.

Jefferson S
　　　　　　　　　　　　　　▽ 23 24 24 $51
The Jefferson, 1200 16th St., NW (M St.), 202-833-6206
■ Considered by some insiders as the "ultimate power-
lunch spot", this "cozy" hotel dining room keeps a low
profile, though its "elegant" New American fare, "intimate
nooks" and unobtrusive service are well known among the
Capitol cognoscenti; its "hushed, historic" atmosphere
also makes the formal afternoon tea a "treat", while sipping
a cocktail in the urbane bar is a "very Washingtonian"
thing to do; N.B. for special events and holidays, the
kitchen recreates dinners from the Thomas Jefferson era.

Jeffrey's at the Watergate S
　　　　　　　　　　　　　　22 23 22 $53
Swissôtel - The Watergate, 2560 Virginia Ave., NW
(New Hampshire Ave.), 202-298-4455
◪ Despite hosting "too many Texans" (including Dubya)
and naming some menu items after the Administration

bigwigs who order them regularly (such as Secretary Evans salad and Condi Rice lemon tart), not to mention its location in a Nixon-era "landmark", this "sophisticated" Southwestern-flavored hotel dining room near the Kennedy Center garners bipartisan support; followers champion the "interesting", "carefully prepared" dishes that pay tribute to the Lone Star State and the "lovely views of the Potomac River", but opponents find it too "impersonal."

Jerry's Seafood   25   13   21 $38

9364 Lanham Severn Rd. (¾ mi. east of Rte. 495, exit 20A), Seabrook, MD, 301-577-0333

◪ Though the tables are now covered with tablecloths, nothing else has changed at this "friendly" Seabrook seafood house – to the great relief of its fans; still starring on the concise menu is the 'crab bomb', a "serious" 10-ounce cake made from the "best" jumbo lump meat, along with "wonderfully" "fresh" fish; wallet-watchers may quibble that given its "out-of-the-way" locale and "rustic" setting, the prices are too "high", but foodies promise it's "worth every penny."

Joe's Noodle House S   18   8   13 $15

1488C Rockville Pike (Congressional Ln.), Rockville, MD, 301-881-5518

◪ Anticipate "many adventures on the menu" at this "no-frills" Rockville "find", whose "authentic" Chinese food (along with some Thai and Korean dishes) attracts a large Asian clientele, as well as locals looking for a "good, cheap" meal; the cooking's the "real deal" here, so don't expect the "spices" to be "toned down" for the American palate (take the chile pepper designations on the menu seriously); doubters, however, shrug "not as exciting as we thought it'd be."

Johnny's Half Shell   23   17   20 $34

2002 P St., NW (bet. 20th & 21st Sts.), 202-296-2021

◪ "Beautifully simple decor and simply great food" is the story at this "fresh and sassy" Dupont Circle seafood bistro whose "dreamy" "crispy oysters", inviting "little touches" (like the homemade malt vinegar for the "great" fries) and "refreshingly casual" vibe have many admirers clamoring for a seat; nitpickers, on the other hand, find the portions "too small" and gripe that the "lovely lighting" doesn't do enough to dress up the "spare" setting.

jordans   –   –   –   E

Ronald Reagan Bldg., 1300 Pennsylvania Ave., NW (13th St.), 202-589-1223

Downtown's "trendy" new power player, Michael Jordan's New American fine-dining venture in the Ronald Reagan Building recasts Palomino Euro Bistro's bi-level circular space into a sophisticated lounge upstairs and a suave ("beige everywhere") dining room below; captained by Daniel Pochron (ex Citronelle), the kitchen turns out "fine, if not memorable", modernized meat and seafood classics; early scouts are looking for a "slam dunk", but some feel the servers are "still warming up."

Kabob Palace ●S

▽ 21 | 5 | 11 | $11

2315 S. Eads St. (23rd St.), Arlington, VA, 703-486-3535

◪ Kebab lovers tailgate cabdrivers to this Crystal City pit stop for "excellent" skewers and other "super-good", "authentic" Pakistani dishes; less palatial surroundings would be hard to find, but the "made-to-order" fare is a "bargain" and provides a culinary trip to "another world"; those who find the ambiance "not particularly welcoming", though, "get it to go."

Kazan

22 | 19 | 22 | $33

Cambridge Corner Shopping Ctr., 6813 Redmond Dr. (Chain Bridge Rd.), McLean, VA, 703-734-1960

■ "Warm and inviting", McLean's "Turkish delight" offers some of the "best" Mediterranean food around, and it's only enhanced by the owner's "personal touch"; look forward to "tasty" meze and "tantalizing" kebabs ("never had such juicy lamb" and "love the swordfish" too), served in an interior that's "attractive" enough "for a business lunch" or out on the new year-round garden patio; factor in "courteous" service and "good-value" prices and it's easy to see why it's been an "old favorite" for decades.

Kaz Sushi Bistro

24 | 18 | 20 | $35

1915 I St., NW (bet. 19th & 20th Sts.), 202-530-5500

◪ Both "cutting-edge" and "traditional", this "artful" Japanese bistro in the Golden Triangle is renowned for its "exemplary sushi" ("try the fabulous salmon with mango sauce") and "original" "East meets West" "little dishes" based on "unusual pairings" (like the "decadent plum wine–infused duck foie gras"); though the decor's a bit "sparse", purists insist that's "the way it should be" so that "nothing distracts from the superb fish"; still, detractors feel it "doesn't live up to its stellar reputation."

KINKEAD'S S

27 | 24 | 25 | $51

2000 Pennsylvania Ctr., 2000 Pennsylvania Ave., NW (I St.), 202-296-7700

■ Voted yet again Washington's Most Popular restaurant, chef-owner Bob Kinkead's "winning" New American brasserie is lauded for maintaining its "high standards"; as Foggy Bottom's "power food" HQ, it's a "professionally run" "special-occasion" destination that delivers "absolutely astounding" seafood dishes and a "superior" wine list in a "supercharged atmosphere"; "a class act in all aspects", it's "hands down" one of the "best" establishments in the capital, even if "the elite" get "preferential" treatment.

Konami [S] ▽ 22 | 19 | 21 | $27

8221 Leesburg Pike (Chain Bridge Rd.), Tysons Corner, VA, 703-821-3400

◪ In bustling Tysons Corner, this "convenient" neighborhood Japanese provides a "serene" refuge with its "pleasant" garden dining; the sushi is very "decent", though "not the best", but the prices are "reasonable" (the "box lunches" are a "great value") and the staff "young and eager."

Kramerbooks & Afterwords Cafe ◐ [S] 17 | 15 | 15 | $21

1517 Connecticut Ave., NW (bet. Dupont Circle & Q St.), 202-387-1462

◪ A "great hangout for the college and twentysomething crowd", especially on weekends (when it's open 24 hours), this "funky" Dupont Circle bookstore/cafe has long been a "DC favorite", offering groupies a "can't-miss combo of books, people-watching" and varied live entertainment; there is a "basic" American menu, but "don't expect great food", particularly at a place that serves cocktails by the pitcher; it's "always crowded" "late at night, so be prepared for a wait during that busy time."

Krupin's [S] 18 | 10 | 15 | $18

4620 Wisconsin Ave., NW (bet. Brandywine & Chesapeake Sts.), 202-686-1989

◪ While longtimers "miss Mel", the late founder of this Upper NW "time warp", his brother Morty is upholding the family tradition by presiding over some of DC's "best" Jewish-style provisions – matzo ball soup, corned beef and pastrami, and "smoked fish fresh from Brooklyn" – while trading "insults" with the customers; though it brings back "nostalgic moments" for some "lost New Yorkers", "disappointed" mavens sniff a mere "shadow of a real NY deli."

Kuna ▽ 22 | 17 | 21 | $26

1324 U St., NW (bet. 13th & 14th Sts.), 202-797-7908

■ Italophiles marvel over the "unbelievably low prices for a pleasant dinner" at this "refreshing" "addition to the New U" scene, where the ever-changing menu "doesn't over-promise" but does deliver "farmhouse cooking at its best"; "hospitable" Mark Giuricich (the owner, "chief cook and dishwasher") cultivates a "personal" atmosphere and always manages to find a "minute to jam" with his patrons, who plead "we really like this place, but it's so small, so please don't tell anyone about it."

LA BERGERIE [S] 25 | 22 | 24 | $49

218 N. Lee St. (bet. Cameron & Queen Sts.), Alexandria, VA, 703-683-1007

■ "Formal yet comfortable", this "understated" Old Town grande dame continues to "beautifully present" "refined"

Classic French cuisine in a "timeless" setting; the menu is as "outstanding" as ever, but now it's been "enlivened" with some modern updates (don't worry, the "wonderful soufflés" are still available), while the "attentive", "professional" staff still tends to all details; long cherished by Alexandria's "old guard", it has been discovered in recent years by their offspring as a "sophisticated" way to "impress a date."

La Brasserie S

21 | 17 | 20 | $38

239 Massachusetts Ave., NE (bet. 2nd & 3rd Sts.), 202-546-9154

◪ See "senators at lunch, neighbors at dinner" at this "little bit of France" on Capitol Hill, where a "warm-weather" meal on the "beautiful, flower-filled" terrace transports one to Paris; devotees are always happy to dine on its "very good" bistro renditions, but dissenters who find the fare "lackluster" ("once fine, it's now predictable") judge it "not worth the price."

La Chaumiere

24 | 23 | 23 | $42

2813 M St., NW (bet. 28th & 29th Sts.), 202-338-1784

◪ Reminiscent of a French country inn, this Georgetown Gallic is "a wintertime treat when the fireplace is roaring", but at any time of year visitors will be rewarded with rustic, "old-fashioned" cooking like "delicious" quenelles and "fantastic cassoulet", as well as "hard-to-find" dishes such as calf's brains and tripe; the few who find it "stodgy" and "not inviting unless you're known", however, caution that the "warmth ends at the hearth."

La Colline

22 | 19 | 22 | $43

400 N. Capitol St., NW (bet. D & E Sts.), 202-737-0400

◪ Perennially a "safe bet for a business power gathering on Capitol Hill" or a "political fund-raiser", this "lobbyists' haunt" pleases with "dependable", "not too complicated" Gallic food, enough "space between the tables" and smooth service; virtually everyone agrees that owner and "schmoozer"-in-chief Paul Zucconi is a "charmer", but some gourmands dismiss the "tired, boring" "French fare without flair."

La Côte d'Or Cafe S

22 | 21 | 21 | $45

6876 Lee Hwy. (bet. Washington St. & Westmoreland Rd.), Falls Church, VA, 703-538-3033

◪ One of the few upscale French options in Northern Virginia, this "welcoming" bistro is a "great place to celebrate a birthday" or "just blow your diet in a spectacular way", satisfying with "delicious, if girth-enhancing", cooking turned out in a series of "cute" "rabbit-warren" rooms; adding to the merriment is the "caring" owner, who "sings on occasion", but frugal sorts complain that it's too "pricey" considering the "hit-or-miss" dishes and "oddball" (read: "low-rent") Falls Church location.

Lafayette **S**   – | – | – | VE

Hay Adams Hotel, 800 16th St., NW (H St.), 202-638-2570
From this legendary dining room in the Hay Adams Hotel, you can get a close-up view of the White House – that is, if you're not too busy scoping out the A-list clientele; recently reopened, with its timeless elegance fully restored, its New American menu (with a European accent) refreshed and its seasoned staff as poised and dignified as ever, this landmark powerhouse beckons anew.

La Ferme **S**   22 | 24 | 22 | $45

7107 Brookville Rd. (Shepherd St.), Chevy Chase, MD,
301-986-5255
◪ "Though it feels dated", this "lovely" French farmhouse in Chevy Chase "delivers" "reliable", "traditional" "country" fare in a room appointed with "beautiful" flowers and a "blazing fireplace" or out on the "delightful" terrace; the staff "treats" everyone "well", making it a "comfortable" retreat for its "wealthy" (predominantly "older") clientele; the younger demographic, however, frowns upon the "unimaginative" cooking and "stodgy" ambiance.

La Fourchette **S**   21 | 18 | 20 | $35

2429 18th St., NW (bet. Columbia & Kalorama Rds.),
202-332-3077
◪ Supping at this veritably French bistro in Adams Morgan is "like having dinner with family – and the family is glad you're there"; it's "quaint", "cramped, loud and rushed, but somehow it all combines to form a lively canvas for great, authentic French cuisine", which explains why it's been a "solid" "favorite for more than 20 years."

La Madeleine
French Bakery & Café **S**   16 | 16 | 13 | $17

3000 M St., NW (30th St.), 202-337-6975
7607 Old Georgetown Rd. (Commerce Ln.), Bethesda, MD,
301-215-9142
Mid-Pike Plaza, 11858 Rockville Pike (Montrose Rd.),
Rockville, MD, 301-984-2270
500 King St. (Pitt St.), Alexandria, VA, 703-739-2854
Bailey's Crossroads, 5861 Crossroads Center Way
(Columbia & Leesburg Pikes), Falls Church, VA, 703-379-5551
1833 Fountain Dr. (bet. Baron Cameron Ave. &
New Dominion Pkwy.), Reston, VA, 703-707-0704
1915C Chain Bridge Rd. (Leesburg Pike), Tysons Corner, VA,
703-827-8833
◪ Heavy traffic at these "faux" French bakery/cafes signals that there's a "lot to be said about a reliable chain that serves fresh bread with marmalade as a free attraction" to begin a "hearty" meal, provides a "comfortable" place for socializing and is priced "reasonably"; on the other hand, there's less to be said about the "controlled pandemonium" of the cafeteria lines and the "disorganized" help.

La Miche   23   20   22 $45
7905 Norfolk Ave. (St. Elmo Ave.), Bethesda, MD, 301-986-0707
◪ When new chef-owner Jason Tepper took over this "charming" bit of provincial "France in Bethesda", he pledged to keep preparing the "great" bourgeois "classics" exactly the way the "high-brow, blue-hair" clientele likes them; while he's smart enough not to fix what isn't broken (retaining the "dependable" kitchen crew and "gracious" staff), he also plans to offer more seafood choices with updated sauces; N.B. the post-*Survey* change may outdate the above Food score.

Landini Brothers S   20   18   19 $36
115 King St. (Union St.), Alexandria, VA, 703-836-8404
◪ "Pretend the host" at this "roomy" Old Town Italian fixture "has been your best friend for nearly 30 years – everybody does" (from movers and shakers to "tourists"), and it's easy to do so because the staff is so "jovial"; the "clubby" feel ("downstairs is the place to be") and traditional "home cooking" win it many friends, though bashers dismiss it as a "trap" and only go with "out-of-town guests whose tastes aren't too discriminating."

L'AUBERGE CHEZ FRANÇOIS S   28   27   28 $59
332 Springvale Rd. (Beach Mill Rd.), Great Falls, VA, 703-759-3800
■ A "magical" "pleasure from apéritif to soufflé", this "truly special" Country French "treat" set on "lovely" bucolic grounds in Great Falls has "epitomized" "romantic" dining for generations; in "cozily" rustic quarters whose "charm can't be beat" and out in the "glorious" garden, an "informed" but "not snotty" staff brings to table "hearty", "outstanding" Alsatian dishes; despite the "reservations hassle", the "experience as a whole" is so "superb" that you're sure to "leave feeling tingly" all over.

L'AUBERGE PROVENÇALE S   25   26   25 $66
13630 Lord Fairfax Hwy. (Rte. 50), Boyce, VA, 540-837-1375
◪ "French country dining with a Virginia hunt country address" is the appeal of this "delightful escape" set in a "lovely", antique-filled manor house circa 1753 that "oozes charm" and "easy elegance"; devotees laud the "rich" dishes and "polished" service and recommend an "overnight stay" in the inn (if only to "get the fantastic breakfast"), but a "disappointed" minority feels it "doesn't live up to its reputation."

Lauriol Plaza S   21   21   17 $25
1835 18th St., NW (S St.), 202-387-0035
◪ "Packed nightly", this "fun" Dupont Circle East "hot spot" hosts a perpetual Latin "fiesta" attended by the "beautiful, young people" (as well as "suburbanites cashing in on the [free] parking") who soak up the scene on the "irresistible"

rooftop deck; the "wait" is "ridiculous" ("you could get a law degree in the time it takes to get a table on the weekend"), but aficionados who praise the "tasty" Mexican-Spanish dishes and "sneakily strong margaritas" are clearly willing to endure all to join the action.

Lavandou S   21 19 19 $38

3321 Connecticut Ave., NW (bet. Macomb & Newark Sts.), 202-966-3002

Bringing "a ray of Provençal sunshine" to Cleveland Park, this "intimate" "neighborhood" bistro pleases with its "full-flavored" French fare and "pretty" decorative touches; habitués advise that it's "best to go" "for lunch" or early on "weekday evenings", when it's "quieter" and the service is less "rushed", but critics who object to "heavy-handed seasoning" at any time dub it "more of a Lavandon't."

LEBANESE TAVERNA S   23 18 20 $26

2641 Connecticut Ave., NW (bet. Calvert St. & Woodley Rd.), 202-265-8681

Congressional Plaza, 1605 Rockville Pike (Congressional Ln.), Rockville, MD, 301-468-9086

1101 S. Joyce St. (Army Navy Dr.), Arlington, VA, 703-415-8681

5900 Washington Blvd. (McKinley Rd.), Arlington, VA, 703-241-8681

"Friendly and inviting", this "wonderful" family-run chainlet is a "must stop on the ethnic dining circuit" due to its "delicious", "properly garlicky" Middle Eastern cooking; its broad menu and Lebanese sampler platters work for groups, kids and "picky eaters" alike, service is "cordial" and the tabs "won't break the bank", but some surveyors feel that as it expands, the dishes are starting to taste "a little prefab" while the service is becoming "slower."

Legal Sea Foods   19 16 18 $32

2020 K St., NW (bet. 20th & 21st Sts.), 202-496-1111
704 Seventh St., NW (bet. G & H Sts.), 202-347-0007 S
Montgomery Mall, 7101 Democracy Blvd. (I-270), Bethesda, MD, 301-469-5900 S
2301 Jefferson Davis Hwy. (23rd St.), Arlington, VA, 703-415-1200 S
Ronald Reagan Washington Nat'l Airport (Terminal C), Arlington, VA, 703-413-9810 S
Tysons Galleria, 2001 International Dr. (Chain Bridge Rd.), Tysons Corner, VA, 703-827-8900 S

Schools of supporters rave about the "straightforward New England–style seafood" prepared by this MA-based chain, notably its "great chowdah, fried clams and raw bar"; critics, however, carp about "basic food at above-basic prices" dished out in a "corporate"-feeling atmosphere but concede that "if you can't be in Boston, this mass-production operation can fill the need."

Le Gaulois | 23 | 20 | 20 | $36 |

1106 King St. (bet. Fayette & Henry Sts.), Alexandria, VA, 703-739-9494

◪ "Just what a French bistro should be" according to its loyal coterie, this Old Town "sleeper" features a "deep menu of classic dishes and seasonal treats" (the cassoulet is a "standout") at a "good" value; in the wintertime, opt for "civilized" dining by the "fireplace" (where "conversation" is actually possible), and in the summer, eat out in the "pretty garden", but expect to encounter that Gallic "attitude" that some consider "rude."

Le Petit Mistral [S] | 22 | 17 | 20 | $43 |

6710 Old Dominion Dr. (Chain Bridge Rd.), McLean, VA, 703-748-4888

◪ McLean's "cozy French retreat" is a "bustling, intimate" "storefront" whose "haute" bistro fare reflects a "lot of care in the preparation"; devotees cherish it as "a *petit* treasure" and especially tout the "great" weekday lunch and early-dinner prix fixe "values", but a few detractors maintain that its "success has bred indifference in the food and service."

Le Refuge | 23 | 19 | 20 | $39 |

127 N. Washington St. (bet. Cameron & King Sts.), Alexandria, VA, 703-548-4661

◪ With enough "genuine" French cafe "ambiance to satisfy any Francophile", this Old Town "favorite" is a "wonderfully quaint" place to savor "traditional, satisfying" bourgeois cooking; habitués expect to have "their neighbor's elbow in their plate" (these quarters are "claustrophobic") and take the "rushed" pace in stride, but critics sniff it "hasn't had a new idea since the '80s."

Le Relais [S] | 25 | 23 | 23 | $52 |

Seneca Square Shopping Ctr., 1025 Seneca Rd. (Georgetown Pike), Great Falls, VA, 703-444-4060

◪ A "dream come true" for sophisticated Northern Virginia suburbanites, this "dressy" Great Falls French "treasure" "stylishly" showcases "marvelous" dishes that "taste as good as they look", along with a "fabulous wine list", in "beautiful, contemporary" surroundings; though the prices are on the "regal" side, its affluent clientele is willing to pay for such "top quality", even if a few respondents report an occasionally "ragged" performance.

Le Rivage [S] | 18 | 19 | 20 | $37 |

1000 Water St., SW (9th St.), 202-488-8111

◪ Arena Stage subscribers anoint this veteran New French "favorite" "the restaurant of choice" on the SW waterfront, "depending" upon it for "well-prepared" seafood served by a staff that "makes one feel special" (and pays attention to curtain times); the dishes may "lack imagination", but

the "wonderful" view of the sunset and the boats in the
marina without doubt make them taste that much better.

Les Halles ●◐ S   19 17 17 $37
1201 Pennsylvania Ave., NW (12th St.), 202-347-6848
◪ "Legitimately French", this "convivial" "late-night"
Downtown meat market pulls off the "authentic brasserie"
look, providing a "charming" backdrop for "comforting
classics" like hanger steak with "perfect pommes frites";
it's a "reliable" source for a "protein kick", plus it's "fun"
to watch the walking "scenery" from the sidewalk tables,
but you better "bring patience" (and a "megaphone") and
brace yourself for "Parisian snobbery."

Le Tarbouche   23 24 22 $40
1801 K St., NW (18th St.), 202-331-5551
■ "Intriguingly" appointed with a luminous blue-hued, tent-
ceilinged dining room, "romantic nooks" and a "sexy",
"candlelit" bar, this K Street "scene" is a "beautiful",
"exotic" place for a rendezvous; the "bold" yet "refined"
Nouvelle Mediterranean dishes, based on "unusual spices
and ingredients", are presented "with style" by a "polite"
staff, making for a "really interesting diversion."

Levante's S   17 17 16 $26
1320 19th St., NW (Dupont Circle), 202-293-3244
7262 Woodmont Ave. (Elm St.), Bethesda, MD, 301-657-2441
◪ Off Dupont Circle and in Bethesda, this pair of popular
gathering spots looks to the Levant for its "expansive"
Mediterranean menu, bright blue-and-yellow color scheme
and "lively" sidewalk seating; the "fun little pizzas" called
pidas are crowd-pleasers, but "everything else is quite
dull", the interior is "distractingly noisy" and the service
runs "hot and cold"; the bottom line according to many: "if
you can't sit outside, don't bother."

LIGHTFOOT S   22 26 21 $38
11 N. King St. (Market St.), Leesburg, VA, 703-771-2233
◪ Housed in a "gorgeously restored bank" in Leesburg, this
"roomy yet private"-feeling New American cafe shows off
chef/co-owner Ingrid Gustafson's "deft touch" with the
"freshest ingredients" (she runs a farmer's market), which
results in "serious food out in the boondocks"; "somewhat
chilly" service notwithstanding, gourmands are happy to
"indulge in some top-notch, albeit a bit pricey", courses.

Little Saigon S   ▽ 23 13 18 $22
*6218B Wilson Blvd. (Patrick Henry Dr.), Falls Church, VA,
703-536-2633*
◪ Falls Church's Vietnamese community knows about the
"absolutely authentic" cooking at this "hole-in-the-wall"
near the Eden Center, even if many food lovers have yet to
discover it; the "interesting and extensive" menu runs the

gamut from "great jicama rolls" to "excellent fish", offering countless "great-value" possibilities that make it easy to overlook the lack of decor.

Little Viet Garden S   20 15 17 $20
3012 Wilson Blvd. (Garfield St.), Arlington, VA, 703-522-9686
◢ "Twinkly lights" around the "festive" garden patio help make Clarendon's young gentry "forget that it's surrounded by busy streets" at this buzzing Vietnamese venue; at a "good price", customers get "fresh food that isn't too heavy" ("love the lemongrass chicken" and "good" spring rolls), but skeptics who find it "a bit hit-or-miss" "wonder why there are few Vietnamese customers" here.

Louisiana Express Co. S   20 9 16 $19
4921 Bethesda Ave. (Arlington Rd.), Bethesda, MD, 301-652-6945
◢ Proving that folks will "gladly sit on straight-back chairs" in "shanty" digs for a "quick dose" of "yummy" Bayou cooking that "packs a punch" (notably the "goody, goody gumbo"), this low-down spot is "unlike anything else in Bethesda" and "you won't mistake it for something by Emeril" either; amenities are few, but it delivers a "bargain taste of Louisiana."

Luigino S   21 19 20 $36
1100 New York Ave., NW (bet. 11th & 12th Sts.), 202-371-0595
◢ Italian food mavens "don't dismiss" this "bona fide" citizen of the red, white and green just because it's so convenient to the Convention Center goings-on and looks a bit "antiseptic" from the sidewalk; inside is an "enjoyable lunch spot (it's much less lively at dinner)" where one can "sit by the window and watch the passersby" while dining on "wonderful" pastas (if you're eating alone, you'll feel "comfortable" at the convivial counter); a few dissenters, however, report food as "uneven" as the service.

Luna Grill & Diner   18 16 17 $19
1301 Connecticut Ave., NW (N St.), 202-835-2280
4024 28th St. S. (Quincy St.), Arlington, VA, 703-379-7173 S
◢ "Diner food with aspirations" is what to expect at this pair of "cool" American eateries off Dupont Circle and in Arlington, where the dishes range from "greasy to organic", as exemplified by its "addictive" sweet potato fries; its young and hungry regulars advise "sticking with the blue- or green-plate specials", slung by servers who are "cute", "cocky" or "characters" (or all of the above), but critics cavil that "nothing quite tastes as it sounds" on the menu.

MAESTRO S   27 28 28 $69
Ritz-Carlton Tysons Corner, 1700 Tysons Blvd. (International Dr.), Tysons Corner, VA, 703-917-5498
■ Open only since last year, this "exquisite" "gourmet heaven" at Tysons Corner's Ritz-Carlton is already a "top

contender" in the "fine-dining" stakes; "genius chef" Fabio Trabocchi, who dares to "take risks", orchestrates a "world-class" "symphony of Italian flavors" from a "gorgeous open kitchen" that only "adds to the evening entertainment"; enhanced by a "luxuriously" appointed space and an "impeccable" staff, it adds up to an "ultimate dining performance" that's "worth every penny" of admission.

Majestic Cafe 🅂   23 21 21 $36
911 King St. (Patrick St.), Alexandria, VA, 703-837-9117
◪ "Chef Susan Lindeborg does it again", this time in Old Town, where she has "re-created an atmospheric" art deco–style cafe from the "WWII" era; it's a "chic" spot to "be seen in" while partaking of "some of the classiest" Southern-accented New American cooking "you'll ever have" (save room for the "fabulous" old-fashioned layer cake); it may need to "work out a few kinks", but groupies already want to "sell our kitchen and eat every meal here."

MAKOTO 🅂   27 24 25 $53
4822 MacArthur Blvd., NW (Reservoir Rd.), 202-298-6866
■ Anticipate a "genuine Japanese experience" at this "peaceful little enclave" in the NW Palisades, designed for those "willing to be adventurous" (after removing their shoes); while the prix fixe menu offers a "great introduction for the novice", presenting a series of "tiny jewels", sushi connoisseurs swoon over the "sweet" morsels of raw fish that are "fresh beyond description"; legions attest that this is "as good as any place in Tokyo, at one third the price."

Malaysia Kopitiam 🅂   21 11 19 $21
1827 M St., NW (bet. 18th & 19th Sts.), 202-833-6232
◪ "A fascinating blend of Chinese and Indian" influences, among others, characterizes the "spicy appeal" of Malaysia, and at this "dumpy" Golden Triangle basement, the dishes "explode with scents and flavors"; the "caring", hospitable hosts want you to love their native cuisine, so follow their recommendations, or just point to what looks "interesting" in the "great picture-book menu"; enthusiasts insist that "everything is good" and pretty "cheap", thus it's hard to go wrong.

Mamma Lucia 🅂   19 12 17 $22
4976 Elm St. (bet. Arlington Rd. & Woodmont Ave.), Bethesda, MD, 301-907-3399
Olney Village Mart, 18224 Village Mart Dr. (Olney-Sandy Spring Rd.), Olney, MD, 301-570-9500
Federal Plaza, 12274 Rockville Pike (Twinbrook Pkwy.), Rockville, MD, 301-770-4894
◪ When you need to feed an SUV-load of "suburban" tykes "cheap and fast", this Italian trio "gets the job done" with its "decent" NY-style pizzas and "hearty", "surprisingly tasty" pastas; sure, they're usually "crowded" and "noisy"

and the service can be "haphazard", but it's an "easy, satisfying" pick for a "casual" meal, even if detractors quibble "nothing remarkable."

M & S Grill S   19 | 19 | 19 | $32
600 13th St., NW (F St.), 202-347-1500
☑ "Lunch reservations are hard to get" at this "clubby" Downtown grill because its "private booths", "comfortable" seats and "business" ambiance set just the right tone for the office crowd; though the service is "spotty", the American menu is "varied" and relatively "reasonably" priced, while the happy-hour bar-food deals and "even better martinis" make it equally marketable in the evening.

Mannequin Pis S   23 | 16 | 19 | $40
18064 Georgia Ave. (Olney-Sandy Spring Rd.), Olney, MD, 301-570-4800
☑ For a "touch of Brussels" in Olney, fans seek out this "small", "hard-to-find" bistro that "proves that Belgian cuisine can give French a run for its money" (Belgium "wins hands down on the beers"); you may well agree after "scarfing" down its "mouthwatering mussels" (prepared in 15 different ways) and pommes frites, though foes denounce "inconsistent" dishes served in "cramped", "chaotic" digs.

MARCEL'S S   26 | 25 | 25 | $58
2401 Pennsylvania Ave., NW (24th St.), 202-296-1166
■ Robert Wiedmaier's "brilliant", "inventive" French dishes tweaked with a Flemish flair (the "boudin blanc is incredible") and "lavishly presented" have earned him a devoted following at this "plush", "sophisticated" West End "star" that may "look stuffy, but isn't" (though it is "accoustically challenged"); he and his "courtly" crew woo guests with "tip-top wine selections", "great" live music nightly in the bar and even complimentary "limousine service to and from the Kennedy Center", while still keeping the focus "on the food."

Mar de Plata ◐ S   21 | 16 | 20 | $34
1410 14th St., NW (bet. P St. & Rhode Island Ave.), 202-234-2679
☑ A "welcome face on 14th Street" for Studio and Source Theatre ticket-holders, as well as Logan Circle denizens, this "warm, friendly" Spanish "find" features a simple setting but "flashy, provocative" tapas and seafood specialties; detractors, however, find the food and atmosphere "dull" and feel the staff "doesn't seem to care", adding that the "prices are pretentious for the area."

Market St. Bar & Grill S   20 | 19 | 20 | $38
Hyatt Regency Reston, 1800 Presidents St. (Market St.), Reston, VA, 703-709-6262
☑ "Better than average hotel food" is the word on this Reston fallback; everyone agrees that the New American

menu is "inventive", but whereas fans say it's "pleasant", foes counter it "doesn't always succeed" ("it tries too hard to be clever") and that combined with "inconsistent" service, it adds up to "mediocre fine dining"; P.S. the "live jazz" on weekends is worth checking out.

Mark's Duck House ◐ [S] 22 | 9 | 16 | $23

Wilson Ctr., 6184A Arlington Blvd. (Patrick Henry Dr.), Falls Church, VA, 703-532-2125

◪ One of the "most authentic Hong Kong–style" restaurants in Northern Virginia, this Annandale Chinese "dive" is patronized by knowledgeable "food lovers" (a "healthy majority" of whom are Asian), who gather to "discover exotic dishes" (ask for translations of the Chinese language listings) and to seek comfort in favorites like "delightful dim sum", "awesome Peking duck" and "excellent roast pig"; "don't expect a high-end setting, just great" fare.

Mark's Kitchen [S] – | – | – | I

7006 Carroll Ave. (Laurel St.), Takoma Park, MD, 301-270-1884

In Takoma Park, this funky "local favorite" run by committed, "kid-friendly" people offers an "unlikely but delightful menu" of American and Korean diner food, from a grilled-cheese-and-bacon sandwich and spinach salad to the "best kimchi" and teriyaki chicken (it's a "vegetarian delight" too); "not only is the food delicious, but it really feels like it's good for me", though it has become so discovered that some regulars "don't even dare try to get in for Sunday breakfast."

Matisse [S] 20 | 22 | 19 | $44

4934 Wisconsin Ave., NW (42nd St.), 202-244-5222

◪ "Lovely" and "romantic", this Upper NW New French–Mediterranean is considered a virtual standout given it's location in a "part of town" with many sophisticated diners but "few good places" to eat; while nobody disputes its "understated elegance", doubters who reserve judgment call it "potentially wonderful" – citing "decor that's better than the food", "service on the too neighborhood-y" side and "Downtown-fancy" prices.

Matuba [S] 22 | 14 | 19 | $25

4918 Cordell Ave. (Old Georgetown Rd.), Bethesda, MD, 301-652-7449

2915 Columbia Pike (Walter Reed Dr.), Arlington, VA, 703-521-2811

◪ "Dependable" and "unpretentious", this long-running Japanese twosome in Bethesda and Arlington makes sushi an everyday family affair, presenting "well-made" selections in "child-friendly", "feel-like-home" surroundings; the menu also offers a wide range of traditional cooked dishes and "good lunch-box specials", all at "reasonable" prices, but the cognoscenti sniff "volume over quality."

Maxim – – – E
1725 F St., NW (bet. 17th & 18th Sts.), 202-962-0280
"Infused with "old-world elegance"", this "hospitable" newcomer transports guests to Eastern Europe with its "interesting" Russian and Georgian specialties (including "amazing" broiled sturgeon and beef stroganoff) and exclusive regional wines; the convivial bar is a happy-hour fixture, while on Thursday–Saturday nights, when the musicians tune up and the crowd hits the dance floor, the "international" clientele shows Downtown how to party.

MCCORMICK & SCHMICK'S S 21 21 20 $37
1652 K St., NW (bet. 16th & 17th Sts.), 202-861-2233
7401 Woodmont Ave. (bet. Montgomery Ln. &
Old Georgetown Rd.), Bethesda, MD, 301-961-2626
11920 Democracy Dr. (bet. Discovery & Library Sts.),
Reston, VA, 703-481-6600
Ernst & Young Bldg., 8484 Westpark Dr. (Leesburg Pike),
Tysons Corner, VA, 703-848-8000
◼ Thirtysomethings socialize at the bar at these popular seafood houses over happy hour, while business meals are dignified by "old-school" dark-wood-and-brass environs and curtained booths; "afishionados" praise the kitchen's "sure hand" with "fresh" fish and the "fabulous" oysters, but critics crab that the operation is more "production-line than custom-order" and caution about a "hectic" pace and "sometimes hyper waiters."

Mediterranee 23 18 22 $35
3520 Lee Hwy. (Monroe St.), Arlington, VA, 703-527-7276
◼ Tucked away in Cherrydale, this "homey" French-Mediterranean is "surprisingly popular" due to its "generous servings" of "high-quality" dishes and "VIP treatment" for all guests; "from the street, you'd never guess what a charming place" it is inside – brightened with colorful curtains, tablecloths and dried flowers – leading devotees to urge "try it", because this is one "terrific neighborhood place" and a "great" value to boot.

Meiwah S 22 18 19 $24
1200 New Hampshire Ave., NW (M St.), 202-833-2888
◼ Geared to the West End's worker bees, this "busy" business-class Chinese is a "semi-fancy" "staple" that's a satisfying lunch option thanks to its broad menu of "distinctive" dishes with lots of "vegetarian picks"; fans recommend it as a "good place to experiment with unusual foods", but purists decry it as a "no-chopsticks" kind of place ("unless you ask for them") with "bland" chow.

MELROSE S 26 24 25 $53
Park Hyatt Washington, 1201 24th St., NW (M St.), 202-955-3899
■ "Efficient for lunch, delightful for dinner", this "light and airy" "special-occasion" destination in the West End is an

"oasis of calm", soothing with an "impressive" fountain-bedecked patio and "thoughtful" service; "talented" chef Brian McBride "does equally well cooking for a table of two or for a banquet", turning out "fabulous" New American fare; to the many fans who can't wait to "dine and dance the night away" on weekends, this "class act" "belies the hotel restaurant curse."

Mendocino Grille & Wine Bar S   22 20 21 $41
2917 M St., NW (bet. 29th & 30th Sts.), 202-333-2912
◪ California reveries are fulfilled at this modish, open-to-the-street Georgetown "gem" where "superbly chosen" "flights" of West Coast wines hook up with "innovative", "appealing" New American dishes suitable for a laid-back lunch or "romantic" dinner alike; even oenophiles let the "knowledgeable", if "slightly pretentious", staff advise on the "excellent" list, but note that at "peak times" the "poor acoustics" make it hard to "hear across the table."

Meskerem ◑S   22 19 18 $23
2434 18th St., NW (bet. Belmont & Columbia Rds.), 202-462-4100
◪ "Scooping up" "subtly spiced" savory stews with "spongy" injera bread is a "fun" "adventure" at this mainstream Ethiopian "escape" in Adams Morgan, where diners "eat with their hands"; many favor the "colorful, upper-level" space with low, cushioned seats or the window perches, both of which allow for prime "people-watching", but wherever your table, you'll be served by "beautiful", "helpful" waitresses (who may not "speak English well"), even if opponents "don't see what the fuss is about."

Meze ◑S   ▽ 19 18 17 $24
2437 18th St., NW (bet. Belmont & Columbia Rds.), 202-797-0017
◪ "Cheap grazing and chic people-gazing" draw in the "beautiful people" at this "hip" late-night "newcomer" in Adams Morgan; it's a "stylish", "sophisticated" haunt with "tasty" Mediterranean–Middle Eastern tapas (plus a few entrees) and an "excellent" martini menu, but those who proclaim it "mediocre all around" feel that it "isn't yet up to snuff."

Mezza 9 S   ▽ 21 20 20 $37
Hyatt Arlington, 1325 Wilson Blvd. (Nash St.), Arlington, VA, 703-276-8999
◪ A "great place to get to know someone" or to "seal" a business deal, this "peaceful", often "overlooked" Rosslyn hotel dining room pleases with an "interesting" Med menu full of "flavorful" "little dishes to share", while in the morning breakfast is "presented with all the niceties", from "fresh-squeezed orange juice" to "fresh-cut" flowers on the table; still, demanding types find it "not so exciting", especially for the price.

Michael's 18 | 18 | 18 | $38

Giant Shopping Ctr., 6825K Redmond Dr. (Old Dominion Dr.), McLean, VA, 703-288-4601

◪ Bringing a "chic and fresh" approach to a shopping mall in McLean, this upscale modern Italian features a "nice variety" of "solid" dishes enlivened by "exciting" specials; at its convivial bar and well-appointed tables, you'll always find tony locals meeting "old friends for good conversation", though detractors mark it down for "inconsistent" cooking.

Mimi's American Bistro 🌙 [S] 18 | 20 | 20 | $28

2120 P St., NW (bet. 21st & 22nd Sts.), 202-464-6464

◪ Offering a "good" meal and "campy" cabaret "for the price of one", this Mediterranean-flavored New American "gathering place" off Dupont Circle showcases a "talented" performing staff that "livens up" the joint with "show tunes" while serving your meal; boosters swear that somehow the "gimmick" works – as long as you're in the mood for "loud" singing and boisterous high jinks – but party-poopers grouch that the "novelty can't overcome the boring food."

Minh [S] – | – | – | I

2500 Wilson Blvd. (Cleveland St.), Arlington, VA, 703-525-2828

A multinational clientele fills the tables at this new Clarendon Vietnamese that's garnering good buzz thanks to its extensive menu of fresh, authentic dishes, served in a softly lit room that's as suitable for a business deal as a date.

Mi Rancho [S] 19 | 15 | 18 | $20

19725A Germantown Rd. (Middlebrook Rd.), Germantown, MD, 301-515-7480

8701 Ramsey Ave. (Cameron St.), Silver Spring, MD, 301-588-4872

◪ Amigos say that the "homestyle" Mexican food featured at this "bustling" pair in Germantown and Silver Spring is prepared with a "lot of heart", from the "standout" fajitas to the "so good *carne asada*"; "cheery" and "appropriately tacky", it's an "unpretentious" place that's "friendly to kids" and "reasonably priced", but fusspots are "not impressed."

Moby Dick ⊄ 21 | 7 | 13 | $13

1300 Connecticut Ave., NW (N St.), 202-833-9788

1070 31st St., NW (bet. K & M Sts.), 202-333-4400 [S]

7027 Wisconsin Ave. (Leland St.), Bethesda, MD, 301-654-1838 [S]

105 Market St. (Kentlands Blvd.), Gaithersburg, MD, 301-987-7770 [S]

Fairfax Town Ctr., 12154 Ox Rd. (Main St.), Fairfax, VA, 703-352-6226 [S]

6854 Old Dominion Dr. (Chain Bridge Rd.), Tysons Corner, VA, 703-448-8448 [S]

◪ "Looking for great kebabs?" – then sail over to one of these "no-nonsense", "eat 'n' run" Persian "dives" that are praised for their "fantastic" "fresh-baked bread", "delicious" hummus, "juicy" skewers and "awesome daily specials"; some find that the "family atmosphere of years past now seems more institutionalized", but plenty of addicts remain convinced that this is "about as good as it gets for fast, fresh", "cheap" grub.

Mon Ami Gabi [S] – | – | – | M

7239 Woodmont Ave. (Bethesda Ave.), Bethesda, MD, 301-654-1234

SRO since day one, this handsome, spacious French bistro evokes the Champs-Elysées with its belle epoque details and elegant rolling wine carts; the menu brims with well-priced Gallic classics (including seafood platters and eight versions of steak frites), while its prime Bethesda Row location guarantees opportune people-watching, especially from the sidewalk cafe.

Monocle 16 | 18 | 20 | $35

107 D St., NE (1st St.), 202-546-4488

◪ Say what you will about this "aging" institution and its "ordinary" American food, but where else can you see "nearly as many senators as at a State of the Union address" and eavesdrop on history being made while eating lunch?; of course, you may feel like an "outsider" in this "clubby" enclave, but just "say hi to Bob the bartender", order the "decent crab cakes" and settle in for some of the "best" people-watching in town.

Montmartre [S] 23 | 20 | 20 | $39

327 Seventh St., NW (Pennsylvania Ave.), 202-544-1244

■ At their "delightful addition to Capitol Hill", Bistrot Lepic alumni Stephane Lezla and Christopher Raynal add a Gallic accent to prettied-up quarters in a onetime post office; the "skillful" kitchen turns out "delicious" bistro classics as well as updated interpretations, enriching the neighborhood scene and helping its many new *amis* dining at its outdoor tables pretend that Pennsylvania Avenue runs through the Left Bank.

Morrison-Clark Inn [S] 24 | 24 | 23 | $48

Morrison-Clark Inn, 1015 L St., NW (bet. 11th St. & Massachusetts Ave.), 202-898-1200

◪ With its "lovely presentations", "charming Victorian drawing room feel" and "attentive" ways, this New American hotel dining room Downtown promises a "blissfully sedate", "grown-up" experience; to its enchanted coterie, it's "always a special place" to visit, but faultfinders report a "mixed performance."

MORTON'S OF CHICAGO [S] 24 | 21 | 23 | $53

3251 Prospect St., NW (Wisconsin Ave.), 202-342-6258
Washington Sq., 1050 Connecticut Ave., NW (L St.), 202-955-5997

(continued)

(continued)
MORTON'S OF CHICAGO
Reston Town Ctr., 11956 Market St. (Reston Pkwy.), Reston, VA, 703-796-0128
Fairfax Sq., 8075 Leesburg Pike (Aline Rd.), Tysons Corner, VA, 703-883-0800

■ Virtually synonymous with "great steaks", "mean" martinis and fine cigars, this national chain of prime "porterhouse palaces" exemplifies the "glorification of excess", hauling out steaks of such "monster size" that you may feel like you're in a "*Honey, I Shrunk the Kids*" sequel; well-hoofed carnivores who are members of the "boys' business club" sigh that the "tender" "beef is pure heaven", though a surprising number confess that the "unbelievable" Godiva cake is the "real reason" they come.

Mr. K's S　　23 | 23 | 24 | $44
2121 K St., NW (bet. 21st & 22nd Sts.), 202-331-8868

☑ "Ceremonious, leisurely and elegant", this haute Chinese relic on K Street with a "high-class French ambiance" is an "over-the-top" "anachronism" that's guaranteed to "amaze" guests; while a majority still considers it the "Cadillac of Chinese cuisine", foes yawn that it's just like "yesterday's newspaper", though even they concede that it might be worth the trip just for the "coffee brewed at your table via a fascinating mad scientist's contraption."

Murasaki S　　– | – | – | M
4620 Wisconsin Ave., NW (Brandywine St.), 202-966-0023

Upper NW sushi fanciers quickly discovered this "modest but pleasant" new find where Hiro Higashigama fashions "pristine" raw fish into interesting creations; Japanese diplomats and business types can also choose from a broad range of traditional appetizers, noodles and tempura dishes, while seriously adventurous eaters can request off-menu specialties (some featuring internal organs and other unfamiliar ingredients).

Myanmar S　　▽ 21 | 9 | 18 | $18
7810 Lee Hwy. (Hyson Ln.), Falls Church, VA, 703-289-0013

■ Treating curious appetites to a rare opportunity to sample Burmese cooking, this young émigré to Falls Church is a "tiny", family-run place with an "excellent" menu that lists more than 100 dishes ("what a variety!"); deftly integrating hot, sour, salty, bitter and sweet tastes, the dishes add up to an "unusual" and satisfying meal; in sum: "sweet smiles + great value = great find."

Mykonos Grill S　　21 | 21 | 20 | $30
Congressional Plaza, 121 Congressional Ln. (Rockville Pike), Rockville, MD, 301-770-5999

☑ Escape to the "Aegean Islands" at this sunny re-creation of a Hellenic cafe just off Rockville Pike, where the "pretty" setting provides an "evocative" (if "somewhat artificial") backdrop for "good" traditional Greek food and welcoming hospitality; despite some quibbles about "uninspired" cooking, most of its suburban "neighbors" appreciate this "reasonably priced" option.

Nam's of Bethesda [S] 20 | 16 | 20 | $25

4928 Cordell Ave. (Old Georgetown Rd.), Bethesda, MD, 301-652-2635

■ "Delicate" soups, "tasty" pho and "mouthwatering" grilled fish are just some of the "authentic", "wholly pleasurable" menu choices at this "quiet Vietnamese retreat" in Bethesda; the "courteous" servers make "helpful recommendations" about the "well-seasoned" specials and the tables are "nicely spaced", resulting in an "all-around good experience" that merits a return visit.

Nam Viet [S] 22 | 12 | 18 | $21

3419 Connecticut Ave., NW (bet. Macomb & Porter Sts.), 202-237-1015

1127 N. Hudson St. (Wilson Blvd.), Arlington, VA, 703-522-7110

■ "Years of eating experience confirm the remarkable consistency" of these Vietnamese veterans in Cleveland Park and Arlington, which comfort with "down-to-earth" cooking including "rich pho" soups, "delicious rice noodles with subtle sauces" and "crispy red snapper that'll thrill the whole table"; granted, the digs are "lackluster", but the "wonderful" food compensates, even if a few nitpickers find it "Americanized."

Napa Thai [S] – | – | – | M

4924 St. Elmo Ave. (Norfolk Ave.), Bethesda, MD, 301-986-8590

Though it's named after the Thai word for 'sky' (the walls are covered with images of faraway galaxies) and not the Napa Valley, the "pleasant patio" at this attractive Bethesda newcomer does give it a certain "Californian" feel; the "excellent" menu, however, is fairly traditional and offers a "wide variety of choices" (don't miss the "best chicken and coconut milk soup" or the "incredible deep-fried or steamed whole fish"), plus the service is "accommodating" and "polite."

Nathan's [S] 17 | 18 | 17 | $34

3150 M St., NW (Wisconsin Ave.), 202-338-2000

◪ Georgetown's "classic", "well-polished" saloon hosts a grown-up bar scene up front and a "dark and mysterious" back room, which provides the local gentry with a "perfect rendezvous" to conduct business or romance; regulars, who have long been content with the "solid" American pub grub (especially the "good" burgers), say that the new management's recently "upgraded" steakhouse menu is "igniting sparks of flavor", which may appease opponents who deem this DC "tradition" "undistinguished."

Negril ▽ 18 | 8 | 14 | $13

2301G Georgia Ave., NW (Bryant St.), 202-332-3737 ⊄
18509 N. Frederick Ave. (Wheatfield Dr.), Gaithersburg, MD, 301-926-7220
Mitchellville Plaza, 12116 Central Ave. (Rte. 193), Mitchellville, MD, 301-249-9101
965 Thayer Ave. (Georgia Ave.), Silver Spring, MD, 301-585-3000

◪ West Indian expats and Jamaican food "addicts" satisfy their cravings with the "homey meat patties and peas 'n' rice", "great" jerk, curried chicken and other Caribbean comfort foods prepared at this "simple", self-serve quartet; the digs aren't much to look at (other than the "hand-painted tables" at the Gaithersburg outlet), but the portions are so generous you'll have "enough for lunch the next day."

Neisha Thai [S] 22 | 20 | 20 | $25

Zulmore Plaza, 6037 Leesburg Pike (Glen Carlyn Rd.), Bailey's Crossroads, VA, 703-933-3788
7924LB Tysons Corner Ctr. (Chain Bridge Rd.), Tysons Corner, VA, 703-883-3588

◪ Designed to "break into your shopping-mall coma", these suburban Siamese twins with a "creative license" spin "trendy" riffs on the standards (think "awesome passion beef" and "tangy" tilapia with lime) amid "cave-like" surroundings; while bashers tag them "Thai light" for "watered-down curries" that are "not in the same class" as nearby (and more traditional) Duangrat's and Rabieng, supporters retort the food is "yummy", "they make you feel like a welcome guest" and "there's never a wait."

New Fortune ◐ [S] 22 | 14 | 15 | $21

16515 S. Frederick Ave. (Westland Dr.), Gaithersburg, MD, 301-548-8886

■ "Packed on Sundays" with large parties sampling its "wonderful", "authentic" dim sum (available daily), this "cavernous" Hong Kong–style banquet hall in Gaithersburg sends out "more rolling carts than you know what to do with", each steered by "friendly" servers who "get excited when you pick something exotic"; at lunch and dinner, expect an enormous, "interesting" menu starring "unusual" seafood specialties and, perhaps, live entertainment from the "karaoke" performers and "wedding parties" that are often present.

New Heights [S] 24 | 22 | 22 | $46

2317 Calvert St., NW (Connecticut Ave.), 202-234-4110

◪ "Artistic" and "adventurous", this "light-filled" Woodley Park "favorite" makes guests feel they're dining on the "cutting edge – even though it's been around forever"; savor "delicious new takes" on New American dishes paired with "well-chosen" wines and served by an "informed" staff in a "lovely", "serene" room (downstairs, "stunning woodwork" marks one of the "most beautiful bars in the city"); while frequent "chef and staff changes" are blamed for some "disappointments", most believe it "reaches new heights each time."

Neyla [S] | 22 | 24 | 20 | $36

3206 N St., NW (Wisconsin Ave.), 202-333-6353

◩ "Dramatic in an *Arabian Nights*" way, this "trendy" Mediterranean scene in Georgetown is alive with attractive thirtysomething "urbanites" sharing "winning" Lebanese-style meze, sipping "fun" papaya martinis and soaking up the "sensuous" atmosphere at either the convivial communal table or in the "Casbah"-like dining room; though the noise level is akin to a "747 taking off", the service is "gracious" and the courtyard is one of the most pleasant around.

Nick & Stef's Steakhouse | 20 | 19 | 19 | $46

MCI Ctr., 601 F St., NW (6th St.), 202-661-5040

◩ Appreciated for its "sophisticated" "elegance", this MCI Center steakhouse is a palace of meat that even a "vegetarian could love"; while its dry-aged rib-eye is "fine", its "refreshingly" "inventive sides" ("blue cheese mashed potatoes, sautéed spinach with shallots, roasted beets") and "divine Caesar salad" nearly steal the show; critical carnivores, however, find it a "mite" too "pricey" for the quality and caution that it can get awfully quiet here on non-event nights.

Nick's Chophouse [S] | ▽ 20 | 22 | 18 | $45

700 King Farm Blvd. (Frederick Rd.), Rockville, MD, 301-926-8869

◩ Early settlers "welcome" this citified fine-dining venture to their Montgomery County enclave; dressed up with elaborate floral arrangements, the "bright", airy room is a comfortable place to dine on "good", if "pricey", steaks, veal chops and fish, while a late-supper menu is available until 1 AM nightly in the "great" lounge; though it's so far "inconsistent" (it "needs some work"), patrons are optimistic that it'll grow up to be "a keeper."

Niwano Hana [S] | ▽ 20 | 16 | 20 | $24

Wintergreen Plaza, 887 Rockville Pike (Edmonston Dr.), Rockville, MD, 301-294-0553

◩ Sharply divided camps war over this Rockville Pike Japanese, with proponents praising its "fresh" sushi, "innovative rolls and tofu dishes", as well as its genuine "hospitality" and "good value", while opponents complain that the "menu is limited" and "not very authentic"; even so, the fact that it's usually "jammed" should be an indication of its merits.

Nizam's 🄢 | 22 | 17 | 21 | $33 |

Village Green Shopping Ctr., 523 Maple Ave. W. (Nutley St.), Vienna, VA, 703-938-8948

☑ "Real" doner kebab (available on Tuesdays and Friday–Sunday) is the leading "star" at this bright Turkish fixture, though the "tasty" meze is equally "worth" a pilgrimage around the Beltway to Vienna; diplomats and world travelers join locals in the ornate rooms for "dependably delicious" specialties delivered by a "professional" team, easily forgiving minor flaws like the "crowded tables."

NORA | 25 | 23 | 24 | $53 |

2132 Florida Ave., NW (bet. Connecticut & Massachusetts Aves.), 202-462-5143

☑ "Eat luxuriously and don't feel guilty" at Nora Pouillon's "outstanding" New American quartered in a "charming" carriage house above Dupont Circle; her "feel-good" ethic – create "beautiful" dishes based on "first-rate" "organic" products – is not only beneficial "for both your health and the environment", it also results in a "memorable" "feast"; though a "senator may well be at the next table", the staff will "make you feel like the center of attention", though foes don't buy the "arrogantly" PC philosophy.

OBELISK | 27 | 22 | 26 | $60 |

2029 P St., NW (bet. 20th & 21st Sts.), 202-872-1180

☑ For gourmands who love food and wine, this "exquisite" Dupont Circle Northern Italian "treasure" is home to "36 of the best seats in town"; the "superb" five-course prix fixe menu changes daily, but it's always "thoughtfully" conceived and combines an "element of surprise along with authentic" touches; though the seating is a bit "tight" and a few beaus feel that the decor is akin to an "old flame that could use some new makeup", the "first-rate" service team really "cares about doing it right."

Occidental 🄢 | 22 | 23 | 22 | $45 |

Willard Complex, 1475 Pennsylvania Ave., NW (14th St.), 202-783-1475

☑ At this Downtown "political version of Sardis" in NYC, "VIP" photographs on the walls illustrate its motto 'where statesmen dine', while "belle epoque" appointments lend a "classy, historic" resonance to the ambiance; by most accounts, the recently "improved" New American menu is now a "match" for the "attentive" (if "stuffy") service, but even if some think the tab is "not worth it", watching the comings and goings of power brokers from the patio is a most enjoyable way to pass the time.

OCEANAIRE SEAFOOD ROOM 🄢 | 23 | 23 | 22 | $47 |

1201 F St., NW (bet. 12th & 13th Sts.), 202-347-2277

☑ With all of that genre's "excesses", this "sleek '30s-style" Downtown American provides the equivalent of a "steakhouse experience for fish" lovers, showing off "bird bath"–size martinis, "super-size" entrees, a single side dish that's "enough for four" people and flaming desserts; fin fanatics are hooked by the "up-to-date" menu ("great" crab cakes and oysters), welcoming this "alternative in a city swimming" with beef barns, but dissenters object to the too "slick" "commercial" feel and Titanic prices.

Old Angler's Inn S   21   24   20 $51

10801 MacArthur Blvd. (Clara Barton Pkwy.), Potomac, MD, 301-365-2425

☑ Bosky "summer evenings under the stars", along with cocktails by the blazing fire in the wintertime, have nurtured countless "romances" over the years at this "quaint" Great Falls "hideaway"; while the New American menu can't rival the "picturesque" setting, admirers laud the "fine" surprise tasting menus, but detractors deem the food and service "indifferent" and note that the upstairs dining room is quite "charmless."

Old Ebbitt Grill ◑ S   20   22   20 $33

675 15th St., NW (bet. F & G Sts.), 202-347-4801

☑ "Who knows which Cabinet secretary will stop by for lunch" at this handsome "must-see" "legend" Downtown; a "powerhouse" at breakfast too and a "tradition" late at night at its four bars, this is a "classic" saloon with "brass and wood everywhere" and "well-prepared" all-American food on the menu; though spoilsports hiss "tired and touristy", with way "too many Republicans" in the house, you "can't get more DC" than here.

Old Glory BBQ S   18   16   17 $22

3139 M St., NW (bet. 31st St. & Wisconsin Ave.), 202-337-3406 ◑
6208 Multiplex Dr. (bet. Lee Hwy. & Rte. 28), Centreville, VA, 703-266-4066

☑ Clamorous collegians "craving BBQ" crowd this open-to-the-street Georgetown crib for its "solid ribs" slathered with a "pick-your-own" housemade sauce and other "hearty" grub; after the meal, belly up to the vintage carved bar (stocked with 79 varieties of bourbon), hauled up from Memphis and reputedly the same one where Elvis tucked into some 'cue, and chat with the "great bartenders"; N.B. at press time, a new outpost was set to open in Centreville.

Olives   23   22   20 $44

World Center Bldg., 1600 K St., NW (16th St.), 202-452-1866

☑ Just a few blocks from the White House, this multi-tiered "'in' place with an uptown feel" is Todd English's "stylish" tribute to contemporary Mediterranean cooking; the downstairs space is "beautiful" (and quieter), but "all the twentysomethings" head to the "hip upstairs" level, where solo diners can snag a seat at the bar facing the exhibition kitchen; though the "original" menu and "models"/servers get mixed reviews, few sniff at the "world-shattering warm chocolate cake."

Oodles Noodles   20 | 15 | 17 | $19
1120 19th St., NW (bet. L & M Sts.), 202-293-3138
4907 Cordell Ave. (bet. Norfolk Ave. & Old Georgetown Rd.), Bethesda, MD, 301-986-8833 S
◩ "Consistently good" and "healthy fast food" leaves customers "feeling full but not stuffed" at these Asian noodle houses in the Golden Triangle and Bethesda; despite "long lines", "crowded" seating and an "impersonal you come, you eat, you leave" atmosphere, wallet-watchers proclaim it a no-brainer – "big portions" and "lots of variety for not much cash."

Oriental East S   ▽ 20 | 9 | 15 | $19
1290 East-West Hwy. (Colesville Rd.), Silver Spring, MD, 301-608-0030
◩ "Extraordinary dim sum" choices turn this ordinary-looking Silver Spring Chinese into a "madhouse" on weekends; dinnertime is less hectic and the meal is nearly as "good – if you order right", meaning ask for the translated Chinese specialty menu and don't settle for the "same old Cantonese options"; expect, however, "gruff" treatment at any time.

Ortanique   ▽ 22 | 23 | 21 | $40
730 11th St., NW (bet. G & H Sts.), 202-393-0975
◩ "Fabulously" decorated with tropical hues and a colorful saltwater aquarium, this "beautiful", romantic two-tiered space Downtown exudes "great" island atmosphere; "equally as exotic" as the setting is its Nuevo Latino 'cuisine of the sun' (think Bahamian black grouper with a citrus sauce), which helps fill an "underserved" Caribbean niche in town; it's "new and still working out the kinks", but early enthusiasts expect it to "bloom."

Oval Room   22 | 23 | 23 | $46
800 Connecticut Ave., NW (bet. H & I Sts.), 202-463-8700
◩ Recently revamped, this "elegant" New American's "sparkling new" decor causes Democrats to quip that the "transition is better here than in the Oval Office" nearby; its strategic location, as well as a staff that "makes you feel like a player" and a patio wherein "to see and be seen", pulls in the "power lunch" crowd, and "if you're in the mood to dress up" for dinner, "this is your place"; as for the food, partisans approve of the "exciting" menu, but some opponents veto it as too "variable."

PALENA   25 | 23 | 22 | $60
3529 Connecticut Ave., NW (Porter St.), 202-537-9250
◩ At their "refined" Cleveland Park venue, Frank Ruta's seasonal New American dishes (inspired by the cuisines

of France and Italy) "awaken taste buds you didn't even know existed", while Ann Amernick's "fabulous" desserts are legendary; everything is "painstakingly prepared" (read: "slowly") and served in a "serene" room by a staff that's either "attentive" or "forgetful" (depending on the night); though most can't wait to "return", a few skeptics conclude "for all the lineage, not enough impact for the money."

PALM S   24 | 20 | 23 | $51

1225 19th St., NW (bet. M & N Sts.), 202-293-9091
1750 Tysons Blvd. (International Dr.), Tysons Corner, VA, 703-917-0200
☑ Locus of the definitive "power lunch", this "rough-and-tumble" chain is famed for its "outstanding" NY strip steaks and "amazing lobsters", as well as its "frenetic pace" and customer "abuse" (our "waiter kept us laughing all night"); while it's true that "regulars" and "VIPs" are pampered with "especially nice treatment" at the Golden Triangle branch and the Tysons Corner outlet (a "romper room") draws "tons of kids", if you think of the place as a "caricature of itself", "it's a kick."

Panino   ▽ 24 | 21 | 22 | $42

9116 Mathis Ave. (Sudley Rd.), Manassas, VA, 703-335-2566
■ "Don't be put off" by its "blue-collar" "strip-mall" locale, because inside this "unexpected spot" the kitchen turns out "first-rate" Northern Italian cooking; it's a "real find" for "fine" dining in "handsome" environs, and the entire experience is so "wonderful" that supporters are convinced it's the "best Manassas has to offer."

Panjshir   ▽ 24 | 14 | 19 | $23

924 W. Broad St. (West St.), Falls Church, VA, 703-536-4566
224 Maple Ave. W. (Lawyers Rd.), Vienna, VA, 703-281-4183 S
■ Among Northern Virginia's "best" and most accessible ethnic options, this pair of "non-threatening" Afghan "gems" is a "favorite among guests timid about exotic" foods; based on familiar ingredients like lamb, rice and pumpkin and "mild in spiciness", the "downright good" dishes are turned out in a "low-key" storefront setting by "affable" folks at such budget-friendly prices that it's easy to dine here "a lot."

Paolo's S   18 | 18 | 17 | $29

1303 Wisconsin Ave., NW (N St.), 202-333-7353 ☽
Reston Town Ctr., 11898 Market St. (Reston Pkwy.), Reston, VA, 703-318-8920
☑ "Prime" locales make these "trendy" Cal-Ital cafes in Georgetown and Reston "buzzing" "hangouts" that are best enjoyed out on the "lively" patio ("fine" "people-watching"); the "superb" giveaway breadsticks and olive dip are "worth filling up on", which is a good thing because there can be a "wait" for your "decent" pasta, pizza or salad to arrive at the table; though the majority finds them

an "easy" pick for a bite, critics dismiss the "predictable" menu and "amateur-hour" service.

Parkway Deli S   20 10 19 $17

Rock Creek Village Shopping Ctr., 8317 Grubb Rd.
(East-West Hwy.), Silver Spring, MD, 301-587-1427
◼ Montgomery County mavens are convinced that this "mensch-like" Silver Spring "mecca" is where lox-and-eggs seekers "want to be on Sunday mornings"; upholding deli tradition, the "irreverent" help also dishes up "grandma's chicken soup", "latkes with sour cream" and all the other "classic" Jewish "comfort foods"; most give it a "grade of B", though because it's in the "wrong area code", it can't possibly live up to its detractors' fond "NYC" memories.

Pasta Mia   24 14 14 $20

1790 Columbia Rd., NW (18th St.), 202-328-9114
◼ "Worth" the "hellacious" wait to end up with a "delicious food coma and five days of leftovers", this idiosyncratic Adams Morgan Italian has cultivated a loyal following that simply craves its "unbelievable" "homemade" pastas; note, however, that it's "cramped", with "no frills" and a "temperamental" staff (which fully believes that "good food takes time, so if you don't have it, go somewhere else"), and even diehards admit that they "would never tolerate being treated like cattle anywhere else."

Pasta Plus S   24 13 20 $26

Center Plaza, 209 Gorman Ave. (bet. Baltimore & Lafayette Aves.),
Laurel, MD, 301-498-5100
◼ As its name suggests, this "terrific" "hidden treasure" in suburban Laurel features not only "fabulous", "authentic" pastas but also "great pizzas" and "down-to-earth" Italian entrees; it's "run by a friendly gentleman [from Abruzzi], who knows his business", and the "lines out the door" at his labor of love are "testimony" to his "marvelous" effort.

Peacock Cafe S   21 19 19 $25

3251 Prospect St., NW (bet. Potomac St. & Wisconsin Ave.),
202-625-2740
◼ "Coveted" for its sidewalk tables that allow "great" scoping of the Georgetown street scene, as well as for its "casual" "California" vibe, this "airy", "stylish" New American cafe provides "fresh, light" nourishment to a "Euro" yuppie crowd; some "snubbed" surveyors may bash this "wanna-be" for dishes that "fall short", but plenty of regulars "know the day of the week by its soup schedule."

Peking Gourmet Inn S   25 15 21 $28

Culmore Shopping Ctr., 6029 Leesburg Pike (Glen Carlyn Rd.),
Falls Church, VA, 703-671-8088
◼ Clearly, the Bush presidency isn't hurting business at this "bustling" veteran Chinese in Falls Church, long associated

with Republican Administrations ("check out the political photos on the wall"); it's "well known" for its "phenomenal" Peking duck and specially grown garlic sprouts, but supporters urge first-timers to try other dishes too (like the "crispy" Szechuan beef) because they're commendably "different from the standard fare" found elsewhere.

Penang S   – – – M

1837 M St., NW (19th St.), 202-822-8773
4933 Bethesda Ave. (bet. Clarendon Rd. & Woodmont Ave.), Bethesda, MD, 301-657-2878

Distantly related but separately run, these "attractive" Malaysian newcomers both focus on the "interestingly" "sweet and spicy" blend of Southeast Asian, Chinese and Indian influences that marks their native homeland's cuisine; the seductive lighting and lounge-like seating at the outpost below Dupont Circle give off a supper club feel at night, while a "waterfall wall adds atmosphere" (and moderates the "noise") at the Bethesda branch, but they need to work out some "kinks."

Perry's S   20 22 16 $32

1811 Columbia Rd., NW (18th St.), 202-234-6218

◪ Summertime sushi under the stars on the "awesome" rooftop deck at this "hip" Adams Morgan "scene" is as much about watching the "pretty people" as it is about dining on "creative" Asian fusion cuisine or "acceptable" sushi; downstairs are comfy couches and a "funky" bar, but brace yourself for "attitude" everywhere; P.S. the "risqué" "drag queen brunch" on Sundays is a "must-do."

Persimmon   25 19 22 $43

7003 Wisconsin Ave. (bet. Leland & Walsh Sts.), Bethesda, MD, 301-654-9860

◪ Small can be "beautiful", as proven by this Bethesda New American "find", which "aims for understatement and achieves it"; the kitchen deftly delivers "finely crafted" dishes that are "delicious" and "different", including some of the "best fish around"; boosters believe it "outshines its competition" in town, but exacting types who feel it "needs some oomph" think that it's "pricey for what you get."

Pesce S   24 15 19 $38

2016 P St., NW (bet. Hopkins & 20th Sts.), 202-466-3474

◪ The "chef knows how to cook fish" at owner Regine Palladin's "informal" seafood bistro near Dupont Circle, where "sparkling fresh" fish and "ingenuity, not attitude", rule (the daily selections listed on the chalkboard reflect the "best" the market has to offer); the "exposed brick" setting is as "charming" as ever, but now a handsome "new" polished bar replaces the fish display case, providing a most "welcome" waiting area; still, a few crab about "close quarters" and a sometimes "hurried" atmosphere.

Petits Plats S   21 19 21 $41

2653 Connecticut Ave., NW (Calvert St.), 202-518-0018

◪ Francophiles find "great charm" and "accomplished" "traditional" bistro fare at this "easy-on-the-eyes" "corner" with a beguiling sidewalk cafe on Woodley Park's restaurant row; "warm" and "vibrant", it captures that certain French feel that "many shoot for but miss", and even if the dishes are "a bit inconsistent", the menu offers "many high points" – from "delightful appetizers" to "amazing salads" to "fantastic crème brûlée."

P.F. Chang's China Bistro S   20 20 18 $26

White Flint Mall, 11301 Rockville Pike (Nicholson Ln.), Rockville, MD, 301-230-6933
Tysons Galleria, 1716M International Dr. (Chain Bridge Rd.), Tysons Corner, VA, 703-734-8996

◪ "Chinese with pizzazz" is what you can expect at this "glitzy", "hyper"-paced chain where the stagey "mood" lighting, loud music and "eye appeal" add an "interesting twist" to the familiar; the fare is "tasty", especially the "flavorful lettuce wraps, and the atmosphere "fun", which explains why it's "always crowded", even though most diners recognize that this is "not real Chinese" food; foes, however, snipe that the concept is "wearing thin."

Pho 75 S≠   22 8 16 $13

1510 University Blvd. E. (New Hampshire Ave.), Langley Park, MD, 301-434-7844
771 Hungerford Dr. (Mannakee St.), Rockville, MD, 301-309-8873
1721 Wilson Blvd. (Quinn St.), Arlington, VA, 703-525-7355
3103 Graham Rd. (Arlington Blvd.), Falls Church, VA, 703-204-1490
382 Elden St. (Herndon Pkwy.), Herndon, VA, 703-471-4145

◪ For the "ultimate comfort food on a cold day", order a "beyond-hearty" bowl of pho (aka "Vietnamese penicillin") at this "no-frills" chain, a "complex, flavorful" concoction of broth, noodles, vegetables and meat that "fills you up" without weighing you down; available in a number of "permutations" (the "thin-sliced eye-round is always a safe choice"), it's ladled up "briskly" and "inexpensively" but with "no smiles."

Pike Pizza ◐S   – – – I

4111 Columbia Pike (bet. Quebec & Randolph Sts.), Arlington, VA, 703-521-3010

Though some locals frequent this late-night Arlington joint for its namesake pies, those in-the-know urge "forget the pizzas, try the *saltenas*" (hard-to-find Bolivian pastries filled with spicy chicken or meat); it's a different world here, especially on weekends, when it's "mobbed" by the Bolivian community, which enjoys a "noisy" good time dining on native specialties like chicharrón, fried pork chunks and beef stew while musicians play lively tunes from their homeland.

Pizzeria Paradiso S ・ 25 | 15 | 18 | $21

2029 P St., NW (bet. 20th & 21st Sts.), 202-223-1245

■ Paradise found rhapsodize acolytes of this "civilized" Dupont Circle pizzeria's "heavenly" wood-fired pies – the "best in DC" – made with a "crisp, light" crust and topped with all sorts of "scrumptious" "goodies" (its "great sandwiches and salads are only a bonus"); aside from the "long" prime-time "wait", most surveyors "come with high expectations – and they're fully "met."

Portabellos S ・ – | – | – | M

Cherrydale Shopping Ctr., 2109 N. Pollard St. (Lee Hwy.), Arlington, VA, 703-528-1557

Virginia native Bill Hamrock fills Cherrydale's contemporary-dining void with this New American addition located on the site last occupied by Pasha Cafe; dishes like its signature portobello mushroom stuffed with crab imperial are served in a comfortable, simply decorated space that's equally suitable for a casual bite after work or a festive dinner.

PRIME RIB ・ 27 | 26 | 26 | $57

2020 K St., NW (bet. 20th & 21st Sts.), 202-466-8811

■ Surprisingly "snazzy" for a lobbyists' lair, this "high-class" K Street powerhouse is nearly as famed for its "wonderful" crab imperial as for its "melt-in-your-mouth" prime rib and "reasonably" priced fine wines; amid "gleaming" lacquered walls and "fresh flowers" all about, "gentlemen and ladies" are cosseted with "royal treatment"; though some find the ambiance a bit "stuffy", most appreciate its ageless appeal and advise when you want to "feel like a character in a '50s movie", dress up (jacket and tie required) and come here.

Primi Piatti ・ 22 | 20 | 20 | $42

2013 I St., NW (bet. 20th & 21st Sts.), 202-223-3600

◪ Favored for both a "high-powered lunch" and "corporate entertaining in the PM", this "sophisticated" trattoria brings Italy to Foggy Bottom; the "A-list" settles itself in the "attractive" indoor/outdoor dining space and "thoroughly enjoys" the "first-rate" pastas, "good" veal chop and "fresh fish" specials, but malcontents fault "unremarkable" yet "overpriced" dishes and "spotty", "uppity" service.

Prince Michel S ・ ▽ 26 | 24 | 27 | $65

Prince Michel Vineyards, Rte. 29 S. (bet. Culpeper & Madison), Leon, VA, 540-547-9720

■ Offering a "relaxing", "lovely" "respite" on the way to Charlottesville, this petite winery showcase in "rural" Leon matches the vineyard's "wonderful" vintages with an "elegant" French menu; throughout the operation, there's an obvious "attention to detail" by a "superb" staff that "strives to please", making a trip "worthwhile", and if you "combine a meal with a stay" in one of the luxurious suites, you'll be assured of a "lovely weekend."

Queen Bee S   20 11 17 $21

3181 Wilson Blvd. (Washington Blvd.), Arlington, VA,
703-527-3444

◢ "When you walk in, you realize the interior probably hasn't changed since the '80s", but the "delectable" Vietnamese cooking at this "dingy" Clarendon dowager "keeps people coming back" for more of the "best" spring rolls; many still regard it as a "favorite" "standby", but former friends who feel it's "not what it used to be" say there are now "too many better choices" around.

Rabieng S   25 17 20 $25

Glen Forest Shopping Ctr., 5892 Leesburg Pike (Glen Forest Dr.),
Bailey's Crossroads, VA, 703-671-4222

■ Billed as nearby Duangrat's less fancy (and "less expensive") "country cousin", this "amazing" Bailey's Crossroads Thai is equally distinguished for its "exciting variations" on the standards, delivering "unusual regional dishes" as well as an "innovative" take on Siamese "street food" at its weekend dim sum brunch; there's "never a dull moment" on the plate, making it "worth the big lines."

Rail Stop S   21 17 19 $34

6478 Main St. (Fauquier Ave.), The Plains, VA, 540-253-5644

◢ At this citified "country oasis" in The Plains, the pink-jacket gentry, "tourists" out for a drive and "real-life locals" gather in the "understated", rustic quarters and out on the wood deck for a "solid" American repast; most find it a "charming" place to stop, but some laid-back souls resent being "rushed" over a "perfectly average" meal.

Raku S   20 19 16 $25

1900 Q St., NW (19th St.), 202-265-7258
7240 Woodmont Ave. (Elm St.), Bethesda, MD, 301-718-8681

◢ Boasting "cool" new wave decor, "hip" vibes and "scenic sidewalk cafes", these self-described Asian diners off Dupont Circle and in Bethesda keep the faithful coming with their "something-for-everyone" "finger foods" ("a wonderful adventure in eating"); fans think the concept is an "ingenious idea", but foes dub it "fusion confusion" (they "manage to make simple foods unappealing") and warn of a "meltdown when it gets crowded."

Ray's The Steaks S   – – – M

Colonial Village, 1725 Wilson Blvd. (Rhodes St.), Arlington, VA,
703-841-7297

Chef-owner Michael Landrum (aka Ray) came up with a straightforward business plan for his new American bistro in Arlington: give customers what they want – charbroiled steaks, top-quality burgers, market-catch seafood – and add on thoughtful touches like hot-from-the-oven bread and church-picnic potato salad; in contrast to the homespun cooking, the whitewashed quarters with an open kitchen are rather stripped down, but that just allows diners to focus on the food; clearly, his idea is working.

Red Hot & Blue BBQ S   19 14 16 $20

*Grove Shopping Ctr., 16811 Crabbs Branch Way
(Shady Grove Rd.), Gaithersburg, MD, 301-948-7333
677 Main St. (Rte. 216), Laurel, MD, 301-953-1943
6482 Landsdowne Ctr. (Beulah St.), Alexandria, VA, 703-550-6465
3014 Wilson Blvd. (Highland St.), Arlington, VA, 703-243-1510
4150 Chain Bridge Rd. (Rte. 236), Fairfax, VA, 703-218-6989
Bellwood Commons Shopping Ctr., 541 E. Market St. (Plaza St.),
Leesburg, VA, 703-669-4242
8366 Sudley Rd. (Irongate Way), Manassas, VA, 703-367-7100
1600 Wilson Blvd. (Pierce St.), Rosslyn, VA, 703-276-7427*
◪ When you need a "barbecue fix", this Memphis-style chain of pig palaces is "quick and inexpensive" and replete with the "appropriate" decor (read: "cheesy") for down 'n' dirty "messy" eating; many are satisfied with the "tasty" ribs and pulled pork ("good, solid flavors") teamed with "all the right sides" (willingly braving "indigestion" for the "great", "greasy" onion loaf), but disgruntled connoisseurs quip "no cigar."

Red Sage ◑ⓢ S   21 23 19 $39

605 14th St., NW (F St.), 202-638-4444
◪ At the upstairs chili bar at this "funkadelic" Southwestern fantasy, Downtown dot-pros tuck into a "fast" lunch "with a kick" and "blow off steam" after work; serious business is done on the "lower level", which ("over-the-top" decor notwithstanding) "oozes mellow sophistication" and features a "creative" menu with Nuevo Latino touches; though it "isn't as trendy" as it once was, stalwarts insist that the "quality remains very good", though opponents feel it's "underachieving."

Renato S   19 15 18 $36

10120 River Rd. (Falls Rd.), Potomac, MD, 301-365-1900
◪ "Potomac's rich and famous" "drop in" at this "pricey" Italian "staple" to "see their neighbors and enjoy good pasta, chicken and fish" dishes (the signature penne Norma is "delicious"); "regulars" who regard it as "our home away from home" are "treated very well", but be forewarned that if you're an unknown, you might be made to "feel like a second-class" citizen.

Restaurant 7   – – – E

*8521 Leesburg Pike (Springhill Rd.), Tysons Corner, VA,
703-847-0707*
The artfully designed setting of Tysons Corner's newest notable entry pleasingly showcases chef Mina Newman's New American cooking; already creating quite a buzz, it could well be a trendsetter thanks to its "interesting" bar-, bistro- and fine-dining menu concepts; not only are the

dishes "delicious" but they're cleverly playful too (steak 'n' potatoes here translates to steak tartare with crispy sticks of spuds and a Dijon-caper sauce); keep an eye on this one.

Rhodeside Grill S   16   14   16 $22
1836 Wilson Blvd. (Rhodes St.), Arlington, VA, 703-243-0145
3971 Chain Bridge Rd. (Rte. 236), Fairfax, VA, 703-293-9600
◪ "Unassuming on the outside", this Courthouse-area bar with a "strong neighborhood feel" features "Hopper-like scenes of Arlington and a wacky mural on the back wall" inside, providing an artistic backdrop for "creative", if "a bit erratic", New American dishes that "can surprise you" (the shrimp and grits in "spicy gravy" is "awesome"); N.B. there's an appropriately Fairfax-themed mural at its new clone.

Rico y Rico   ▽ 19   21   19 $41
Rio Entertainment Ctr., 9811 Washingtonian Blvd. (Sam Eig Hwy.), Gaithersburg, MD, 301-330-6611
◪ This "pretty", airy rendezvous replete with a waterside patio and periodic live harp music is Gaithersburg's "Saturday night date" restaurant; not only does it feature contemporary International dishes with "style" (especially the Spanish-style tapas), but it boasts an "excellent wine program", though foes feel it "needs to work out some problems with the menu" and the service.

Rio Grande Cafe S   21   17   18 $23
4919 Fairmont Ave. (Old Georgetown Rd.), Bethesda, MD, 301-656-2981
231 Rio Blvd. (Washingtonian Blvd.), Gaithersburg, MD, 240-632-2150
4301 N. Fairfax Dr. (Glebe Rd.), Arlington, VA, 703-528-3131
Reston Town Ctr., 1827 Library St. (New Dominion Pkwy.), Reston, VA, 703-904-0703
◪ Hungry hordes fortify themselves with "great chips", "smoky" salsa and "out-of-this-world" swirlies during the "long wait" for a table at these wildly "popular" cantinas; once seated, they dig into "dependable" Tex-Mex standards (notably the "area's best fajitas") served at a "decent" price by a "kid-friendly" staff; though it may be a "chain", amigos say it has "its act down", but detractors are turned off by the "zoo-like" atmosphere.

Ritz-Carlton, The Grill   24   25   24 $52
(Pentagon City) S
Ritz-Carlton, Pentagon City, 1250 S. Hayes St.
(bet. Army Navy Dr. & 15th St.), Arlington, VA, 703-412-2760
■ There's "not an 'i' left undotted" at this "elegant" New American–Continental hotel dining room in Pentagon City, where one goes "to be pampered and not rushed"; its "quiet, classy" surroundings are "quite conducive to conducting both serious love or serious business" over lunch or dinner, while its formal afternoon tea and "elaborate" Sunday

brunch provide "terrific" excuses to "get together" with friends; a few windows wouldn't hurt, but nothing's perfect.

Ritz-Carlton, The Grill (Washington, DC) S

20 25 21 $53

(fka Kobalt)

Ritz-Carlton, Washington, DC, 1150 22nd St., NW (bet. L & M Sts.), 202-835-0500

◪ Exemplifying the "Ritz-Carlton's effortlessly elegant style", this New American grill in the West End is as "beautiful" as you've come to expect from such a prestigious hotel chain; as for the food, however, the consensus is that it's generally "good, if not truly outstanding" (though the "superb" Sunday champagne brunch buffet garners praise), leading skeptics to conclude "all style, little substance."

Roberts S

– – – M

Omni Shoreham Hotel, 2500 Calvert St., NW (Connecticut Ave.), 202-756-5300

"Elegant yet comfortable", with soft lights, mirrored walls and a "terrace with a view of the beautifully landscaped grounds", this spacious New American hotel dining room in Woodley Park may not be that well known, but those who have visited it recommend its "interesting" menu, "exceptional" resort-like setting and "moderate prices."

Rocklands S

22 11 15 $17

2418 Wisconsin Ave., NW (Calvert St.), 202-333-2558
4000 Fairfax Dr. (Quincy St.), Arlington, VA, 703-528-9663

◪ "Why heat up your grill" when you can get "bone-sucking good" BBQ ("made like they care"), as well as "great" Texas corn pudding, the "best" baked beans and even some "unusual" "fixings", ready to go from this Georgetown pit?; if you're in the Arlington area, there's a sit-down outpost tucked away inside the CarPool billiards parlor, which offers "tunes, pool and pick-up possibilities" along with the ribs.

Roof Terrace at the Kennedy Center S

17 21 18 $43

Kennedy Ctr., 2700 F St., NW (bet. New Hampshire & Virginia Aves.), 202-416-8555

◪ As "convenient" as can be if you're bound for an event at the Kennedy Center, this rooftop New American lets you "check out the monuments" while you sup; even if the "passable" dinner menu doesn't nearly "live up" to the "spectacular view", the Sunday brunch is totally "terrific", with guests trooping though the kitchen and piling up their plates at food stations along the way.

RT's S

23 14 20 $32

3804 Mt. Vernon Ave. (Glebe Rd.), Alexandria, VA, 703-684-6010

◪ "Tons of character" and "lots of hustle and bustle" (and cholesterol too) distinguish this "time-warp" saloon in

Arlandria, where the "solid" kitchen turns out "fabulous" Louisiana-style cooking (especially "super-fine" seafood like its "awesome Jack Daniel's shrimp") that's heavy on "rich sauces"; fusspots may gripe that it can take a "long time to get your calories here", but if you want a taste of what this town once was, this is the place.

RUTH'S CHRIS STEAK HOUSE [S] 24 | 23 | 23 | $49

1801 Connecticut Ave., NW (S St.), 202-797-0033
7315 Wisconsin Ave. (Elm St.), Bethesda, MD, 301-652-7877
2231 Crystal Dr. (23rd St.), Crystal City, VA, 703-979-7275

◪ At this "classy" temple of meat, they sure know how to put the "sizzle" in steak, so prepare to "sink your teeth into" a "wonderfully" "decadent" "hunk of beef"; "dressing up seems right" in such a luxurious atmosphere (suitable for business entertaining and "special occasions" alike), but critical carnivores feel the experience doesn't "rate the hype or the prices" (though they don't seem to complain if "the company is paying"); P.S. the Crystal City venue affords a "breathtaking view" of DC sparkling with lights.

Saigonnais [S] 22 | 15 | 19 | $24

2307 18th St., NW (bet. Belmont & Columbia Rds.), 202-232-5300

■ You'll find all the familiar "favorites" ("excellent spring rolls", "tasty lemongrass beef") plus more at this "small, comfortable" Adams Morgan Vietnamese where the dishes are made with "high-quality ingredients"; even veterans let the "super-friendly owner" help them choose "something new to try" from the interesting, "varied" menu that reflects Saigon's cosmopolitan culture.

Saigon Saigon [S] – | – | – | M

Pentagon Row, 1101 S. Joyce St. (Army Navy Dr.), Arlington, VA, 703-412-0822

Offering a sliver of serenity amid the new Pentagon Row sprawl, this Vietnamese newcomer pleases the eye with soothing tones, unusual accent pieces and soft lighting, while pleasing the palate with mostly traditional country-style dishes (with "good flavors") complemented by daily specials and a few fusiony touches such as steak flambéed in a Cabernet sauce.

Saint Basil ▽ 20 | 16 | 20 | $34

12050A N. Shore Dr. (Wiehle Ave.), Reston, VA, 703-742-6466

◪ "Hugs aplenty" welcome "regular customers" at this "friendly" New American–Mediterranean "find" in Reston, which draws a local techie crowd with its "unique flavor combinations" based on "fresh", "simple ingredients"; meanwhile, neighbors who not long ago used to just drop in "for a pizza" (currently available only at lunch and on Tuesday nights) but now "end up with a $32 entree" bemoan its upwardly mobile progress.

Sakana 23 | 15 | 18 | $27

2026 P St., NW (bet. 20th & 21st Sts.), 202-887-0900

◪ An open "neighborhood secret" shared by Dupont Circle's old guard and "Gen Y" is the "excellent" sushi prepared at this easy-to-miss basement Japanese; in a "small room that feels like Tokyo", "entertaining chefs" please the cognoscenti with "non-Americanized" raw-fish selections, along with "wonderful seaweed salad", "yummy bento boxes" and "interesting" specials, though detractors conclude "good but not worth going out of your way."

Sakoontra [S] ▽ 21 | 20 | 19 | $23

Costco Plaza, 12300 Price Club Plaza, Bldg. C (Ox Rd.), Fairfax, VA, 703-818-8886

■ "Colorful" and "playful", this "friendly" Fairfax Thai charms youngsters with the tuk-tuk "buggy" (brought over from Bangkok) parked inside the front door while satisfying their elders with "consistently good" food at a "decent" price; boosters swear that everything on the extensive menu is "great", but they especially "love the duck salad."

Sala Thai [S] 19 | 15 | 18 | $22

3507 Connecticut Ave., NW (Ordway St.), 202-237-2777
2016 P St., NW (bet. 20th & 21st Sts.), 202-872-1144
2900 10th St. N. (Washington Blvd.), Arlington, VA, 703-465-2900

◪ Earning a cult following with its "out-of-the-ordinary" dishes filled with "big tastes" (a request for 'Bangkok hot' is taken seriously), this Thai trio is a "treat" according to fans; while the menu is the same at the three branches, the settings are very different – the "subterranean" Dupont Circle flagship has a *Twilight Zone* feel about it, the Arlington outlet is "nice" in a suburban way and the new Cleveland Park addition is modish – though none of that matters to those who find it "nothing special."

Samadi Sweets Cafe [S] ▽ 21 | 10 | 14 | $15

5916 Leesburg Pike (bet. Seven Corners & Skyline St.), Falls Church, VA, 703-578-0606

◪ "Abandon ye diet all who enter" this petite Falls Church Middle Eastern bakery/cafe where you'll find the "most authentic, delectable pastries west of Beirut"; though the savory Lebanese selections are "delicious" (the falafel is the "best" around), the "sweet of tooth" will be most tempted to "skip lunch" or dinner and head straight for the "out-of-this-world" "baklava counter."

Sam & Harry's 24 | 22 | 24 | $50

1200 19th St., NW (bet. M & N Sts.), 202-296-4333
8240 Leesburg Pike (Chain Bridge Rd.), Tysons Corner, VA, 703-448-0088

◪ For most locals, this pair of hometown steakhouses is "the class of its class", and they'll choose it every time over the chain beef barns because the atmosphere is "less pretentious" and you'll always "encounter interesting people" at the bar; while the Golden Triangle cornerstone still pulls in a "power" crowd, the Tysons Corner offshoot is now "quieter after the dot-com bust", but both are known for "mouthwatering" prime cuts backed by an "awesome wine" cellar and "smart" service.

Saveur S

– | – | – | E

2218 Wisconsin Ave., NW (Calvert St.), 202-333-5885
Now run by ambitious new owners, this "charming" Upper Georgetown bistro continues to be a "good date place", even if the proprietors need to "work out some kinks"; as for the updated New French–Californian menu, early reports are that many of the dishes – notably bouillabaisse, rack of lamb with garlic mousseline and tuna with miso sauce – are a "pleasant surprise", while the chocolate fondant is simply "unbelievable."

Sea Catch

21 | 21 | 19 | $42

Canal Sq., 1054 31st St., NW (M St.), 202-337-8855
◪ "Enchanting" summertime dining on a deck overlooking the C&O barge canal hooks in schools of fans at this "civilized" retreat in Georgetown; the seafood menu stars "fresh", "well-prepared" fish, plus there's a "spectacular" raw bar and "good happy-hour deals"; admirers consider it an "excellent choice" for simple grilled finny fare, but skeptical seafarers carp about "too casual" service and too upscale pricing.

SEASONS S

25 | 26 | 26 | $57

Four Seasons Hotel, 2800 Pennsylvania Ave., NW (28th St.), 202-944-2000
■ "Elegant in every respect", this "especially attractive" hotel dining room in Georgetown "maintains the high standards of the Four Seasons"; appointed with every "luxurious" detail, it promises "a wonderful experience" – from the "relaxing" ambiance to the "comfortably spaced tables" to the "impeccable" service; the "toque sits well" on new chef Doug Anderson, whose New American menus are "imaginative" and "superb", and who has made the Sunday brunch more "incredible" than ever.

Sequoia ●S

16 | 24 | 16 | $35

Washington Harbour, 3000 K St., NW (30th St.), 202-944-4200
◪ "Who can resist dining outdoors overlooking the Washington Harbour in the summertime?" ask defenders of this "overpriced hangout" that's "always overrun" with thirtysomethings "looking for someone" at sunset, as well as "tourists" joining the action; clearly, the "uninspired" American menu is merely an "afterthought", but that doesn't deter the many whose main objective is to "people-watch" and take in the "unbelievable" "river view."

Sesto Senso
| 20 | 18 | 18 | $35 |

1214 18th St., NW (bet. Jefferson Pl. & M St.), 202-785-9525
A "high Euro-chic quotient" may explain why this "trendy club" below Dupont Circle doesn't register more strongly on foodies' radar screens, but insiders attest that the Northern Italian menu is "authentic" and "surprisingly affordable" ("don't miss the grilled calamari" or "excellent pastas"); "good for business lunches" during the day, it "turns into Mr. Hyde in the evenings", with a "hip" "bar scene" and "late-night dancing" on the weekends.

701 S
| 23 | 23 | 23 | $45 |

701 Pennsylvania Ave., NW (7th St.), 202-393-0701
For a "great swanky night out" in the Penn Quarter, replete with "caviar and champagne" and "quiet jazz", it's hard to beat this "perpetual" New American favorite where "elegant is done right"; patrons come to be treated like "grown-ups" in a "sophisticated" setting that actually allows for conversation while dining on "tasteful" dishes brought to table by a "knowledgeable" team; delivering "true value for the quality", it "rarely disappoints."

Seven Seas ● S
| 21 | 12 | 17 | $24 |

Federal Plaza, 1776 E. Jefferson St. (bet. Montrose Rd. & Rollins Ave.), Rockville, MD, 301-770-5020
"Ask for the red menu, which has all the good Chinese stuff" (including Taiwanese specialties), advise those in-the-know about this modest Rockville Asian; you can be assured that the "whole fish dishes are terrific" because you can see the ingredients swimming in the tanks, but the more "unusual" seafood selections are worth "trying" too (sushi is also available); critics, however, gripe that the "seedy" digs "need a face-lift" and caution that service isn't as "organized as it should be."

1789 S
| 26 | 25 | 25 | $53 |

1226 36th St., NW (Prospect St.), 202-965-1789
Much, much more than just a "place to take your visiting parents", this "inviting" Federal period piece in Georgetown provides "formality" "without intimidation"; "genius" chef Ris Lacoste deftly "blends" old and new seasonal American recipes into "top-notch" renditions (her "superb" rack of lamb makes sure that "food is the star of the show" here), while the "outstanding" staff "goes out of its way for guests"; it's a "splurge", but the prix fixe menus are a "steal."

Shula's Steak House S
| 20 | 18 | 18 | $46 |

Wyndham City Center, 1143 New Hampshire Ave., NW (M St.), 202-828-7762
Tysons Corner Marriott Hotel, 8028 Leesburg Pike (Old Gallows Rd.), Vienna, VA, 703-506-3256
Owned by Don Shula, the most winning coach in NFL history, these beefy players are "dark", "macho" "shrines"

that score with "too large portions" of "competently" prepared certified angus steaks; boosters approve of the "well-appointed" space, decorated with memorabilia from his legendary Dolphins days, but opponents take a pass on the hokey hand-"painted football menu" and pre-game show of raw meat.

Signatures – – – VE

801 Pennsylvania Ave., NW (9th St.), 202-628-5900

The Penn Quarter's latest lair for lawyers, lobbyists and legislators is this handsome haunt that's abuzz from morning till late at night; the upscale New American menu is designed to please diverse palates without distracting from the matter of doing business, though with luxurious temptations like Kobe beef offered at breakfast, lunch and dinner, that may prove difficult; N.B. the moniker refers to its noteworthy collection of historical memorabilia, many signed, all for sale.

Siné ◐ [S] – – – M

1301 S. Joyce St. (Army Navy Dr.), Arlington, VA, 703-415-4420

Located on Arlington's newly minted Pentagon Row (next to the City Mall), this handsome, spacious establishment provides a number of settings – convivial bars, alcoves and booths, a pair of patios, even fireside tables – in which to hoist a glass (expect a wide selection of brews and malts); for ballast, the kitchen turns out hearty Irish specialties such as shepherd's pie, beer-battered fish 'n' chips and nachos spun with a Celtic twist (they're made with fried potatoes).

Skewers/Cafe Luna [S] 20 16 18 $20

1633 P St., NW (bet. 16th & 17th Sts.), 202-387-7400

◪ Two restaurants in one, this "indispensable" Dupont Circle East staple gives diners an option: head upstairs if you're in the mood for "good" kebabs and other "healthy, tasty" Middle Eastern dishes that are suitable for "sharing", served in "cramped quarters" that are short on decor but long on atmosphere; or stay on the ground floor if you're looking for "quick, fresh" Italian fare like pastas and pizzas; either way, you'll find "interesting people to watch."

Smith & Wollensky ◐ [S] 21 20 21 $48

1112 19th St., NW (bet. L & M Sts.), 202-466-1100

■ Situated on "angus alley" in the Golden Triangle, this "consistently good" Big Apple import appeals to a somewhat "younger" (in spirit, anyway) crowd with its "beautiful cuts" of prime meat, "excellent" wine list and "try-harder" ethic; the "grill has all the cholesterol, at a cheaper price", making it an "informal alternative to the rather stuffy dining room side", while the sidewalk cafe is "wonderful" in clement weather.

Sorak Garden S   ▽ 22 | 16 | 13 | $27

4308 Backlick Rd. (Little River Tpke.), Annandale, VA, 703-916-7600

◪ "One of the better places in the area for Korean food", this spacious, "affordable" Annandale standby features a "great variety" of "tasty", "authentic" dishes including BBQ kalbi, bulgoki and bibimbop; supporters say it's a "lovely food experience", but foes complain about "slapdash" service.

South Beach S   – | – | – | M

7904 Woodmont Ave. (bet. Fairmont & St. Elmo Aves.), Bethesda, MD, 301-718-9737

Bold colors and art deco motifs make a festive backdrop for "gracious" chef-owner John Richardson's "fresh and airy" new Miami beachhead in Bethesda; just as "lively" as the setting is his "creative" menu inspired by the cuisines of Florida and Cuba; in addition to street-level dining, there's an upstairs lounge that features colorful drinks, flavorful bites and salsa dancing (on Thursdays), making it one of the "hottest" late-night scenes around.

Spezie   22 | 20 | 19 | $39

1736 L St., NW (bet. Connecticut Ave. & 18th St.), 202-467-0777

◪ This "worthy newcomer" to DC's "already crowded field of modern Italians" "showcases" owner Enzo Livia's (Il Pizzico) "range" as a chef; at lunchtime, expect to see a crowd of Golden Triangle lawyers and lobbyists congregating over "delicious pastas" in an "elegant" space with lots of elbow room; though there's "nothing really surprising on the menu", advocates say "that doesn't detract from the pleasure of dining here", but faultfinders feel "there's room for improvement."

Spices S   20 | 17 | 18 | $25

3333A Connecticut Ave., NW (bet. Macomb & Ordway Sts.), 202-686-3833

◪ Recently reopened after a mod makeover (a "major improvement"), this "sexy" Cleveland Park "hot" spot offers something "Asian for everybody" – from "yum yum" noodles and stir-fries to curries and sushi – and the "assortment" is so "diverse" you "won't run out of things" to try anytime soon; "be prepared to sit too near" your neighbors, though, and beware that the "engaging" servers can quickly get "overburdened."

Starfish Cafe S   – | – | – | M

539 Eighth St., SE (bet. E & G Sts.), 202-546-5006

Warm and welcoming, this Capitol Hill start-up brings an "upscale" note to a burgeoning neighborhood near the Shakespeare Theatre with its "attractive" tiled bars, exposed brick and colorful art; the "ambitious" seafood-slanted menu ranges from scallop and salmon ceviche to blackened grouper to cornmeal-crusted sea bass, making it a "good place to graze."

Starland Cafe [S] | 18 | 17 | 20 | $30 |

5125 MacArthur Blvd., NW (bet. Arizona Ave. & Dana Pl.), 202-244-9396

◪ Coming up with some "interesting ideas in a contemporary setting", this "relaxing" New American in the Palisades attracts a "mix" of young families, yuppies and their elders; though it's "nothing special", "it's all it has to be", because it gives locals a much-appreciated dining-out option, whether it be a "pleasant" lunch on the terrace, an "imaginatively" presented Friday night dinner (try the "flavorful" fish) accompanied by "live music" or "Sunday brunch served in a sun-filled room."

St. Regis, Library Lounge [S] | – | – | – | E |

St. Regis, 923 16th St., NW (K St.), 202-879-6900

The clubby elegance of this hotel lounge only two blocks from the White House lends dignity to any business or social dealing; the dining room (once the site of Lespinasse) is as stately as ever, but recent management changes have introduced a concise New American menu featuring such dishes as salmon dressed with caviar, NY strip steak and pasta with seafood; N.B. presently, dinner is served only at the bar.

Sushi-Ko [S] | 25 | 17 | 20 | $35 |

2309 Wisconsin Ave., NW (south of Calvert St.), 202-333-4187

◪ A "Washington classic", this "memorable" Upper Georgetown Japanese "challenges your taste buds" with "still squirming" sushi and "divine" omakase meals "intelligently paired" with fine French wines; aesthetes are "disappointed" by the "stripped-down" decor ("not a good mood-setter"), but the majority embraces it as a "standard"-bearer.

Sushi Taro [S] | 24 | 20 | 20 | $32 |

1503 17th St., NW (P St.), 202-462-8999

■ Reputedly the "pick of the Japanese press corps" (and also favored by its Embassy staff), this "busy" Dupont Circle East traditionalist is well respected for its "succulent sushi" (choose from a "wide selection of critters"), "fine tempura" and other "delicious entrees"; whether you sit at the long sushi bar, at a sunny window seat or in the tatami room, the "authentic" experience is like "visiting Tokyo but at a much more reasonable" price.

Sweet Basil [S] | 23 | 19 | 22 | $29 |

4910 Fairmont Ave. (bet. Norfolk Ave. & Old Georgetown Rd.), Bethesda, MD, 301-657-7997

■ Definitely not "ho-hum" Thai, this "sweet" "star" on the Bethesda scene takes a "light", "creative" approach to its native cuisine, exemplified in "nontraditional" dishes like its signature grilled rack of lamb with tamarind sauce and "terrific" chicken curry pot pie; the surroundings are modern yet "not too slick", providing a compatible backdrop for the "delicately seasoned" dishes and leaving admirers eager to return "again and again."

Sweetwater Tavern S   21   19   20 $26
14250 Sweetwater Ln. (Multiplex Dr.), Centreville, VA, 703-449-1100
3066 Gatehouse Plaza Dr. (Old Gallows Rd.), Merrifield, VA, 703-645-8100
45980 Waterview Plaza (Loudon Tech Dr. & Rte. 7), Sterling, VA, 571-434-6500
◪ At these "congenial" cowboy country–themed brewpubs (the "beer sampler is a must") in Northern Virginia, "value-conscious" diners stampede in for "tasty" Southwestern favorites like hickory-smoked babybacks, "drunken" rib-eye steak and the "great chocolate waffle dessert"; popularity notwithstanding, detractors find the menu "predictable", the noise "deafening" and the service too "fast-paced."

Tabard Inn S   22   23   21 $38
Hotel Tabard Inn, 1739 N St., NW (bet. 17th & 18th Sts.), 202-833-2668
◪ "Quirky, charming" and filled with "funky antiques", this Dupont Circle "delight" is as much "about mood" as the "creative" New American food; the courtyard is a "refreshing hideaway" and the dining room is a "genteel" haven, but many "particularly cherish" "rendezvousing" by the "roaring fire" in the lounge while "drinking wine, eating cheese and making the world a better place"; those not smitten, however, snipe about "tired", "uneven" food that's "less than inspiring."

TABERNA DEL ALABARDERO   25   26   25 $52
1776 I St., NW (18th St.), 202-429-2200
■ "Old-world Spain comes alive" at this "gorgeous" "standout" near the World Bank, where "you can be romantic or all business" and still have a "memorable" meal; at the bar, the "international elite sips wine and eats tapas", while earthy regional dishes (including the "best paella this side of Valencia" and "perfect" stews) are served "with flair" in the "sumptuous" dining rooms by a "pampering" staff.

Tachibana S   25   16   19 $32
6715 Lowell Ave. (Emerson Ave.), McLean, VA, 703-847-1771
◪ "Die-hard fans fill the sushi bar" at this "unaffectedly unstylish" McLean Japanese known for its "impressive variety" of "high-quality" selections (check the specials, but don't miss the "best" spicy tuna or scallop roll); the "sashimi lunch is invariably fresh, generously sliced" and more than fairly priced, plus the kitchen turns out "consistently good" cooked dishes, which compensates for the sometimes "indifferent" service.

Tahoga S 21 | 20 | 20 | $44

2815 M St., NW (bet. 28th & 29th Sts.), 202-338-5380

◪ Though the interior, all white walls and polished woods, "can seem stark unless you're in the mood for modern minimalism" (which its regulars are), everyone concurs that the hidden "courtyard is a treat" at this "appealing" Georgetown New American; though the dishes can be "inconsistent", they're generally "vibrant" and "when they're on, they're very on" – and that's often enough to make it a "great lunch place" or "stylish" night out.

Tako Grill S 23 | 17 | 19 | $28

7756 Wisconsin Ave. (Cheltenham Dr.), Bethesda, MD, 301-652-7030

◪ In Bethesda's increasingly cosmopolitan dining hub, this established "neighborhood" favorite continues to please connoisseurs with its "fresh" sushi and sashimi, but it's the other Japanese specialties – "excellent" tempura, nabeyaki and especially the "unique" robatayaki (grilled vegetables, fish or meats) – that draw a wider audience; while a few fear that "overpopularity has taken its toll", most feel that it has actually "improved" over the years.

Tandoori Nights S – | – | – | M

106-108 Market St. (Kentlands Blvd.), Gaithersburg, MD, 301-947-4007

Fanciful murals, svelte appointments, a modish bar and a menu of healthfully prepared Indian favorites distinguish this "classy" new addition to the cosmopolitan Kentlands Market Square dining mix; choices abound for meat lovers and vegetarians alike, presented in an upscale atmosphere that works for both socializing and business, leading locals to proclaim it a "don't miss."

Taqueria Poblano S ▽ 23 | 14 | 19 | $17

2400B Mt. Vernon Ave. (Oxford Ave.), Alexandria, VA, 703-548-8226

■ "Colorful and cheerful", this "family"-friendly Del Ray Mexican outpost is "full of charm"; its "fantastic" tacos and other "delicious" "California-style" items reflect the LA-raised owner's commitment to "authenticity" and quality; though the compact quarters can get "too crowded", the dining is "delightful in the summertime, when you can sit outside" in the sidewalk cafe.

Tara Thai S 21 | 20 | 19 | $24

4828 Bethesda Ave. (bet. Arlington Rd. & Woodmont Ave.), Bethesda, MD, 301-657-0488
12071 Rockville Pike (Montrose Rd.), Rockville, MD, 301-231-9899
4001 Fairfax Dr. (bet. Quincy & Randolph Sts.), Arlington, VA, 703-908-4999
7501E Leesburg Pike (Pimmit Dr.), Falls Church, VA, 703-506-9788

(continued)

Tara Thai

226 Maple Ave. W. (bet. Lawyers Rd. & Pleasant St.), Vienna, VA, 703-255-2467

◪ "Radioactive" "under-the-sea" decor and "pretty plates" are the eye-catching attractions at these wildly popular Thai mainstays whose "well-priced", "solid" fare provides a "satisfying experience" for the "masses"; critics may knock their success, citing "sanitized" flavors and a "rushed" "fast-food" feel, but the heavy traffic gives them some credibility.

Taste of Morroco [S] — – – – M

3211 Washington Blvd. (Wilson Blvd.), Arlington, VA, 703-527-7468

An "intimate" refuge in Clarendon near "otherwise drab Wilson Boulevard", this "charming" Moroccan "transports guests to Casablanca" with its comfortable seating on pillowed banquettes, congenial belly dancer (on weekends) and "yummy" food (especially the "savory" couscous and b'steeya); it's "reasonably priced" and worth "checking out."

Taste of Saigon [S] — 24 17 20 $26

410 Hungerford Dr. (Beall Ave.), Rockville, MD, 301-424-7222
8201 Greensboro Dr. (International Dr.), Tysons Corner, VA, 703-790-0700

■ Providing an "oasis" of "comfort" in "sterile" suburban office parks in Rockville and Tysons Corner, this Vietnamese twosome "feeds you well and treats you well"; its distinctive black-pepper sauce "on anything" is so "delicious" that addicts can't bring themselves to "experiment with the rest" of the "huge", "wonderful" menu; it's a "superb value" too.

Teaism — 19 17 15 $16

800 Connecticut Ave., NW (H St.), 202-835-2233
400 Eighth St., NW (D St.), 202-638-6010 [S]
2009 R St., NW (Connecticut Ave.), 202-667-3827 [S]

◪ "Stress relief" is dispensed at this trio of "Asian-esque" teahouses, which function as "college coffeehouses for post-post-grads, only with no coffee" available; instead, expect "huge mugs of satisfying chai" and a limited menu of "interesting" small plates and bento boxes presented in "coolly" "rustic" settings "best" visited during "off-times" if you're seeking a "soul-cleansing" break; nitpickers, though, quibble "a little too light on the service that would make for a truly tranquil place."

TEATRO GOLDONI — 24 25 22 $50

1909 K St., NW (bet. 19th & 20th Sts.), 202-955-9494

◪ At this "sophisticated", "eye-catching" "carnival" on K Street, chef-owner Fabrizio Aielli promises the "'in' crowd" a "full evening of entertainment", showing off his "artistic", Venetian-inspired Nuovo Italian cooking (his lobster risotto is "amazing") in a "gorgeous", "theatrical" space decorated with a wall of vintage masks and colorful glass panels that pay homage to Harlequins; fans applaud this "feel-good" "star", but critics pan it as "hit-or-miss", reserving special barbs for the "pretentious" service.

Temel 🅂   ▽ 24 | 19 | 21 | $28 |
3232 Old Pickett Rd. (Old Lee Hwy.), Fairfax, VA, 703-352-5477
■ "Let's keep this one a secret" plead those in-the-know about this "hidden jewel" tucked away in a nondescript Fairfax "strip mall" ("another case of don't judge a book by its cover"); it's a "real surprise" for "delicious, authentic" Turkish meals served in an "attractive, comfortable" space (replete with "relaxing" waterfalls) by "hospitable" people at a "good value."

Tempo 🅂   23 | 19 | 22 | $38 |
4231 Duke St. (Gordon St.), Alexandria, VA, 703-370-7900
☑ Some of the "best fine-dining for the money" can be had at this Alexandria "winner" where "imaginatively prepared" French and Italian "classics" are presented in a "converted gas station"; despite the "noisy" acoustics and occasionally "overwhelmed" service, "regular customers feel really appreciated" and just "love" the "unpretentious" ambiance.

TENPENH   25 | 25 | 23 | $45 |
1001 Pennsylvania Ave., NW (10th St.), 202-393-4500
☑ "Atmosphere and attitude" reign at one of Downtown's most glamorous "destinations", a "dramatic" pastiche of Pan-Asian visuals and victuals where the "beautiful people" are part of the show; don't think for a second, though, that the food is secondary, because Jeff Tunks will "astonish" your taste buds with his "clever, creative" plays on the cuisines of Thailand, Vietnam, China, the Philippines and beyond, presenting his dishes as works of "art" on a plate; still, holdouts hoot "too bad you can't eat hipness."

Terrazza   22 | 19 | 21 | $41 |
2 Wisconsin Circle (Western Ave.), Chevy Chase, MD, 301-951-9292
☑ "Hidden away" on the terrace level of a Friendship Heights office building, this "spacious" Northern Italian caters to discriminating palates with the "best" grilled calamari, "great" pumpkin agnolotti and "first-rate" saltimbocca; the unconverted, however, feel that "something's flat" about some of the dishes and caution that while there's "lots of room", it gets "loud" fast if "large parties" are present.

T.H.A.I. 🅂   23 | 21 | 21 | $24 |
Village at Shirlington, 4029 28th St. S. (Randolph St.), Arlington, VA, 703-931-3203
☑ At this eye-catching Thai in Shirlington, the "modern" design, theatrical lighting and bold colors form an "arty"

backdrop for the kitchen's "inventive", "spicy" plates; though traditionalists may shake their heads, partisans insist that the "truly beautiful dishes taste as good as they look" and give kudos too to the "sweet staff that aims to please"; P.S. the "big bowl lunch special is a bargain."

Thai Basil S   ▽ 19 | 15 | 19 | $22

14511 Lee Jackson Memorial Hwy. (Airline Pkwy.), Chantilly, VA, 703-631-8277

■ "Hard to find but well worth the effort", this "authentic Thai surprise south of Dulles airport" in Chantilly justifies the journey with its "consistently" "fine" dishes ("try the curries" and what may be the definitive version of pad Thai), some of which are "not found on menus" elsewhere; though the digs are a little "plain", they're brightened up by artifacts from the homeland.

Thaiphoon S   19 | 17 | 16 | $23

2011 S St., NW (20th St.), 202-667-3505

◪ "As exciting as a good first date" (and as "crowded as Bangkok"), this "slick" Thai bistro above Dupont Circle seduces with its "hip, urban" "energy" and "well-designed" space, not to mention its "extensive", "satisfying" menu; detractors, though, deem the dishes "underwhelming" and don't like getting "squeezed" into a too "closely packed table", nor the "hurry-up attitude."

Thanh Thanh S   ▽ 22 | 17 | 21 | $19

11423 Georgia Ave. (University Blvd.), Wheaton, MD, 301-962-3530

■ Achieving pure "depths of flavor", this Vietnamese "treasure" in Wheaton "will change your whole sense of what fish" should taste like after one bite (also a must is the "memorable crispy quail" and "phenomenal pho"); "charming" and unassuming, not even a "small language barrier" detracts from the "pleasant" experience, making it a "great", "cheap" "escape" that's "so not DC."

That's Amore S   16 | 15 | 17 | $27

1699 Rockville Pike (Halpine Rd.), Rockville, MD, 301-881-7891
15201 Shady Grove Rd. (Research Blvd.), Rockville, MD, 301-670-9666
46300 Potomac Run Plaza (Cascades Pkwy.), Sterling, VA, 703-406-4900
Danor Plaza, 150 Branch Rd., SE (Maple Ave.), Vienna, VA, 703-281-7777

◪ "Mega-size" platters of Southern Italian food (with "garlic in everything") dished up *famiglia* style (individual portions are available too) plus handy suburban locales make these "festive" (or "hectic") "mass-market" halls useful for "family" dining; while they attract heavy traffic, though, gourmands shrug the "food didn't make me feel the love."

Thyme Square S
19 | 18 | 18 | $28

*4735 Bethesda Ave. (Woodmont Ave.), Bethesda, MD,
301-657-9077*

☑ A "cheery" pit stop for cyclists and other "healthy types",
this New American "vegetarian's dream" just "off the bike
path" in Bethesda features a "wide range" of "interesting"
dishes based on organic ingredients and wholesome
cooking techniques (no deep-frying, for example); for all
its good intentions, however, many find the preparations
too "erratic" ("either delicious or a dud") and the service
"eager" but rather "untrained", leading sympathizers to
"want it to be better than it is."

Timpano Italian Chophouse S
18 | 18 | 18 | $32

*12021 Rockville Pike (Montrose Rd.), Rockville, MD,
301-881-6939*

☑ "Sinatra would feel right at home" at this "dark" "Las
Vegas"-in-the-suburbs Italian steakhouse in Rockville
that's filled with martini sippers and swing-night strutters
(Thursday–Saturday); while many concede that the food is
"pretty good", sticklers caution that there's "more ambiance
than authenticity" (expect a "theme-park feel") at work at
this "wanna-be."

Tivoli
22 | 19 | 21 | $37

*1700 N. Moore St. (bet. 19th St. & Wilson Blvd.), Rosslyn, VA,
703-524-8900*

☑ "Year after year", a mature audience in Rosslyn has
regarded this "step-back-in-time" as a "comfortable
friend" thanks to its "consistently well-served" Continental
and Northern Italian dishes, "fine European" pastries and
award-winning wine list; though the "rich" fare may be
"a diet-destroyer" and the room a bit "dated", loyalists
insist it's an "underrated", "often overlooked" "treat" for
a "traditional" meal.

Toka Cafe
– | – | – | E

1140 19th St., NW (M St.), 202-429-8652

White-on-white color treatments, reflective surfaces and
cleverly sculpted spaces transform the basement setting
of this Golden Triangle upstart into a stylish place replete
with a glowing blue bar that's ideal for after-work socializing,
while the French- and Italian-inflected Eclectic menu offers
something a little different from the other eateries nearby.

Tono Sushi S
19 | 14 | 19 | $26

2605 Connecticut Ave., NW (Calvert St.), 202-332-7300

☑ "If you're on a budget, go for the soups" or the "great
bento box lunch" deal at this "laid-back" Woodley Park
Japanese, which is also known for preparing the "best"
soft-shell crab roll; detractors admit to "decent sushi at a
decent price" but find it "boring all around", though the
"outdoor seating" may be its "redemption."

Tony & Joe's Seafood Place S
15 | 20 | 15 | $32

Washington Harbour, 3000 K St., NW (30th St.),
202-944-4545

◪ "Wear Prada" if you go to this "singles'" see-and-be-seen scene set on the banks of the Potomac, which boasts a "delightful location" with a "fantastic view of the harbor"; on Friday nights in the summertime, it's like a "frat party with heels and ties", and though "they could do better" in the way of the seafood menu and the service, it doesn't seem to matter much to those focused on the "waterfront setting" and people-watching.

Tony Cheng's S
20 | 14 | 17 | $25

619 H St., NW (bet. 6th & 7th Sts.), 202-842-8669

◪ "Throngs of white-collar types flock to this fun" all-you-can-eat Mongolian BBQ near the MCI Center at lunchtime and compete to see "who can load their bowl the highest"; groups and kids find the concept a "hoot", but serious eaters head to the "upstairs seafood restaurant" where they feel the daily dim sum is the "real star of the venue"; despite "cheesy" decor, this is a "piece of old Chinatown" that should be seen "before it disappears."

Topaz Bar S
▽ 20 | 24 | 19 | $26

Topaz Hotel, 1733 N St., NW (bet. 17th & 19th Sts.), 202-393-3000

◪ Providing a "trendy" backdrop, with "cool" (or "odd") mood lighting that shifts from iridescent red to blue to green, this "hip" new lounge attracts the "somewhat young" to Dupont Circle; the Asian-flavored New American menu highlights "adventurous small plates" (make that "tiny" dishes) that are a "mix of awesome and so-so", but many "would go again" just for the "inventive" cocktails.

TOSCA S
26 | 24 | 23 | $53

1112 F St., NW (bet. 11th & 12th Sts.), 202-367-1990

◪ Downtown's "rising star" is this "svelte" showroom where chef Cesare Lanfranconi (ex Galileo) masterminds "fabulous" Northern Italian fare that achieves a "refined" "balance of traditional and contemporary" styles, with many dishes inspired by his native Lombardy; his tasting menu is particularly "heavenly" and the "sophisticated" dining room is "a place to dress up for" and feel oh so "Cary Grant", but it's "still finding its way" and a few discordant notes can be detected in the "arrogant" service.

Tragara S
21 | 20 | 21 | $45

4935 Cordell Ave. (bet. Norfolk Ave. & Old Georgetown Rd.),
Bethesda, MD, 301-951-4935

◪ At this "special-occasion" Northern Italian in Bethesda, your "delicious" Dover sole is filleted at the table and your crêpes suzette is flambéed for all to see; its wealthy clientele appreciates the "upscale" menu, "fancy" surroundings and "private party" expertise, but as dissenters see things, the kitchen is getting "tired" while the staff is busy "trying to look elegant rather than be elegant."

Tryst ●S   16 20 13 $15
2459 18th St., NW (bet. Belmont & Columbia Rds.), 202-232-5500
◪ Whether for lattes at breakfast, "chunky sandwiches" at lunch, the "city's best chai" in the late afternoon or cocktails during the "meat market" action late at night, this "funky" coffeehouse is the "perfect social hangout" in Adams Morgan ("if you can tolerate the smoke"); nobody – "including the staff" – is "in a hurry" here, so sink into a "beat-up sofa" or perch on a "stool at the counter" and settle in for a spell.

Tuscarora Mill S   23 22 21 $34
Market Station, 203 Harrison St., SE (Loudoun St.), Leesburg, VA, 703-771-9300
■ "Tuskies", as it's affectionately called by Leesburg's "'in' crowd", is a little "like *Alice's Restaurant*" in that "you can get anything you want" to eat or drink – "lite plates", American "comfort food scaled up", "wonderful" "wine flights (great fun)", "very good beers" – all "dependably" "splendid"; "interestingly" quartered in a "charming", "beautifully" restored grain mill, it's rustic in a tony way, with a "warm" atmosphere, and "worth the drive."

2 Amys S   22 14 17 $22
3715 Macomb St., NW (Wisconsin Ave.), 202-885-5700
◪ Peter Pastan's (of Obelisk renown) "very special" new Italian gift brings wood-fired artisanal pies (crafted according to exacting standards set by the Verrace Pizza Napoletana trade association) to this sunny, tiled venue in Northwest DC; his "dedication" to the "authenticity" of the art is obvious, even if those weaned on Domino's find these refined pizzas a bit "bland" and "not crunchy enough"; the consensus: "on its way to greatness, but it needs to work out a few kinks."

219 S   19 21 19 $37
219 King St. (Fairfax St.), Alexandria, VA, 703-549-1141
◪ Evoking the "atmospheric" "French Quarter", this "charming" Old Town fixture sets the stage for a "tasty" New Orleans experience with its cozy downstairs bar, "great" "upstairs jazz" lounge, "lovely" drawing rooms and "romantic" all-weather terrace; most say it's a "safe bet" for "acceptable" Cajun-Creole food, but purists proclaim it a Big Easy "knockoff."

Two Quail S   21 23 21 $39
320 Massachusetts Ave., NE (bet. 3rd & 4th Sts.), 202-543-8030
◪ Nearly everyone "succumbs" to this "romantic" Capitol Hill "darling", which manages to endear with "eccentric", "cluttered" parlors (a cross "between Laura Ashley and a

Paris bordello") that are favored for "private conversations" and "proposals" of all sorts; "starry-eyed lovers" who have enjoyed "many happy returns" here cherish it as a "one-of-a-kind" "favorite" with "fine" American vittles (the "signature dish is quite good", natch), but lonely hearts are unmoved by it all.

Udupi Palace S   23 | 11 | 18 | $18

1329 University Blvd. E. (New Hampshire Ave.), Langley Park, MD, 301-434-1531

◪ "Authentic and delicious, not to mention cheap", a meal at this "sweet" Langley Park Indian is a "singularly satisfying" vegetarian experience; though the decidedly unpalatial site "isn't much to look at" (it "feels like a bingo hall"), the kitchen knows what it's doing with a "stunning blend of exotic spices", with special praise reserved for its "fabulous dosas", "delicious" curries and "beautiful" desserts.

Uni S   21 | 17 | 17 | $28

2122 P St., NW (bet. 21st & 22nd Sts.), 202-833-8038

◪ "Modern sushi in a mod setting" is the calling card of this new wave "adult" Japanese off Dupont Circle, where "fresh fish" can be matched with "imaginative" small plates and trendy saketinis; though a few sense that it's "trying too hard to be hip", groupies retort that what it "lacks in quality it makes up for in originality."

Union St. Public House S   17 | 18 | 17 | $25

121 S. Union St. (bet. King & Prince Sts.), Alexandria, VA, 703-548-1785

◪ Downstairs at this all-purpose Old Town tavern near the waterfront, a young local crowd meets over microbrews and "upscale" bar food and has a "boisterous" "good" time; upstairs, the "broad" Southern-accented American menu and "English pub" rusticity make it a destination for families and "tourists", who begin a meal with oysters from the "reliable" raw bar and follow with ribs or chicken smoked over "real wood."

U-topia ●S   18 | 19 | 17 | $25

1418 U St., NW (bet. 14th & 15th Sts.), 202-483-7669

◪ "Creativity" flows freely at this "funky", "late-night" New U social center where there's "cool rotating art" on the walls, "groovy" live jazz in the air and International food on the plates; the fare is "pleasant, if unmemorable", and the staff "friendly" though "s-l-o-w", but fans "return often just for the music" and "eclectic people-watching."

Vegetable Garden S   20 | 13 | 18 | $18

11618 Rockville Pike (bet. Nicholson Ln. & Old Georgetown Rd.), Rockville, MD, 301-468-9301

◪ Those who opt to "go meatless" salute this Rockville alchemist's ability to turn tofu into "good" approximations of their favorite Asian chicken and meat dishes; its "organic and macrobiotic" Vegetarian options make it an "'in' spot among the granola crowd", but critics who conclude that the menu pictures make the food "look more appetizing" than it tastes advise "BYOS (bring your own seasonings)."

Vida S　　　– | – | – | M |
1120 20th St., NW (bet. L & M Sts.), 202-293-5433
High ceilings, bold colors and a handsome tequila-lined bar welcome suits at lunchtime and hipsters in the evening to this festive Nuevo Latino addition in the Golden Triangle; the spacious courtyard patio is an inviting happy-hour hangout and there's a dance club upstairs, but the kitchen is very serious; top toque Hector Guerra's (ex Galileo) menu moves from burritos, fajitas and other familiar favorites to specialties including Spanish seafood paella, grilled Argentinean steak and Chilean lamb stew.

VIDALIA S　　　26 | 23 | 24 | $51 |
1990 M St., NW (bet. 19th & 20th Sts.), 202-659-1990
◪ Look forward to "a little love on every plate" and an "explosion of tastes" in your mouth at this "stylish" Dixie-influenced New American in the Golden Triangle; despite its basement setting, it delivers a "top-notch" "culinary adventure when you want something both delicious and a little different" (think pork short ribs with new turnips and baby carrots), but be forewarned that the service can be "slow"; P.S. turn "luxury dining" into a "deal" with the prix fixe lunch.

Vignola S　　　19 | 12 | 16 | $24 |
113A N. Washington St. (bet. Beall Ave. & Middle Ln.), Rockville, MD, 301-340-2350
◪ In Rockville, this "family-run" "neighborhood" Italian deli offers "great" lunchtime subs and "homemade" pastas that are ordered at the counter for carryout or a casual "eat-in" meal; it morphs into a full-service restaurant at night, while on weekends, "live music adds some charm" to the "simple" space; exasperated Italophiles, however, are "lukewarm" about the results, citing merely "passable" food and service that's "seriously lacking."

Village Bistro S　　　21 | 15 | 19 | $31 |
Colonial Village, 1723 Wilson Blvd. (Quinn St.), Arlington, VA, 703-522-0284
■ "Tucked" away in an "unassuming" Arlington strip mall, this Continental bistro establishes its own "neighborhood atmosphere" with a "quirky" touch and "rough"-edged quarters that somehow make people feel at home (as does the "personable owner"); the "extensive" seafood-slanted menu is "satisfying and well-priced" and the service "accommodating", leading regulars who "go weekly" to "only hope" this "quiet" "hidden treasure" "stays a secret."

Visions 🅂   14   20   14 $16
*1927 Florida Ave., NW (bet. Connecticut Ave. & 19th St.),
202-667-0090*
☑ Featuring a "winning" script for "one-stop dating", this
Eclectic cafe "conveniently" set in the Visions cinema house
above Dupont Circle offers a diverse menu of "modestly
priced" Mediterranean and Middle Eastern tapas, snacks
and beverages (alcoholic and otherwise) along with
showings of independent flicks; even if the mostly pre-made
eats are "only so-so" and the service is "disorganized", it's
still a "great alternative to movie concession stands."

Vivo! ◗🅂   20   17   19 $33
1509 17th St., NW (bet. P & Q Sts.), 202-986-2627
☑ Just "like a trattoria in Northern Italy", only it's in Dupont
Circle East, applaud admirers of this "charming" eatery that
turns out "delicious" pastas (notably the homemade
agnolotti) and specialties from the wood-burning oven;
something of a "sleeper", it's one of Roberto Donna's (of
Galileo fame) projects and said to be a "training ground"
for his up-and-coming chefs, but despite its credentials
"disappointed" detractors demand to know "is mediocrity
contagious on 17th Street?"

Warehouse Bar & Grill 🅂   19   17   19 $31
*214 King St. (bet. Fairfax & Lee Sts.), Alexandria, VA,
703-683-6868*
☑ Caricatures of local movers and shakers decorate the
walls of this two-story Cajun-Creole seafood pub near Old
Town's waterfront, where the drill is to sit upstairs at a
"window table", order the "awesome she-crab soup" and
"reliably good" crawfish étouffée, and save room for the
"absolute best chocolate crème brûlée"; though some feel
it has grown "indifferent" over the years, loyalists still find
it a "comfortable" respite.

Washington Cafe & Grill ▽   24   20   24 $21
1025 Vermont Ave., NW (K St.), 202-347-7700
■ Sarajevo's loss is Downtown's gain, as Bianca and
Dxevad Topic bring their native Bosnian recipes to this
"wonderful" brick-walled enclave; *chivapichichi* (spiced
sausages), the specialty of the house, along with some
wines from Montenegro, draw expats from Southern
Europe for home cooking, live music and fellowship (on
weekends, it's an unofficial community center).

Washington Harbour Club 🅂   –   –   –   E
3000 K St., NW (31st St.), 202-339-9494
Snazzy and sophisticated, this sweeping new Georgetown
addition on the Potomac waterfront is anchored by a
mesmerizing wall-size aquarium filled with brilliantly hued
tropical fish; providing a tony backdrop for everything from
a high-end business meal (the booths are equipped with

Internet access) to late-night cocktails, it features an upscale Southeast Asian–accented New American menu, while more casual bites are served in its bars and lounges.

Wazuri [S] – | – | – | M

1836 18th St., NW (bet. Swann & T Sts.), 202-797-4930

Providing a culinary adventure inspired by the African diaspora, this warm-toned, art-filled addition is a one-of-a-kind experience in Adams Morgan; the far-reaching menu touches upon the regional cooking of Africa, Brazil, the Caribbean, Indonesia and beyond, and it's offered on two townhouse levels, out on the sidewalk patio and (best of all) up on the tree-shaded rooftop deck; overseeing all is Kojo Davis, who knows how to make everyone feel at home.

West End Cafe [S] – | – | – | E

One Washington Circle Hotel, 1 Washington Circle, NW (New Hampshire Ave.), 202-293-5390

The "post"-event place for Kennedy Center patrons and theatergoers, this West End supper club recently reopened after a suave hotel redo; now running the versatile New American kitchen is talented toque George Vetch (ex Oval Room), whose internationally inflected dishes are served in a greenhouse dining room; N.B. the renowned jazz piano music in the bar can be heard again starting in the fall.

WILLARD ROOM 24 | 27 | 25 | $59

Willard Inter-Continental Washington,
1401 Pennsylvania Ave., NW (14th St.), 202-637-7440

◪ A place to "spoil" someone special with "timeless" "elegance, fine dining and history", this "magnificent" "Edwardian" hotel dining room Downtown is a "culinary wonderland" that makes you "feel like you've arrived"; amid "stunning" surroundings with "ornate" appointments, an "impeccable" service team brings to table "marvelous" New American–New French fare, leading legions to avow that it's "*the*" place to "celebrate" an occasion, despite the "stuffy" ambiance.

Willow Grove Inn [S] ▽ 24 | 25 | 22 | $51

14079 Plantation Way (Rte. 15), Orange, VA, 540-672-5982

■ Nestled on dozens of acres in the rolling foothills of the Blue Ridge Mountains in Virginia's plantation country (not far from Montpelier or Monticello), this "antebellum" "charmer" "beautifully" reflects innkeeper Angela Mulloy's "personal touch"; amid "period" furnishings like heirloom quilts and handwoven rugs, a "friendly" staff serves an "excellent" seasonal menu of updated regional Southern fare.

Wok & Roll [S] – | – | – | I

604 H St., NW (bet. 6th & 7th Sts.), 202-347-4656

In ever-changing Chinatown, this au courant Asian addition near the MCI Center offers "good food at a good price" in simple, smart surroundings; not only does it serve traditional Chinese and Japanese crowd-pleasers (including roast duck and sushi), but it makes the "best bubble tea in DC" and it's open till 3 AM on weekends.

Woo Lae Oak S   23 | 17 | 19 | $29

River House, 1500 S. Joyce St. (15th St.), Arlington, VA, 703-521-3706

◪ Reputedly, every Korean president to visit Washington has dined at this "authentic" Seoul stalwart in Arlington, a veritable "headquarters for Korean VIPs on expense accounts" and "homesick" expats; the wide-ranging menu features many "serious" specialties, though novices tend to stick to easy-to-like choices such as the "BBQ grilled tableside" (a "must-have"), the "best bulgoki" and a "great seafood pancake"; be warned, though, of "slow", "curt" service and some language barriers.

Wurzburg Haus S   20 | 15 | 19 | $25

Red Mill Shopping Ctr., 7236 Muncaster Mill Rd. (Shady Grove Dr.), Rockville, MD, 301-330-0402

◪ "Lovers of traditional German food" make frequent "pilgrimages" to this "old-world" Bavarian outpost in Rockville for a "tempting" "taste" of bratwurst, boar and Wiener schnitzel "done properly" ("hardly a vegetable in sight") and washed down with "great imported beers"; on weekends, an accordion player adds to the "lively", "kid-oriented" atmosphere, but note that there are "few alternatives for those on low-fat diets."

Yama S   – | – | – | M

328 Maple Ave. W. (Nutley St.), Vienna, VA, 703-242-7703

"They do everything right" say ardent admirers about this traditional Japanese in Vienna, which many insist prepares the "best sushi in Northern Virginia" (the competition "doesn't even come close"); aside from its "interesting selection" of "super-fresh" raw fish, it also features a broad, affordably priced menu of "very good" cooked dishes; any surprise that it's "always busy"?

Yanÿu S   24 | 24 | 21 | $47

3433 Connecticut Ave., NW (bet. Macomb & Ordway Sts.), 202-686-6968

◪ Take an "exotic adventure to Asia" by visiting this "refreshingly different", "ultra-modern" "sophisticate" in Cleveland Park, where the "refined", "highly delectable" plates (inspired by the cuisines of China, Malaysia, Vietnam and beyond) are simply a "revelation" (the "Peking duck is unparalleled"); as "beautiful" as the presentations is the "serene" room, and though some complain that the prices are as "pretentious" as the ambiance, devotees promise that the "divine tasting menu is worth" it all.

Yoko S
▽ 23 | 16 | 22 | $27

*Hunter Mill Plaza, 2946J Chain Bridge Rd. (Hunter Mill Rd.),
Oakton, VA, 703-255-6644*

Yoko II S

*Herndon Center V, 332 Elden St. (Herndon Pkwy.),
Herndon, VA, 703-464-7000*

■ Situated in "unassuming" suburban "shopping centers" in
Northern Virginia, this pair of "family-friendly" Japanese
eateries earns a "key spot in the sushi rotation" of many
appreciative locals due to its "consistently good" raw fish
and special rolls, as well as its extensive sake selection,
all at an equally "good" price.

Yosaku S
22 | 14 | 20 | $30

4712 Wisconsin Ave., NW (Chesapeake St.), 202-363-4453

■ Some easily recognized faces salute this modest Upper
NW "pleaser" as "one of the best unknown Japanese
restaurants" in town thanks to its "always fresh" (if not
cutting-edge) sushi, "authentic shabu-shabu" and "solid"
udon noodles; the digs may be "plain", but it's a "favorite
no-special-occasion" kind of "neighborhood" place.

Zed's S
20 | 17 | 19 | $25

1201 28th St., NW (M St.), 202-333-4710

◪ Set in an "inviting" townhouse in Georgetown, this "white-
tablecloth" Ethiopian decorated with fresh flowers and
carved artifacts has a certain "class" about it; it's an
"enduring presence due to its tasty", vegetarian-friendly
cooking (beginning with the "best ever" injera bread) and
"respectful" service, but a handful of critics blast the
"beginner" seasoning and gripe that the "dressy-ish digs
don't suit the eating-with-your-hands" experience.

Washington, DC Indexes

Indexes list the best of many within each category.

CUISINES

Afghan
Afghan
Faryab
Panjshir

African
Wazuri

American (New)
Addie's
Arbor
Ardeo
Ashby Inn
Bardeo
Bistro Bistro
Black's Bar
Blue Iguana
Boulevard Woodgrill
Brasserie at Watergate
Butterfield 9
Cafe Bethesda
Carlyle Grand Cafe
Cashion's Eat Pl.
Caucus Room
Chef Geoff's
Coeur de Lion
Colorado Kitchen
Colvin Run Tavern
Corduroy
DC Coast
Dean & DeLuca
eCiti Cafe
Elysium
Equinox
Evening Star
Fairfax Room
Felix
Four & Twenty Blackbirds
Grapeseed

Greenwood
Grille 88
Inn at Little Washington
Jefferson
jordans
Kinkead's
Lafayette
Lightfoot
Majestic Cafe
Market St. B&G
Melrose
Mendocino Grille
Mimi's American
Morrison-Clark Inn
New Heights
Nora
Occidental
Old Angler's Inn
Oval Room
Palena
Peacock Cafe
Persimmon
Portabellos
Restaurant 7
Rhodeside Grill
Ritz, Grill (Pent. City)
Ritz, Grill (Wash. DC)
Roberts
Roof Terrace at Kennedy Ctr.
Saint Basil
Seasons
701
1789
Signatures
Starland Cafe
St. Regis, Library Lounge
Tabard Inn
Tahoga

Thyme Square
Topaz Bar
Vidalia
Washington Harbour Club
West End Cafe
Willard Room

American (Traditional)
Artie's
Bailiwick Inn
Ben's Chili Bowl
Bob & Edith's
Boulevard Woodgrill
Broad St. Grill
Cafe Deluxe
Cheesecake Factory
Clyde's
Colorado Kitchen
Daily Grill
Diner
District ChopHse.
Firehook Bakery
Franklins
Hard Times Cafe
Kramerbooks & Afterwords
Luna Grill
M & S Grill
Mark's Kitchen
Monocle
Nathan's
Oceanaire Sea. Rm.
Old Ebbitt Grill
Rail Stop
Ray's The Steaks
Sequoia
Tuscarora Mill
Two Quail
Union St. Public Hse.

Asian
Big Bowl
Ching Ching Cha

Oodles Noodles
Raku
Seven Seas
Teaism
Vegetable Garden
Wok & Roll

Asian Fusion
Asia Nora
Cafe Japoné
Kaz Sushi Bistro
Perry's

Bakeries
Bread Line
Firehook Bakery
La Madeleine
Samadi Sweets

Barbecue
Ben's Whole Hog BBQ
Green Field
Hee Been
Old Glory BBQ
Red Hot & Blue BBQ
Rocklands
Tony Cheng's
Woo Lae Oak

Belgian
Bistrot Belgique
Mannequin Pis
Marcel's

Bolivian
Pike Pizza

Bosnian
Washington Cafe

Brazilian
Coco Loco
Green Field
Grill from Ipanema

Burmese
Burma
Myanmar

Cajun/Creole
Black's Bar
B. Smith's
Louisiana Express Co.
RT's
219
Warehouse B&G

Californian
California Tortilla
Paolo's
Saveur

Caribbean
Caribbean Feast
Islander Caribbean
Negril
Ortanique

Chinese
A&J
China Star
City Lights
Eat First
Fortune
Full Kee
Full Key
Good Fortune
Hollywood East
Hope Key
Hunan Lion
Hunan Palace
Joe's Noodle House
Mark's Duck Hse.
Meiwah
Mr. K's
New Fortune

Oriental East
Peking Gourmet Inn
P.F. Chang's
Seven Seas
Wok & Roll

Coffeehouses/Dessert
Bread Line
Cheesecake Factory
Firehook Bakery
Kramerbooks & Afterwords
Tryst

Coffee Shops/Diners
Ben's Chili Bowl
Bob & Edith's
Diner

Continental
Bailiwick Inn
Ritz, Grill (Pent. City)
Tivoli
Village Bistro

Cuban
Banana Café
Cubano's
Havana Breeze
South Beach

Delis/Sandwich Shops
Chutzpah
Krupin's
Parkway Deli
Vignola

Dim Sum
A&J
Fortune
Good Fortune
Mark's Duck Hse.
New Fortune

Oriental East
Rabieng

Eclectic/International
Acropolis
Bar Rouge
Bread Line
C.F. Folks
Cities
Inn at Glen Echo
Rico y Rico
Signatures
Siné
Toka Cafe
U-topia
Visions

Ethiopian
Duken
Meskerem
Zed's

Floridian
South Beach

French
Brasserie at Watergate
Chez Marc
Jean-Michel
La Bergerie
La Chaumiere
La Colline
La Côte d'Or
La Ferme
La Miche
L'Auberge Chez François
L'Auberge Provençale
Le Gaulois
Le Refuge
Le Relais
Les Halles

Mediterranee
Prince Michel
Tempo

French (Bistro)
Bistro Bis
Bistro Français
Bistro 123
Bistrot du Coin
Bistrot Lepic
La Brasserie
La Chaumiere
La Fourchette
La Madeleine
Lavandou
Le Gaulois
Le Petit Mistral
Mon Ami Gabi
Montmartre
Petits Plats

French (New)
Brasserie Monte Carlo
Cafe 15
Citronelle
Gerard's Place
Le Relais
Le Rivage
Marcel's
Matisse
Saveur
Willard Room

German
Wurzburg Haus

Greek
Acropolis
Mykonos Grill

Hamburgers
Addie's
Carlyle Grand Cafe

Clyde's
Five Guys
Nathan's
Occidental
Ray's The Steaks

Indian/Pakistani
Amma Vegetarian
Bombay Bistro
Bombay Club
Bombay Palace
Bombay Tandoor
Cafe Taj
Connaught Place
Delhi Dhaba
Haandi
Heritage India
Jaipur
Kabob Palace
Tandoori Nights
Udupi Palace

Irish
Fadó Irish Pub
Siné

Italian
(N=Northern; S=Southern;
N&S=includes both)
Al Tiramisu (N&S)
Argia's (N&S)
Arucola (N&S)
Barolo (N)
Buca di Beppo (N&S)
Cafe Milano (N&S)
Café Mileto (S)
Centro Italian (N)
Cesco (N)
Coppi's (N&S)
Da Domenico (N)
Dolce Vita (N&S)
Etrusco (N)

Faccia Luna (N&S)
Filomena Rist. (N&S)
Finemondo (N&S)
Fontina Grille (S)
Galileo (N&S)
Generous George's (N&S)
Geranio (N&S)
Il Borgo (N&S)
Il Cigno (N&S)
Il Pizzico (N&S)
Il Radicchio (N&S)
I Matti (N)
i Ricchi (N)
Kuna (N&S)
Landini Brothers (N)
Luigino (N&S)
Maestro (N&S)
Mamma Lucia (N&S)
Michael's (N&S)
Obelisk (N)
Panino (N)
Paolo's (N&S)
Pasta Mia (N&S)
Pasta Plus (N&S)
Primi Piatti (N&S)
Renato (N&S)
Sesto Senso (N)
Skewers/Cafe Luna (N&S)
Spezie (N&S)
Teatro Goldoni (N&S)
Tempo (N&S)
Terrazza (N)
That's Amore (S)
Timpano Italian (N&S)
Tivoli (N)
Tosca (N)
Tragara (N)
2 Amys (N&S)
Vignola (N&S)
Vivo! (N)

Jamaican
Negril

Japanese
Acropolis
Cafe Japoné
Hakuba
Hama Sushi
Hinode
Ichiro Hibachi
Kaz Sushi Bistro
Konami
Makoto
Matuba
Murasaki
Niwano Hana
Perry's
Sakana
Sushi-Ko
Sushi Taro
Tachibana
Tako Grill
Tono Sushi
Uni
Wok & Roll
Yama
Yoko
Yosaku

Jewish
Krupin's
Parkway Deli

Korean
Hee Been
Mark's Kitchen
Sorak Garden
Woo Lae Oak

Latin/South American
Andale
Banana Café

Cafe Atlantico
Chi-Cha Lounge
Coco Loco
Crisp & Juicy
El Mariachi
El Pollo Rico
Gabriel
Green Field
Grill from Ipanema
Gua-Rapo
Lauriol Plaza
Ortanique
Pike Pizza
Red Sage
Vida

Lebanese
Bacchus
Lebanese Taverna
Neyla
Samadi Sweets

Malaysian
Malaysia Kopitiam
Penang

Mediterranean
BeDuCi
Bistro Bistro
Brasserie Monte Carlo
Cafe Midi
Café Olé
Cafe Promenade
Kazan
Lebanese Taverna
Le Tarbouche
Levante's
Matisse
Mediterranee
Meze
Mezza 9

Mimi's American
Neyla
Olives
Saint Basil

Mexican/Tex-Mex
Andale
Austin Grill
Burrito Bros.
Burro
Cactus Cantina
California Tortilla
El Mariachi
Guajillo
Lauriol Plaza
Mi Rancho
Rio Grande Cafe
Taqueria Poblano
Vida

Middle Eastern
Bacchus
Faryab
Kabob Palace
Kazan
Lebanese Taverna
Le Tarbouche
Meze
Moby Dick
Samadi Sweets
Skewers/Cafe Luna
Temel

Mongolian
Tony Cheng's

Moroccan
Taste of Morroco

Noodle Shops
A&J
China Star

Full Key
Joe's Noodle House
Oodles Noodles
Pho 75

Nuevo Latino
Cafe Atlantico
Gabriel
Gua-Rapo
Ortanique
Red Sage
Vida

Pan-Asian
Asia Nora
Cafe Asia
Joe's Noodle House
Malaysia Kopitiam
Spices
TenPenh
Yanÿu

Persian
Moby Dick

Peruvian
Crisp & Juicy
El Pollo Rico

Pizza
Arucola
Café Mileto
Coppi's
Dolce Vita
Faccia Luna
Fontina Grille
Generous George's
Il Radicchio
Levante's
Mamma Lucia
Pasta Plus
Pike Pizza

Pizzeria Paradiso
Saint Basil
2 Amys

Pub Food
Clyde's
Siné
Union St. Public Hse.

Puerto Rican
Banana Café

Russian
Maxim

Salvadoran
El Mariachi

Seafood
Andaman
Black's Bar
Blue Point Grill
DC Coast
Grillfish
Jerry's Seafood
Johnny's Half Shell
Kinkead's
Legal Sea Foods
Le Rivage
McCormick & Schmick's
Oceanaire Sea. Rm.
Palm
Pesce
Prime Rib
Ray's The Steaks
RT's
Sea Catch
Seven Seas
Starfish Cafe
Tony & Joe's
Village Bistro
Warehouse B&G

Southern/Soul
B. Smith's
Florida Ave. Grill
Georgia Brown's
Majestic Cafe
Vidalia
Willow Grove Inn

Southwestern
Jeffrey's at Watergate
Red Sage
Sweetwater Tavern
Vidalia

Spanish
Andalucia
Gabriel
Jaleo
Lauriol Plaza
Mar de Plata
Taberna del Alabardero

Steakhouses
Angelo & Maxie's
Blackie's
Bobby Van's
Capital Grille
Caucus Room
District ChopHse.
Fleming's
Ichiro Hibachi
Les Halles
Morton's of Chicago
Nick & Stef's
Nick's Chophse.
Palm
Prime Rib
Ray's The Steaks
Ruth's Chris
Sam & Harry's
Shula's Steak Hse.

Smith & Wollensky
Timpano Italian

Tapas

Andaman
Bardeo
Bar Rouge
Café Olé
Chi-Cha Lounge
Gabriel
Grapeseed
Jaleo
Mar de Plata
Meze
Mezza 9
Rico y Rico
Taberna del Alabardero
Topaz Bar
Visions

Tearooms

Ching Ching Cha
Teaism

Thai

Andaman
Bangkok Blues
Benjarong
Busara
Crystal Thai
Duangrat's
Haad Thai
Napa Thai
Neisha Thai
Rabieng
Sakoontra
Sala Thai

Sweet Basil
Tara Thai
T.H.A.I.
Thai Basil
Thaiphoon

Turkish

Cafe Divan
Kazan
Nizam's
Temel

Vegetarian

Amma Vegetarian
Cafe Taj
Mark's Kitchen
Meiwah
Minh
Thyme Square
Udupi Palace
Vegetable Garden

Vietnamese

Green Papaya
Huong Que
Little Saigon
Little Viet Garden
Minh
Nam's of Bethesda
Nam Viet
Pho 75
Queen Bee
Saigonnais
Saigon Saigon
Taste of Saigon
Thanh Thanh

LOCATIONS

WASHINGTON, DC

Capitol Hill
Banana Café
Barolo
Bistro Bis
B. Smith's
Burrito Bros.
Caucus Room
Firehook Bakery
Il Radicchio
La Brasserie
La Colline
Monocle
Montmartre
Starfish Cafe
Two Quail

**Chinatown/Penn Quarter/
MCI Center**
Andale
Angelo & Maxie's
Austin Grill
Burma
Cafe Atlantico
Capital Grille
Coco Loco
District ChopHse.
Eat First
Fadó Irish Pub
Full Kee
Haad Thai
Jaleo
Luigino
Nick & Stef's
701
Signatures
Teaism

Tony Cheng's
Wok & Roll

Downtown
Bar Rouge
Bobby Van's
Bread Line
Butterfield 9
Cafe 15
Coeur de Lion
Corduroy
DC Coast
Dean & DeLuca
Finemondo
Georgia Brown's
Gerard's Place
Havana Breeze
Jefferson
jordans
Les Halles
M & S Grill
Maxim
Morrison-Clark Inn
Occidental
Oceanaire Sea. Rm.
Old Ebbitt Grill
Ortanique
Red Sage
Shula's Steak Hse.
St. Regis, Library Lounge
Teaism
TenPenh
Tosca
Washington Cafe
Willard Room

Northeast
Colorado Kitchen

Upper NW
Arucola
Cafe Deluxe
Café Olé
Cheesecake Factory
Chef Geoff's
Delhi Dhaba
Greenwood
Krupin's
Makoto
Matisse
Murasaki
Negril
Starland Cafe
2 Amys
Yosaku

West End
Asia Nora
Blackie's
Marcel's

Meiwah
Melrose
Ritz, Grill (Wash. DC)
West End Cafe

Woodley Park/ Cleveland Park
Ardeo
Bardeo
Cactus Cantina
Firehook Bakery
Lavandou
Lebanese Taverna
Nam Viet
New Heights
Palena
Petits Plats
Roberts
Sala Thai
Spices
Tono Sushi
Yanÿu

NEARBY MARYLAND

Bethesda/Chevy Chase
Andalucia
Andaman
Austin Grill
Bacchus
Black's Bar
Brasserie Monte Carlo
Cafe Bethesda
Cafe Deluxe
California Tortilla
Centro Italian
Cesco
Clyde's

Delhi Dhaba
Faryab
Grapeseed
Green Papaya
Grillfish
Haandi
Hard Times Cafe
Heritage India
Hinode
Jaleo
Jean-Michel
La Ferme
La Madeleine

La Miche
Legal Sea Foods
Levante's
Louisiana Express Co.
Mamma Lucia
Matuba
McCormick & Schmick's
Moby Dick
Mon Ami Gabi
Nam's of Bethesda
Napa Thai
Oodles Noodles
Penang
Persimmon
Raku
Rio Grande Cafe
Ruth's Chris
South Beach
Sweet Basil
Tako Grill
Tara Thai
Terrazza
Thyme Square
Tragara

Gaithersburg/
Shady Grove/Olney

Buca di Beppo
Café Mileto
China Star
Hakuba
Hunan Palace
Mamma Lucia
Mannequin Pis
Mi Rancho
Moby Dick
Negril
New Fortune
Red Hot & Blue BBQ

Rico y Rico
Rio Grande Cafe
Tandoori Nights

Hyattsville/College Park/
Lanham/Laurel

Franklins
Hard Times Cafe
Jerry's Seafood
Negril
Pasta Plus
Pho 75
Red Hot & Blue BBQ
Udupi Palace

Potomac/Glen Echo

California Tortilla
Inn at Glen Echo
Old Angler's Inn
Renato

Rockville/White Flint

A&J
Addie's
Andalucia
Benjarong
Bombay Bistro
California Tortilla
Caribbean Feast
Cheesecake Factory
Crisp & Juicy
El Mariachi
Fontina Grille
Green Field
Hard Times Cafe
Hinode
Ichiro Hibachi
Il Pizzico
Joe's Noodle House
La Madeleine

Lebanese Taverna
Mamma Lucia
Mykonos Grill
Nick's Chophse.
Niwano Hana
P.F. Chang's
Pho 75
Seven Seas
Tara Thai
Taste of Saigon
That's Amore
Timpano Italian
Vegetable Garden
Vignola
Wurzburg Haus

Silver Spring/Wheaton

Crisp & Juicy
Cubano's
El Pollo Rico
Full Key
Good Fortune
Hollywood East
Mark's Kitchen
Mi Rancho
Negril
Oriental East
Parkway Deli
Thanh Thanh

NEARBY VIRGINIA

Alexandria

Afghan
Austin Grill
Blue Point Grill
Clyde's
Elysium
Evening Star
Faccia Luna
Firehook Bakery
Five Guys
Generous George's
Geranio
Haad Thai
Hard Times Cafe
La Bergerie
La Madeleine
Landini Brothers
Le Gaulois
Le Refuge
Majestic Cafe
Red Hot & Blue BBQ

RT's
Taqueria Poblano
Tempo
219
Union St. Public Hse.
Warehouse B&G

Arlington

Big Bowl
Bob & Edith's
Boulevard Woodgrill
Cafe Asia
Crisp & Juicy
Crystal Thai
Delhi Dhaba
El Pollo Rico
Faccia Luna
Hard Times Cafe
Hope Key
Il Radicchio
Kabob Palace

Lebanese Taverna
Legal Sea Foods
Little Viet Garden
Luna Grill
Matuba
Mediterranee
Minh
Nam Viet
Pike Pizza
Portabellos
Queen Bee
Rio Grande Cafe
Ritz, Grill (Pent. City)
Rocklands
Ruth's Chris
Saigon Saigon
Sala Thai
Siné
Tara Thai
Taste of Morroco
Woo Lae Oak

Fairfax/Springfield/
Annandale
A&J
Artie's
Austin Grill
Bailiwick Inn
Blue Iguana
Bombay Bistro
Chutzpah
Connaught Place
Dolce Vita
Five Guys
Hard Times Cafe
Hee Been
Jaipur
Mark's Duck Hse.
Moby Dick

Red Hot & Blue BBQ
Rhodeside Grill
Sakoontra
Sorak Garden
Temel
Yoko

Falls Church/
Baileys Crossroads
Argia's
Bangkok Blues
Broad St. Grill
Crisp & Juicy
Duangrat's
Fortune
Full Kee
Haandi
Huong Que
La Côte d'Or
La Madeleine
Little Saigon
Myanmar
Neisha Thai
Panjshir
Peking Gourmet Inn
Pho 75
Rabieng
Samadi Sweets
Tara Thai

Great Falls
L'Auberge Chez François
Le Relais

Leesburg/Middleburg/
The Plains
Lightfoot
Rail Stop
Red Hot & Blue BBQ
Tuscarora Mill

Manassas/Centreville/ Prince William County

Ben's Whole Hog BBQ
Bistrot Belgique
Chez Marc
Five Guys
Hard Times Cafe
Old Glory BBQ
Panino
Red Hot & Blue BBQ
Sweetwater Tavern

McLean

Cafe Taj
Il Borgo
Kazan
Le Petit Mistral
Michael's
Tachibana

Reston/Herndon/Chantilly

Angelo & Maxie's
Big Bowl
Clyde's
Delhi Dhaba
Fortune
Hama Sushi
Hard Times Cafe
Il Cigno
La Madeleine
Market St. B&G
McCormick & Schmick's
Morton's of Chicago
Paolo's
Pho 75
Rio Grande Cafe
Saint Basil
Sweetwater Tavern
Thai Basil
That's Amore
Yoko

Rosslyn/Courthouse

Guajillo
Gua-Rapo
Mezza 9
Pho 75
Ray's The Steaks
Red Hot & Blue BBQ
Rhodeside Grill
Tivoli
Village Bistro

Shirlington

Bistro Bistro
Carlyle Grand Cafe
T.H.A.I.

Tysons Corner/Vienna

Amma Vegetarian
Bistro 123
Bombay Tandoor
Burrito Bros.
Busara
Cafe Deluxe
Capital Grille
Clyde's
Colvin Run Tavern
Da Domenico
Daily Grill
eCiti Cafe
Fleming's
Hunan Lion
Konami
La Madeleine
Legal Sea Foods
Maestro
McCormick & Schmick's
Moby Dick
Morton's of Chicago
Neisha Thai

Nizam's
Palm
Panjshir
P.F. Chang's
Restaurant 7
Sam & Harry's

Shula's Steak Hse.
Sweetwater Tavern
Tara Thai
Taste of Saigon
That's Amore
Yama

VIRGINIA COUNTRYSIDE

Ashby Inn
Four & Twenty Blackbirds
Inn at Little Washington

L'Auberge Provençale
Prince Michel
Willow Grove Inn

SPECIAL FEATURES

(Restaurants followed by a † may not offer
that feature at every location.)

Breakfast

(See also Hotel Dining)

Ben's Chili Bowl

Bob & Edith's†

Bread Line

Daily Grill†

Diner

Florida Ave. Grill

La Colline

Louisiana Express Co.

Old Ebbitt Grill

Signatures

Teaism

Brunch

A&J

Arbor

Artie's

Ashby Inn

Austin Grill

Banana Café

Bistro Bis

Bombay Club

B. Smith's

Cafe Atlantico

Cafe Promenade

Carlyle Grand Cafe

Cashion's Eat Pl.

Cheesecake Factory

Clyde's

Coeur de Lion

Colorado Kitchen

Evening Star

Felix

Four & Twenty Blackbirds

Gabriel

Georgia Brown's

Grille 88

Inn at Glen Echo

Kramerbooks & Afterwords

Le Relais

Maestro

Majestic Cafe

Market St. B&G

Mark's Duck Hse.

Melrose

Morrison-Clark Inn

New Heights

Old Ebbitt Grill

Oriental East

Paolo's

Parkway Deli

Peacock Cafe

Perry's

Portabellos

Rabieng

Rail Stop

Restaurant 7

Rhodeside Grill†

Ritz, Grill (Pent. City)

Ritz, Grill (Wash. DC)

Seasons

Sequoia

Seven Seas

Starland Cafe

Tabard Inn

Thyme Square

Tony & Joe's

219

Willow Grove Inn

Washington, DC – Special Feature Index

Buffet Served
(Check availability)
Ben's Whole Hog BBQ
Bombay Bistro
Bombay Palace
Bombay Tandoor
Cafe Promenade
Cafe Taj
Coco Loco
Connaught Place
Delhi Dhabat
Filomena Rist.
Georgia Brown's
Green Field
Haandit
Hee Been
Ritz, Grill (Pent. City)
Tony Cheng's

Business Dining
Addie's
Angelo & Maxie'st
Argia's
Artie's
Bacchus
Barolo
Bistro Bis
Bobby Van's
Bombay Club
Bombay Tandoor
Butterfield 9
Cafe 15
Cafe Promenade
Capital Grille
Caucus Room
Citronelle
Colvin Run Tavern
DC Coast
Equinox
Fairfax Room

Finemondo
Fleming's
Fontina Grille
Gabriel
Galileot
Georgia Brown's
Gerard's Place
Haad Thait
Hakuba
i Ricchi
Jaipur
Jeffrey's at Watergate
jordans
Kaz Sushi Bistro
Kinkead's
Konami
Lafayette
Legal Sea Foodst
Le Relais
Maestro
M & S Grill
Marcel's
Market St. B&G
McCormick & Schmick's
Melrose
Mezza 9
Michael's
Monocle
Morton's of Chicago
Occidental
Oceanaire Sea. Rm.
Old Ebbitt Grill
Olives
Oval Room
Palm
Prime Rib
Primi Piatti
Red Sage
Restaurant 7
Ritz, Grill (Pent. City)

Ritz, Grill (Wash. DC)
Ruth's Chris
Sam & Harry's
Seasons
701
Signatures
Smith & Wollensky
Spezie
St. Regis, Library Lounge
Taberna del Alabardero
Tahoga
Tandoori Nights
Taste of Saigon
Teatro Goldoni
Tivoli
Tosca
Tuscarora Mill
Vidalia
Washington Harbour Club
Willard Room

Catering

Al Tiramisu
Amma Vegetarian†
Andale
Bacchus
Ben's Whole Hog BBQ
Bread Line
Burrito Bros.†
Cafe Midi
Cafe Milano
California Tortilla
Caribbean Feast
C.F. Folks
Chutzpah
Citronelle
Clyde's†
Dean & DeLuca
Firehook Bakery
Hard Times Cafe†

Il Radicchio
Islander Caribbean
Jeffrey's at Watergate
Kazan
Krupin's
Lafayette
La Madeleine†
Lebanese Taverna
Louisiana Express Co.
Malaysia Kopitiam
Market St. B&G
Mark's Kitchen
Old Ebbitt Grill
Old Glory BBQ
Red Hot & Blue BBQ†
Red Sage
Rocklands
St. Regis, Library Lounge
Tivoli
Washington Cafe
Wurzburg Haus
Yanÿu
Zed's

Chef's Table in Kitchen

Citronelle
Galileo
Marcel's
Matisse
Tosca

Child-Friendly

(Besides the normal fast-food
places; * children's menu
available)
Arucola
Austin Grill†
Big Bowl†
Cactus Cantina
Clyde's†
Filomena Rist.

Franklins
Generous George's*
Hard Times Cafe†
Lebanese Taverna†
Legal Sea Foods†
Mamma Lucia†
Mark's Kitchen
Matuba
Red Hot & Blue BBQ†
Rio Grande Cafe*
Rocklands†
Tara Thai
2 Amys

Delivery/Takeout
(D=delivery, T=takeout)
Addie's (T)
Al Tiramisu (T)
Andale (T)
Andalucia (T)
Angelo & Maxie's (T)
Arbor (T)
Ardeo (T)
Argia's (T)
Arucola (D,T)
Austin Grill (T)
BeDuCi (T)
Ben's Whole Hog BBQ (T)
Big Bowl†
Bistro Bistro (T)
Black's Bar (T)
Blue Iguana (T)
Bobby Van's (T)
Bombay Club (T)
Boulevard Woodgrill (T)
Brasserie at Watergate (T)
Bread Line (T)
Cafe Deluxe (T)
Cafe Milano (T)
Café Mileto (D,T)

Café Olé (T)
Capital Grille (T)
Caucus Room (T)
Centro Italian (T)
Cesco (T)
Cheesecake Factory†
Cities (T)
Clyde's (T)
eCiti Cafe (T)
Finemondo (T)
Fontina Grille (T)
Gabriel (T)
Galileo†
Georgia Brown's (T)
Heritage India†
Jaleo (T)
Jeffrey's at Watergate (T)
Jerry's Seafood (T)
Johnny's Half Shell (T)
Kaz Sushi Bistro (T)
Konami (T)
La Brasserie (D,T)
Lavandou (T)
Lebanese Taverna (T)
Legal Sea Foods†
Le Relais (T)
Le Tarbouche (T)
Lightfoot (T)
Luigino (T)
M & S Grill (T)
McCormick & Schmick's (T)
Melrose (T)
Mendocino Grille (D,T)
Mon Ami Gabi (T)
Montmartre (T)
Nick's Chophse. (T)
Oceanaire Sea. Rm. (T)
Old Ebbitt Grill (T)
Oval Room (T)
Palm (T)

Pesce (T)
Pizzeria Paradiso (T)
Red Sage (D,T)
Renato (T)
Restaurant 7 (T)
Rocklands†
Saint Basil (T)
Sam & Harry's†
Seasons (T)
Sesto Senso (D,T)
701 (T)
Smith & Wollensky (T)
Teatro Goldoni (T)
TenPenh (T)
Tivoli (T)
2 Amys (T)
Vidalia (T)

Dessert

Bread Line
Carlyle Grand Cafe
Cashion's Eat Pl.
Chef Geoff's
Citronelle
DC Coast
Dean & DeLuca†
Firehook Bakery
Galileo†
Inn at Little Washington
Johnny's Half Shell
jordans
Kinkead's
Kramerbooks & Afterwords
Majestic Cafe
Melrose
Obelisk
Palena
Restaurant 7
Samadi Sweets
1789

TenPenh
Thyme Square
Tivoli
Tragara
2 Amys

Dining Alone

(Other than hotels and places
with counter service)
Al Tiramisu
Bread Line
Cafe Divan
C.F. Folks
Clyde's†
DC Coast
Dean & DeLuca†
Diner
Finemondo
Grapeseed
Johnny's Half Shell
Kaz Sushi Bistro
Kinkead's
Mamma Lucia
Marcel's
Old Ebbitt Grill
Olives
Pizzeria Paradiso
Raku
Rocklands†
Spezie
Teaism
Toka Cafe
Uni
Visions
Washington Harbour Club

Entertainment

(Call for days and times of
performances)
Acropolis (jazz)
Andalucia†

Andaman (jazz)
Banana Café (piano)
Bangkok Blues (varies)
Bar Rouge (DJ)
Ben's Whole Hog BBQ (bands)
Bistro Bistro (bands/guitar)
Blackie's (DJ)
Blue Iguana (DJs)
Bombay Club (piano)
B. Smith's (jazz)
Cafe Milano (DJs)
Café Olé (guitar)
Cafe Promenade (jazz brunch)
Chi-Cha Lounge (bands)
Cities (DJ)
Clyde's†
Coco Loco (Brazilian)
Coeur de Lion (jazz/piano)
Connaught Place (sitar)
Dean & DeLuca†
Dolce Vita (guitar/piano)
Duangrat's (Thai dance)
Duken (Ethiopian)
eCiti Cafe (DJ)
Elysium (piano)
Evening Star (jazz)
Fadó Irish Pub (modern Irish)
Felix (DJ/jazz/piano)
Four & Twenty Blackbirds (harp)
Georgia Brown's (jazz brunch)
Grille 88 (piano bar)
Hakuba (bands)
Il Borgo (piano)
Il Cigno (guitar/vocals)
Inn at Glen Echo (jazz)
Islander Carib. (jazz/piano/vocals)
Jaleo†
Jefferson (piano)
Kinkead's (jazz)
Kramerbooks (varies)

Lafayette (piano)
Le Tarbouche (belly dancer/DJ)
Marcel's (piano)
Market St. B&G (jazz)
Maxim (dancing/vocals)
Melrose (ballroom/jazz)
Meze (Turkish)
Mimi's Amer. (singing waiters)
Ortanique (dancing)
Penang†
Perry's (drag brunch)
Pike Pizza (Latino)
Prime Rib (bass/piano)
Rhodeside Grill†
Rico y Rico (harp)
Ritz, Grill (Wash. DC) (jazz trio/piano)
Sesto Senso (dancing/DJ)
701 (jazz/piano)
Signatures (jazz)
South Beach (DJs)
Starland Cafe (varies)
Taste of Morroco (belly dancer)
Teatro Goldoni (jazz)
Timpano Italian (bands/swing)
Tony & Joe's (vocals)
219 (jazz)
U-topia (blues/jazz)
Vida (DJ)
Vignola (piano)
Washington Cafe (blues/jazz/rock)
Washington Harbour Club (DJ)
West End Cafe (jazz/piano)
Willard Room (piano)
Willow Grove Inn (piano)
Wurzburg Haus (accordion)

Family-Style
Arucola
Buca di Beppo
Green Field

Ichiro Hibachi
Mamma Lucia†
That's Amore
Tony Cheng's

Fireplaces

Al Tiramisu
Ashby Inn
Bistro Bis
Cities
Clyde's†
Coeur de Lion
Duken
Fadó Irish Pub
Fairfax Room
Jefferson
La Chaumiere
La Ferme
La Madeleine†
L'Auberge Provençale
Le Gaulois
Lightfoot
Matisse
Old Angler's Inn
Petits Plats
Sea Catch
1789
Siné
Tabard Inn
Timpano Italian
Vivo!

Historic Places

(Year opened; *building)
1753 L'Auberge Provençale*
1778 Willow Grove Inn*
1800s Bailiwick Inn*
late 1800s Lightfoot*
1851 Willard Room*
1860 Old Angler's Inn*

1860 1789*
1865 Morrison-Clark Inn*
1887 Tabard Inn*
1890 Nora*
1904 Two Quail*
1908 B. Smith's*
1910 Four & Twenty Blackbirds*
1940s Majestic Cafe*

Hotel Dining

Ashby Inn
    Ashby Inn
Bailiwick Inn
    Bailiwick Inn
Four Seasons Hotel
    Seasons
Georgetown Inn
    Daily Grill†
Henley Park Hotel
    Coeur de Lion
Hotel George
    Bistro Bis
Hotel Rouge
    Bar Rouge
Hotel Tabard Inn
    Tabard Inn
Hyatt Arlington
    Mezza 9
Hyatt Regency Reston
    Market St. B&G
Inn at Little Washington
    Inn at Little Washington
Jefferson, The
    Jefferson
Latham Hotel
    Citronelle
Morrison-Clark Inn
    Morrison-Clark Inn
Morrison House
    Elysium

Omni Shoreham Hotel
   Roberts
Park Hyatt Washington
   Melrose
Radisson Barcelo Hotel
   Gabriel
Renaissance Mayflower Hotel
   Cafe Promenade
Ritz-Carlton Pentagon City
   Ritz, Grill (Pent. City)
Ritz-Carlton Tysons Corner
   Maestro
Ritz-Carlton Washington D.C.
   Ritz, Grill (Wash. DC)
Sheraton Four Points
   Corduroy
Sofitel Lafayette Square
   Cafe 15
St. Regis
   St. Regis, Library Lounge
Swissôtel-The Watergate
   Jeffrey's at Watergate
Topaz Hotel
   Topaz Bar
Tysons Corner Marriott
   Shula's Steak Hse.
Westin Embassy Row
   Fairfax Room
Willard Inter-Continental
   Willard Room
Willow Grove Inn
   Willow Grove Inn
Wyndham City Center
   Shula's Steak Hse.

"In" Places

Addie's
Ardeo
Asia Nora
Bardeo

Bar Rouge
Ben's Chili Bowl
Bistro Bis
Bistrot Lepic
Black's Bar
Bread Line
Cafe Deluxe
Cafe Milano
Carlyle Grand Cafe
Cashion's Eat Pl.
Caucus Room
C.F. Folks
Chef Geoff's
Cities
DC Coast
Diner
Duken
eCiti Cafe
Equinox
Evening Star
Four & Twenty Blackbirds
Full Keet
Gabriel
Galileo
Georgia Brown's
Grille 88
Hakuba
Huong Que
Inn at Little Washington
Jaleo
Johnny's Half Shell
Kaz Sushi Bistro
Konami
Kramerbooks & Afterwords
La Chaumiere
La Fourchette
Landini Brothers
Lauriol Plaza
Le Tarbouche
Majestic Cafe

Mimi's American
Mon Ami Gabi
Monocle
Nathan's
Nora
Obelisk
Old Ebbitt Grill
Olives
Oval Room
Palena
Palm
Peking Gourmet Inn
Pesce
Pizzeria Paradiso
Rail Stop
Restaurant 7
RT's
Sam & Harry's†
Sesto Senso
701
Sushi-Ko
Tabard Inn
TenPenh
Topaz Bar
2 Amys
Vidalia
Visions
Willow Grove Inn
Yanÿu

Late Dining

(Weekday closing hour)
Acropolis (12 AM)
Ben's Chili Bowl (2 AM)
Bistro Français (3 AM)
Cafe Japoné (1:30 AM)
Duken (1 AM)
Eat First (2 AM)
Full Kee†
Full Key (1:30 AM)

Good Fortune (1 AM)
Hard Times Cafe†
Hollywood East (1 AM)
Hope Key (1 AM)
Kramerbooks (1:30 AM)
Meze (2 AM)
New Fortune (1 AM)
Old Ebbitt Grill (1 AM)
Old Glory BBQ†
Smith & Wollensky (1:30 AM)
Tryst (2 AM)
Vivo! (2:30 AM)

Meet for a Drink

Acropolis
Artie's
Banana Café
Bardeo
Bar Rouge
Bistro Bis
Black's Bar
Caucus Room
Cities
Clyde's†
Coco Loco
eCiti Cafe
Fairfax Room
Gabriel
Jaleo
jordans
Landini Brothers
Les Halles
Le Tarbouche
Marcel's
Market St. B&G
McCormick & Schmick's
Melrose
Mezza 9
Mimi's American
Nathan's

Old Ebbitt Grill
Olives
Ortanique
Penang†
Red Sage
Restaurant 7
Sequoia
701
Siné
South Beach
Spezie
St. Regis, Library Lounge
Tandoori Nights
Teaism
TenPenh
Toka Cafe
Topaz Bar
Tryst
Visions
Washington Harbour Club

Noteworthy Newcomers
Acropolis
Andale
Bangkok Blues
Bardeo
Bar Rouge
Boulevard Woodgrill
Cafe Divan
Cafe 15
Colorado Kitchen
Colvin Run Tavern
Fairfax Room
Finemondo
Franklins
Grille 88
Guajillo
Gua-Rapo
Ichiro Hibachi
Jaipur

jordans
Kuna
Maxim
Meze
Minh
Mon Ami Gabi
Montmartre
Murasaki
Napa Thai
Ray's The Steaks
Restaurant 7
Saigon Saigon
Signatures
Siné
South Beach
Spezie
Tandoori Nights
Toka Cafe
Topaz Bar
2 Amys
Vida
Washington Cafe
Washington Harbour Club
Wazuri
Wok & Roll

Offbeat
Ben's Chili Bowl
Bob & Edith's†
Ching Ching Cha
Duken
Florida Ave. Grill
Franklins
Greenwood
Johnny's Half Shell
Malaysia Kopitiam
Mark's Kitchen
Matuba†
Maxim

Meskerem
Mimi's American
Perry's
Pike Pizza
Tabard Inn
Teaism
Toka Cafe
Washington Cafe
Wazuri

Outdoor Dining

(G=garden; P=patio;
S=sidewalk; T=terrace;
W=waterside)
Addie's (P)
Arbor (P)
Argia's (P)
Arucola (P)
Ashby Inn (P)
Bacchus (P)
Banana Café (S)
BeDuCi (T)
Bistro 123 (T)
Bistrot Belgique (P)
Black's Bar (P)
Blue Point Grill (P)
Bombay Club (S)
Brasserie at Watergate (T)
Bread Line (S)
Busarat
Cactus Cantina (S)
Cafe Atlantico (S)
Cafe Bethesda (P)
Cafe Deluxet
Cafe 15 (T)
Cafe Japoné (S)
Cafe Milano (P)
Café Mileto (P)
Café Olé (P)
Carlyle Grand Cafe (P)

Cashion's Eat Pl. (S)
Centro Italian (P)
Cesco (P)
C.F. Folks (P)
Chef Geoff's (P)
Dean & DeLuca (P)
Equinox (S)
Etrusco (S)
Evening Star (P)
Faccia Lunat
Firehook Bakeryt
Five Guyst
Fontina Grille (P,S)
Galileot
Gerard's Place (S)
Green Papaya (S)
Grille 88 (S)
Grill from Ipanema (P)
Hakuba (P)
Il Cigno (T,W)
Inn at Glen Echo (T)
Inn at Little Washington (G,P)
Jaipur (T)
Jaleot
jordans (P)
Konami (G)
Kramerbooks (P,S)
La Brasserie (P)
La Ferme (T)
La Fourchette (T)
La Miche (S)
L'Auberge Chez François (G)
L'Auberge Provençale (T)
Lauriol Plaza (P,T)
Lebanese Tavernat
Le Gaulois (G)
Le Rivage (T,W)
Les Halles (P)
Levante's (P)
Little Viet Garden (P)

Luna Grill (P)
Marcel's (P)
Melrose (P)
Meze (P)
Mimi's American (S)
Minh (P)
Mi Rancho (P)
Mon Ami Gabi (P)
Montmartre (P)
Napa Thai (S)
New Heights (S)
Neyla (P)
Occidental (P,S)
Old Angler's Inn (T)
Old Glory BBQ†
Oval Room (S)
Paolo's (P)
Peacock Cafe (P,S)
Penang†
Perry's (T)
Petits Plats (P)
Primi Piatti (S)
Prince Michel (P)
Rail Stop (P)
Raku†
Renato (S)
Rhodeside Grill†
Rico y Rico (P)
Rio Grande Cafe†
Roberts (T)
Roof Terrace at Kennedy Ctr. (T)
Sea Catch (P,T,W)
Sequoia (T)
701 (P)
Siné (P)
Skewers/Cafe Luna (P)
Smith & Wollensky (S)
Starland Cafe (P)
Sweetwater Tavern†
Tabard Inn (G)

Tahoga (G,T)
Tandoori Nights (S)
Tara Thai†
Taste of Saigon (P)
Teaism†
TenPenh (P)
Terrazza (T)
T.H.A.I. (P)
Thyme Square (P)
Toka Cafe (P)
Tony & Joe's (P,W)
Tuscarora Mill (P)
2 Amys (P)
219 (T)
Vida (P)
Visions (P)
Washington Harbour Club (P)
Wazuri (T)
Willow Grove Inn (P,T)
Yosaku (P)
Zed's (P)

Parking

(L=lot, V=valet, *=validated)
Addie's (L)
Al Tiramisu (V)
Andale (V)
Ardeo (V)
Arucola (L)
Asia Nora (V)
Bacchus (V)
Bailiwick Inn (L)
Bardeo (V)
BeDuCi (V)
Bistro Bis (V)
Blackie's (V)
Black's Bar*
Blue Point Grill (L)
Bobby Van's (V)
Bombay Club (V)

Bombay Palace (V)

Boulevard Woodgrill (L)

Brasserie at Watergate (V)

Broad St. Grill (L)

B. Smith's*

Butterfield 9 (V)

Cafe Atlantico (V)

Cafe Bethesda (V)

Cafe Milano (L)

Café Olé*

Cafe Promenade (V)

Capital Grille (V)*

Carlyle Grand Cafe (L)

Cashion's Eat Pl. (V)

Caucus Room (V)

Centro Italian (L,V)

Cesco (V)

Chef Geoff's (L)

Cities (V)

Citronelle (V)

Clyde's†

Coeur de Lion (L,V)

Colvin Run Tavern (V)*

Corduroy (V)*

Da Domenico (L)

DC Coast (V)

Dean & DeLuca†

eCiti Cafe (V)

Elysium (L,V)

Equinox*

Fairfax Room*

Faryab (L)

Felix (L)

Finemondo (V)

Full Kee†

Full Key (L)

Gabriel (V)

Galileo (V)

Georgia Brown's (V)

Gerard's Place (V)

Grapeseed (V)

Greenwood (L)

Heritage India (V)

Hunan Lion (L)

i Ricchi (V)

Jaleo†

Jean-Michel (L)

Jefferson (L,V)

Jeffrey's at Watergate (V)

jordans (V)

Kinkead's (V)

La Bergerie (L)

La Chaumiere*

La Colline*

La Miche (V)

Landini Brothers*

L'Auberge Chez François (L)

Lauriol Plaza*

Le Rivage (V)

Les Halles (L,V)

Le Tarbouche (L)

Lightfoot (L)

Maestro (L,V)

M & S Grill (V)

Marcel's (V)

Melrose (V)

Mezza 9*

Mon Ami Gabi (V)

Monocle (L,V)

Morrison-Clark Inn*

Mr. K's (V)

New Heights (V)

Neyla (V)

Nick & Stef's (V)

Nora (V)

Obelisk (L)

Occidental (V)
Oceanaire Sea. Rm. (V)
Old Ebbitt Grill (V)
Olives (V)
Oval Room*
Palena (L)
Penang (V)
Persimmon (L)
Pesce (V)
Prime Rib (V)
Primi Piatti (L,V)
Red Sage (V)*
Restaurant 7 (L,V)
Ritz, Grill (Pent. City) (V)
Ritz, Grill (Wash. DC) (V)
Roberts (V)
Rocklands†
Ruth's Chris (V)*
Sam & Harry's (L,V)
Sea Catch (L,V)
Seasons (L,V)
Sequoia (L)
Sesto Senso (L,V)
701 (V)
1789 (V)
Smith & Wollensky (V)
Spezie (V)
Sushi-Ko (V)
Sushi Taro (L)
Tabard Inn (L,V)
Taberna del Alabardero (L)
Tahoga (V)
Teatro Goldoni (V)
TenPenh (V)
Terrazza*
Thyme Square (L)
Tivoli (L)
Tosca (V)

Vidalia (V)
Village Bistro (L)
Yanÿu (V)

People-Watching
Acropolis
Arbor
Bar Rouge
Bistro Bis
Bistro Français
Black's Bar
Bob & Edith's†
Bread Line
Cafe 15
Cafe Japoné
Cafe Milano
Cafe Promenade
Carlyle Grand Cafe
Cashion's Eat Pl.
Caucus Room
Cities
Dean & DeLuca†
Diner
eCiti Cafe
Galileo†
Georgia Brown's
Inn at Little Washington
Jaleo
Johnny's Half Shell
jordans
Kinkead's
La Brasserie
La Colline
Lauriol Plaza
Levante's
Meze
Mon Ami Gabi
Monocle
Neyla
Nora

Old Ebbitt Grill
Ortanique
Oval Room
Palm†
Penang†
Primi Piatti
Red Sage
Restaurant 7
Rhodeside Grill
Sam & Harry's†
Seasons
Sequoia
701
Skewers/Cafe Luna
TenPenh
Thaiphoon
Tryst
Vida
Washington Harbour Club

Power Scenes
Ardeo
Bistro Bis
Bobby Van's
Bombay Club
Capital Grille
Caucus Room
Citronelle
Colvin Run Tavern
DC Coast
Equinox
Etrusco
Galileo
Inn at Little Washington
Jeffrey's at Watergate
Kinkead's
La Colline
Le Relais
Maestro
Marcel's

Monocle
Morton's of Chicago
Nick & Stef's
Nora
Occidental
Old Ebbitt Grill
Olives
Oval Room
Palena
Palm
Prime Rib
Restaurant 7
Sam & Harry's
Seasons
701
Signatures
Taberna del Alabardero
Teatro Goldoni
Tosca
Tuscarora Mill
Vidalia
Willard Room

Pre-Theater Menus
(Call for prices and times)
Bistro Français
Bistro 123
Brasserie at Watergate
Cafe Atlantico
Carlyle Grand Cafe
Clyde's
Gabriel
Jeffrey's at Watergate
La Côte d'Or
Lavandou
Le Rivage
Oval Room
Petits Plats
Portabellos
Roof Terrace at Kennedy Ctr.

Saigon Saigon
701
Tivoli
West End Cafe

Private Rooms

(Restaurants charge less at off times; call for capacity)
Andaman
Ardeo
Asia Nora
Barolo
BeDuCi
Bistro Bis
Bistrot Lepic
Blackie's
B. Smith's
Buca di Beppo†
Cafe Milano
Caucus Room
Chef Geoff's
China Star
Colvin Run Tavern
Duangrat's
Equinox
Etrusco
Evening Star
Finemondo
Firehook Bakery†
Galileo
Greenwood
Gua-Rapo
Havana Breeze
Hee Been
Heritage India†
i Ricchi
Kinkead's
La Bergerie
La Brasserie
Lafayette

La Ferme
L'Auberge Provençale
Lebanese Taverna†
Lightfoot
Marcel's
Maxim
Melrose
Mr. K's
New Heights
Nick & Stef's
Nora
Old Ebbitt Grill
Olives
Ortanique
Oval Room
Red Sage
Rico y Rico
Sam & Harry's
701
Signatures
Sorak Garden
Sushi-Ko
Taberna del Alabardero
Tahoga
Teatro Goldoni
Tivoli
Tono Sushi
Tosca
Tragara
Tuscarora Mill
219
Vida
Vidalia
Washington Harbour Club
Yanÿu

Prix Fixe Menus

(Call for prices and times)
Bailiwick Inn
BeDuCi

Bistro Français
Bistro 123
Blue Iguana
Bombay Club
Bombay Palace
Brasserie at Watergate
Cafe Atlantico
Cafe Promenade
Caucus Room
Chez Marc
Ching Ching Cha
Citronelle
City Lights
Coeur de Lion
Colvin Run Tavern
Elysium
Evening Star
Finemondo
Geranio
Greenwood
I Matti
Inn at Little Washington
Jefferson
Jeffrey's at Watergate
La Côte d'Or
La Fourchette
L'Auberge Chez François
L'Auberge Provençale
Le Petit Mistral
Le Rivage
Les Halles
Le Tarbouche
Maestro
Marcel's
Melrose
Morrison-Clark Inn
Obelisk
Oval Room
Palena
Persimmon

Petits Plats
Red Sage
Ritz, Grill (Wash. DC)
Saveur
Seasons
701
1789
Sushi-Ko
Tivoli
Tosca
Vidalia
Willard Room

Quiet Conversation

Asia Nora
Bailiwick Inn
Bombay Club
Butterfield 9
Cafe Bethesda
Caucus Room
Ching Ching Cha
Citronelle
Coeur de Lion
Elysium
Gerard's Place
Heritage India†
Inn at Little Washington
La Ferme
Maestro
Majestic Cafe
Makoto
Melrose
Morrison-Clark Inn
New Heights
Obelisk
Oceanaire Sea. Rm.
Palena
Ritz, Grill (Pent. City)
Roberts
Sea Catch

Washington, DC – Special Feature Index

Seasons
1789
Taberna del Alabardero
Tahoga
Temel
Terrazza
Tosca
West End Cafe
Willard Room

Raw Bars

Black's Bar
Blue Point Grill
Clyde's†
eCiti Cafe
Johnny's Half Shell
Kinkead's
Legal Sea Foods†
Matuba†
McCormick & Schmick's†
Old Ebbitt Grill
Sea Catch
Tony & Joe's

Romantic Places

Al Tiramisu
Asia Nora
Bombay Club
Citronelle
Coeur de Lion
Green Papaya
Inn at Little Washington
La Bergerie
L'Auberge Chez François
Le Refuge
Le Tarbouche
Majestic Cafe
Melrose
New Heights
Nora
Obelisk

Old Angler's Inn
Ortanique
Palena
Seasons
701
1789
Tabard Inn
Taberna del Alabardero
Tahoga
Two Quail
Yanÿu

Senior Appeal

Blackie's
Brasserie Monte Carlo
Chef Geoff's
Colvin Run Tavern
Crystal Thai
Il Borgo
Jean-Michel
Jeffrey's at Watergate
Krupin's
La Bergerie
La Chaumiere
La Ferme
La Miche
L'Auberge Chez François
Le Gaulois
Le Petit Mistral
Le Rivage
Matisse
Michael's
Morton's of Chicago
Nizam's
Oceanaire Sea. Rm.
Parkway Deli
Peking Gourmet Inn
Prime Rib
Prince Michel
Renato

Ritz, Grill (Wash. DC)
Roof Terrace at Kennedy Ctr.
Ruth's Chris
Tako Grill
That's Amore†
Tivoli
Tragara
Willard Room
Wurzburg Haus

Singles Scenes

Acropolis
Angelo & Maxie's†
Arbor
Artie's
Austin Grill
Bardeo
Bar Rouge
Boulevard Woodgrill
Cafe Asia
Cafe Atlantico
Cafe Deluxe
Cafe Japoné
Cafe Milano
Chi-Cha Lounge
Coco Loco
eCiti Cafe
Felix
Grille 88
Gua-Rapo
Kramerbooks & Afterwords
Le Tarbouche
McCormick & Schmick's
Meze
Nathan's
Neyla
Old Ebbitt Grill
Old Glory BBQ†
Paolo's†
Peacock Cafe

Perry's
Red Sage
Rocklands†
Sequoia
Sesto Senso
Siné
South Beach
Sweetwater Tavern†
TenPenh
Timpano Italian
Toka Cafe
Tony & Joe's
Topaz Bar
Tryst
Uni
Union St. Public Hse.
U-topia
Vida

Tea Service

Bailiwick Inn
Ching Ching Cha
Jefferson
Ritz, Grill (Pent. City)
Ritz, Grill (Wash. DC)
Teaism†
Willard Room

Theme Restaurants

Buca di Beppo
Cities
Coco Loco
Green Field
Mimi's American
Red Sage

Transporting Experiences

(Like traveling to another
place and time)
Bar Rouge
Bombay Club

Caucus Room
Ching Ching Cha
Green Papaya
Heritage India†
Inn at Little Washington
L'Auberge Chez François
Makoto
Maxim
Neyla
Red Sage
Tara Thai
Topaz Bar

Views

Gerard's Place
Il Cigno
Inn at Glen Echo
Lafayette
L'Auberge Chez François
Le Rivage
New Heights
Perry's
Rico y Rico
Roof Terrace at Kennedy Ctr.
Ruth's Chris†
Sea Catch
Sequoia
701
Washington Harbour Club

Visitors on Expense Account

Bailiwick Inn
Barolo
Butterfield 9
Cafe 15
Capital Grille
Caucus Room
Citronelle
Colvin Run Tavern
Elysium

Etrusco
Galileo
Gerard's Place
Inn at Little Washington
i Ricchi
Jeffrey's at Watergate
jordans
Kinkead's
Lafayette
Maestro
Marcel's
Michael's
Morton's of Chicago
Mr. K's
Nick & Stef's
Oceanaire Sea. Rm.
Olives
Palena
Palm
Prime Rib
Ritz, Grill (Pent. City)
Ritz, Grill (Wash. DC)
Ruth's Chris
Sam & Harry's†
1789
Signatures
Tosca
Vidalia
Willard Room
Yanÿu

Winning Wine Lists

Ashby Inn
Barolo
Bistro Bis
Bistro Français
Cafe Atlantico
Cafe 15
Capital Grille
Carlyle Grand Cafe

Cashion's Eat Pl.
Caucus Room
Cesco
Citronelle
Colvin Run Tavern
Elysium
Etrusco
Evening Star
Gabriel
Galileo
Gerard's Place
Grapeseed
Inn at Little Washington
Jaleo
Johnny's Half Shell
jordans
Kinkead's
La Chaumiere
La Colline
Le Relais
Maestro
M & S Grill
Marcel's
Melrose
Mendocino Grille
Mezza 9
Mon Ami Gabi
Nathan's
New Heights
Nick & Stef's
Nora
Obelisk
Occidental
Old Ebbitt Grill

Oval Room
Palena
Palm
Prime Rib
Prince Michel
Restaurant 7
Rico y Rico
Sam & Harry's
Seasons
Smith & Wollensky
Sushi-Ko
Taberna del Alabardero
Tivoli
Tosca
Vidalia
Washington Cafe
Willard Room

Worth a Trip

Boyce, VA
    L'Auberge Provençale
Flint Hill, VA
    Four & Twenty Blackbirds
Leon, VA
    Prince Michel
Orange, VA
    Willow Grove Inn
Paris, VA
    Ashby Inn
The Plains, VA
    Rail Stop
Washington, VA
    Inn at Little Washington

Baltimore, Annapolis and the Eastern Shore

Baltimore's Most Popular

www.zagat.com

Baltimore's Most Popular

Each of our reviewers has been asked to name his or her five favorite Baltimore restaurants. The places most frequently named, in order of their popularity, are:

1. Charleston
2. Prime Rib
3. Tio Pepe
4. Helmand
5. Ruth's Chris
6. Morton's of Chicago
7. Linwood's
8. Petit Louis Bistro
9. Ambassador Dining Room
10. Boccaccio
11. Tersiguel's
12. Bicycle
13. Brass Elephant
14. Oregon Grille
15. Polo Grill
16. Black Olive
17. Legal Sea Foods*
18. Hampton's
19. Milton Inn
20. Kali's Court
21. Sotto Sopra
22. Helen's Garden
23. Orchard Market Cafe
24. Antrim 1844
25. Kings Contrivance
26. Blue Agave
27. Louisiana
28. Ixia
29. Samos
30. Corks
31. Fleming's
32. Cafe Zen
33. Amicci's
34. Marconi's*
35. Rudys' 2900*
36. Jeannier's
37. Joy America Cafe
38. Asean Bistro
39. Harryman House*
40. Café Troia
41. Sabatino's*
42. Tapas Teatro*

It's obvious that many of the restaurants on the above list are among the Baltimore area's most expensive, but if popularity were calibrated to price, we suspect that a number of other restaurants would join the above ranks. Given the fact that both our surveyors and readers love to discover dining bargains, we have added a list of 40 Best Buys on page 161. These are restaurants that give real quality at extremely reasonable prices.

---

* Tied with restaurant directly above it

Top Ratings*

Top lists exclude restaurants with low voting.

Top 20 Food Rankings

28 Prime Rib	Helmand
27 Samos	Linwood's
Charleston	Bistro St. Michaels/E
Hampton's	Antrim 1844
Stone Manor	Boccaccio
208 Talbot/E	Tio Pepe
Joss Cafe & Sushi Bar/A	Rudys' 2900
Trattoria Alberto	**25** Les Folies Brasserie/A
26 Milton Inn	Oregon Grille
Lewnes' Steakhouse/A	Tersiguel's

Top Food by Cuisine

American (New)
27 Charleston
Hampton's
26 Linwood's
22 Joy America Cafe
Helen's Garden

American (Traditional)
26 Milton Inn
25 Oregon Grille
Narrows/E
24 Brass Elephant
21 Harryman House

Asian Fusion/Pan-Asian
24 Purple Orchid
23 Asean Bistro
Ixia
Yin Yankee Cafe/A
Eurasian Harbor

Chesapeake Bay
25 Brighton's
24 Pierpoint
23 Harry Browne's/A
22 Marconi's
19 Captain Harvey's

Chinese
24 Szechuan Best
23 Szechuan House
21 Cafe Zen
20 P.F. Chang's

Continental
27 208 Talbot/E
26 Rudys' 2900
24 Northwoods/A
22 Josef's Country Inn
Marconi's

Crab Houses
25 Costas Crab House
23 Cantler's Riverside Inn/A
21 Obrycki's Crab House
Harris Crab House/E
20 Crab Claw/E

French
26 Antrim 1844
25 Tersiguel's
Louisiana
23 Jeannier's
22 Martick's

French (Bistro)
26 Bistro St. Michaels/E
25 Les Folies Brasserie/A
24 Petit Louis Bistro
20 Cafe Normandie/A
Crêpe du Jour

Greek
27 Samos
24 Kali's Court
21 Ikaros
Zorba's Bar & Grill
19 Timbuktu

---

* All restaurants are in the Baltimore area unless otherwise noted
(A=Annapolis and E=Eastern Shore).

Top Food

Italian
27 Trattoria Alberto
26 Boccaccio
24 Sotto Sopra
23 Café Troia
22 La Scala

Seafood
25 O'Learys Seafood/A
   Black Olive
23 Faidley's Seafood
   Pisces
22 Sam's Waterfront Cafe/A

Steakhouses
28 Prime Rib
26 Lewnes' Steakhouse/A
25 Oregon Grille
24 Ruth's Chris
   Morton's of Chicago

Sushi
27 Joss Cafe & Sushi Bar/A
25 Matsuri
24 Edo Sushi
   Sushi Hana
   Tsunami/A

Top Food by Special Feature

Boat-Accessible
25 Narrows/E
23 Cantler's Riverside Inn/A
22 Sam's Waterfront Cafe/A
21 Harris Crab House/E
20 Crab Claw/E

Breakfast*
25 Brighton's
18 Chick & Ruth's Delly
17 Jimmy's
   Baugher's
16 Cafe Hon

Brunch
24 Polo Grill
   Ambassador Dining Room
23 Blue Moon Cafe
   Pisces
19 City Cafe

Business Dining
27 Charleston
   Hampton's
26 Linwood's
   Boccaccio
24 Polo Grill

Historic Places
26 Milton Inn
22 Elkridge Furnace Inn
21 Baldwin's Station
20 Treaty of Paris/A
18 Woman's Industrial Exchange

Hotel Dining
27 Hampton's
   Harbor Court Hotel
25 Brighton's
   Harbor Court Hotel
24 Morton's of Chicago
   Sheraton Inner Harbor
23 Pisces
   Hyatt Regency
20 Windows
   Renaissance Harborplace

Newcomers/Rated
24 Roy's
23 Ixia
20 Babalu Grill
19 Chester's Steakhouse

Newcomers/Unrated
   Cerando's Kitchen & Bistro
   Henry's, an American Bistro
   Red Maple
   Soigné
   Sputnik Cafe/A

Worth a Trip
27 Stone Manor
   Middletown
   208 Talbot/E
   St. Michaels
26 Antrim 1844
   Taneytown
25 Narrows/E
   Grasonville
23 Cantler's Riverside Inn/A
   Annapolis

---

* Other than hotels

Top Food

Top Food by Location

Downtown North/ Charles St./Mt. Vernon
- **28** Prime Rib
- **26** Helmand
- **24** Brass Elephant
    Sotto Sopra
- **23** Tapas Teatro

Fells Point
- **25** Louisiana
    Black Olive
- **24** Pierpoint
    Kali's Court
    Peter's Inn

Inner Harbor
- **27** Hampton's
- **25** Brighton's
- **24** Purple Orchid
- **23** Pisces
- **22** Joy America Cafe

Inner Harbor East/Little Italy
- **27** Charleston
- **26** Boccaccio
- **22** La Scala
- **21** Amicci's
- **20** Sabatino's

Outer Baltimore
- **27** Trattoria Alberto
- **26** Milton Inn
    Linwood's
    Rudys' 2900
- **25** Tersiguel's

South Baltimore
- **25** Bicycle
    Matsuri
- **21** Vespa
    Blue Agave
- **20** SoBo Cafe

Annapolis
- **27** Joss Cafe & Sushi Bar
- **26** Lewnes' Steakhouse
- **25** Les Folies Brasserie
    O'Learys Seafood
- **24** Northwoods

Eastern Shore
- **27** 208 Talbot
- **26** Bistro St. Michaels
- **25** Narrows
- **21** Harris Crab House
- **20** Michael Rork's

Top 20 Decor Rankings

28 Hampton's
   Antrim 1844
27 Stone Manor
   Milton Inn
   Brighton's
26 Ixia
   Brass Elephant
   Oregon Grille
   Charleston
   Prime Rib
   Louisiana
   Eurasian Harbor
25 Linwood's
   Aldo's
   Ambassador Dining Room
   Elkridge Furnace Inn
   Sotto Sopra
24 Pisces
   Roy's
   Joy America Cafe

Outdoors

Ambassador Dining Room
Cantler's Riverside Inn/A
Carrol's Creek/A
Crêpe du Jour
Harris Crab House/E
Helen's Garden
Joy America Cafe
Linwood's
L.P. Steamers
Narrows/E
River Watch
Tapas Teatro

Romance

Ambassador Dining Room
Cafe de Paris
Charleston
Columbia/E
Hampton's
Helen's Garden
Milton Inn
208 Talbot/E
Woman's Industrial Exchange
Ze Mean Bean Cafe

Rooms

Ambassador Dining Room
Brass Elephant
Cafe de Paris
Columbia/E
Eurasian Harbor
Hampton's
Inn at Perry Cabin/E
Milton Inn
Sascha's 527
Woman's Industrial Exchange

Views

Brighton's
Gertrude's
Hampton's
Inn at Perry Cabin/E
Joy America Cafe
L.P. Steamers
Phillips
Pisces
River Watch
Windows

Top 20 Service Rankings

27 Prime Rib	**24** Northwoods/A
Hampton's	Lewnes' Steakhouse/A
26 Charleston	Tersiguel's
208 Talbot/E	Marconi's
Antrim 1844	Les Folies Brasserie/A
25 Milton Inn	Ambassador Dining Room
Boccaccio	Brass Elephant
Linwood's	Helmand
Brighton's	Aldo's
Stone Manor*	Oregon Grille

---

* Tied with restaurant directly above it

Best Buys

Top 20 Bangs for the Buck

List derived by dividing the cost of a meal into its ratings.

1. Woman's Industrial Exchange
2. Samos
3. Attman's Deli
4. Chick & Ruth's Delly/A
5. Holy Frijoles
6. Blue Moon Cafe
7. Faidley's Seafood
8. Jimmy's
9. Baugher's
10. Szechuan Best
11. Szechuan House
12. SoBo Cafe
13. Cafe Zen
14. Cafe Hon
15. Crêpe du Jour
16. Duda's Tavern
17. Suzie's Soba
18. Holly's/E
19. Banjara
20. Helmand

Other Good Values

Barn
Bill's Terrace Inn
Chameleon Café
City Cafe
Costas Crab House
Fuji
Helen's Garden
Ikaros
Jalapeño/A
John Steven, Ltd.
Kelly's
L.P. Steamers
Martick's
Peppermill
River Watch
Ruby Lounge
Sabatino's
Szechuan
Timbuktu
Zorba's Bar & Grill

Baltimore, Annapolis and the Eastern Shore Restaurant Directory

Baltimore

	F	D	S	C
Aldo's [S]	24	25	24	$45

306 S. High St. (Fawn St.), 410-727-0700

◪ "Expensive but worth it" say surveyors smitten by this "posh", "family-run" Southern Italian in Little Italy, which delivers "beautiful food in a beautiful setting" by a staff that pampers "everyone like royalty"; those who "love it go back" often for a "truly gourmet", "elegant evening" out that "gets better" with the years, but detractors think "they take themselves too seriously" and object to their "dog and pony show."

	F	D	S	C
AMBASSADOR DINING ROOM [S]	24	25	24	$28

3811 Canterbury Rd. (bet. 39th St. & University Pkwy.), 410-366-1484

■ Known for "distinctive, complex" Indian food "at its best", this "regal" "gem" in Homewood near the Hopkins campus "appeals even to people who think they don't like Indian"; "cushy and intimate inside", with "magical" garden dining outside, it provides "a return to the days of the Raj", replete with "marvelously" "gracious" service that helps make it a "romantic" "special-occasion kind of place."

	F	D	S	C
Amicci's [S]	21	15	19	$24

231 S. High St. (bet. Fawn & Stiles Sts.), 410-528-1096

◪ "Solid pastas at prices that are hard to beat" ensure "long lines" at this "simple", "laid-back" Italian "find" with "no pretensions"; supporters swear it's "just as good as many other places in Little Italy, only with college-student decor", but they gladly overlook the "minimalist", "cramped" digs because "you can't go wrong" with the "super" food.

	F	D	S	C
Angelina's [S]	18	11	16	$27

7135 Harford Rd. (Rosalie Ave.), 410-444-5545

◪ "Long considered to make the best crab cakes in the city", this "homey" "neighborhood" Italian quartered in an "ancient row house" in Northeast Baltimore has been feeding generations for half a century; "disappointed" diners, however, who lament that the once "highly touted" "baseball-size" signature item is now "no big deal" and caution that the rest of the menu is "hit-or-miss" yet "overpriced" conclude that it's "living on its reputation."

	F	D	S	C
ANTRIM 1844 [S]	26	28	26	$60

30 Trevanion Rd. (Rte. 140), Taneytown, 410-756-6812

■ "Romantics" "swoon" over this "historic" country inn "wonderfully" "secluded" in the Catoctin Mountains near

Gettysburg; it takes visitors back "to a more genteel era" with its "elegant" interior, "gorgeous" gardens, veranda dining and "impeccably courteous" service; admirers predict that new chef Michael Gettier's "superb" French-accented Chesapeake-style menu "will make it one of the top destinations in Maryland"; though "you may need a bank loan and three hours" for dinner, it's "worth" it.

Asean Bistro S　　　　　　　　23 | 22 | 21 | $27

8775 Centre Park Dr. (Rte. 108), Columbia, 410-772-5300

◪ Far "less stereotypical" than what you'd expect of a "strip-mall" establishment, "consummate restaurateur" Jesse Wong's "fancy" Pan-Asian bistro in Columbia appeals with a "great variety of dishes presented with artistic flair" in "spiffy" surroundings; a few frugal types who deem it "a little pricey", though, quip "a piano player shouldn't make Chinese food cost this much."

Atlantic S　　　　　　　　21 | 23 | 19 | $36

American Can Company Bldg., 2400 Boston St. (Hudson St.), 410-675-4565

◪ Luring a "hip crowd" to Canton, this "chic" seafood house with "big city" decor is a "visual pleasure" with a waterfall indoors and a pondside patio outside; as for the New American menu, it's "a bit of a lottery – some dishes are very good, others only fair" – as is the service, which swings between "spunky" and "surly"; be forewarned too of the "terrific din (be ready to yell)", especially when there's live entertainment (jazz trio, Latin quartet).

Attman's Delicatessen S　　　　23 | 9 | 15 | $12

1019 E. Lombard St. (bet. Central Ave. & Fallsway), 410-563-2666

◪ "If you get a yen for a hot corned beef sandwich, pastrami or a fat hot dog", head right over to this "classic Jewish-style deli" in East Baltimore, "stand in line, place your order" with the "colorful countermen" and carry your meal to the "tacky" dining room that "hasn't changed in years"; granted, it's located in a "bleak" area east of Downtown, but it's "worth the drive from Washington" to "hit that certain spot."

Austin Grill S　　　　　　　　16 | 15 | 16 | $21

American Can Company Bldg., 2400 Boston St. (Hudson St.), 410-534-0606

See review in Washington, DC Directory.

Babalu Grill S　　　　　　　　20 | 21 | 18 | $31

32 Market Pl. (Water St.), 410-234-9898

■ "Deliberately hip" and "always packed", this "Nuevo Latino" supper club near the Inner Harbor is a hot new "place to see and be seen", attracting a "20s-to-30s" crowd with its throbbing music and salsa and merengue dance lessons; fans think it's off to a "good start", even if skeptics feel it's "trying too hard to be trendy."

Baldwin's Station S   21 22 21 $34
7618 Main St. (Rte. 32), Sykesville, 410-795-1041

☑ "Trains still go by" the "beautiful historic station" at the "rural" Carroll County crossroads of Sykesville, "worth a detour" for "imaginative" New American dining with "a bit of sophistication" (but "kids are welcome"), as well as for the "picturesque" view of the Patapsco River from the "deck alongside the tracks"; the "folk musicians on Wednesday evenings" add a sweet touch, but disgruntled passengers report that the experience is derailed by "unpredictable quality" and service that can be "lacking."

Banjara S   23 18 21 $22
1017 S. Charles St. (bet. Cross & Hamburg Sts.), 410-962-1554

■ "Blissful" Indian food "where you'd least expect it" – South Baltimore – awaits at this "cozy", "candlelit" (read: "dark") nook, a "great date" place with "excellent" dishes served by a "hospitable", "accommodating" staff in a "traditionally" decorated room; regulars swear they've "never had a bad meal here."

Barn S   ▽ 19 12 18 $25
9527 Harford Rd. (Joppa Rd.), Parkville, 410-882-6182

■ Apparently, "the Baltimore Colts haven't departed" the building, because at this "raucous basement crab house" tucked under a Parkville bar north of the Beltway, photos of Johnny Unitas and other former players still reign; amid a "wall-to-wall warm community feeling", fans tackle piles of "big and delicious" steamed crabs served year-round on long tables covered with paper; it's a "great place to spend an evening" talking sports, politics and philosophy.

Baugher's S   17 12 18 $15
289 W. Main St. (Rte. 31), Westminster, 410-848-7413

☑ "Step back in time" at this American "tradition" in Westminster, embraced by many loyalists for its "simple" "country" food and "what-a-bargain" prices; "genuinely nice" "farmers' daughters and sons serve plain meals" "just like mom used to cook", followed by "wholesomely decadent desserts" of "homemade ice creams and pies"; though skeptics sniff "nothing spectacular", at least "you won't leave hungry."

Bertha's S   17 16 16 $24
734 S. Broadway (Lancaster St.), 410-327-5795

☑ "Dark" and "funky", this "classic" "watering hole" pioneered the gentrification of now "tourist-filled" Fells Point, and it "still looks like a place where Captain Ahab's crew might walk in"; the seafood-slanted menu stars its "world-famous mussels", though schools of critics carp that the bivalves are as "gritty" as the "grungy" decor, adding that it's "totally" "resting on its laurels"; "love it or hate it, you have to at least try" it.

Bicycle 25 | 20 | 22 | $35

1444 Light St. (Fort Ave.), 410-234-1900

◪ Addicts "would pedal 100 miles" to this "very hip" South Baltimore "storefront" for the chance to savor chef-owner Barry Rumsey's "playful perfection", exemplified by his Thai-style rockfish baked in banana leaves and teamed with chutney, red curry sauce and black sticky rice; the other dishes on the Eclectic menu are equally "complex and interesting", making this "tiny" "husband-and-wife"-run bistro a true "foodie haven", but better "reserve weeks in advance" and perhaps "bring earplugs."

Bill's Terrace Inn [S] ▽ 23 | 12 | 18 | $28

200 Eastern Blvd. (Mace Ave.), Essex, 410-687-5994

◪ "There's no Bill, no terrace and no inn", but there is "great food worth waiting for" at this "straightforward" crab house in old Essex; catering to a "true Bawlmer crowd", it serves "terrific steamed crabs" in the proper manner – dumped on paper-covered tables, accompanied by mallets and pitchers of beer; there are "no tourists" and "no atmosphere" either ("decor? – ha!"), just "real serious" eating "year-round."

Black Olive [S] 25 | 18 | 22 | $44

814 S. Bond St. (Shakespeare St.), 410-276-7141

◪ Be "transported to the Mediterranean" at this "charming" renovated row house in Fells Point, which is "heaven for serious seafood lovers"; "meet your treat before you eat" by taking the "fish tour" given by the "friendly owners", then have the "amazingly fresh" fare (including "exotic types that'll wow even aficionados") "simply prepared"; some wallet-watchers carp "sooo good but sooo pricey", but those who are hooked "always leave happy."

Blue Agave [S] 21 | 20 | 19 | $29

1032 Light St. (Cross St.), 410-576-3938

◪ At this "festive" hot spot in "revitalized" South Baltimore, the kitchen prepares "solidly good" "real" Mexican ("not American Mexican") dishes with a "nouveau twist", though the cocktails at the "superb" bar (stocked with a "wide variety of tequilas", it makes "amazing margaritas" that'll "make you smile") can eclipse the food; it often gets "too loud for conversation", you may feel a "bit rushed" and the service is "hit-or-miss", but even so, amigos plead "don't tell how good it is – it's already hard enough to get reservations."

Blue Moon Cafe [S] 23 | 16 | 17 | $15

1621 Aliceanna St. (bet. Bond St. & Broadway), 410-522-3940

■ "Go early or wait long", especially during Sunday brunch, at this "tiny" "hippie" cafe set in an old Fells Point house, but it's "worth" it because it "raises breakfast to real-meal" status; it's "hard to decide" between the "best cinnamon buns in the world", "excellent crab omelets", "phenomenal" eggs Benedict and other "superior" American fare, served by "down-to-earth" folks; the "portions are huge" and the prices "low", but note its "odd hours" (Thursday–Saturday, it's open overnight).

BOCCACCIO S
| 26 | 23 | 25 | $46 |

925 Eastern Ave. (bet. Exeter & High Sts.), 410-234-1322
■ "Memories of the meal linger for days" rhapsodize admirers of this "extraordinary" Northern Italian "paradise", a "longtime favorite" of many; the "delicate", "delicious and different" dishes ("not the standard" suspects) are served amid "beautiful", "inviting" quarters by an "impeccable" team, so though "it'll cost you" big ("thank God for expense accounts"), it's "first-class in every way" and it fully "deserves its reputation as one of Little Italy's best."

Brass Elephant S
| 24 | 26 | 24 | $41 |

924 N. Charles St. (bet. Eager & Read Sts.), 410-547-8480
■ Dating from Charles Street's grand era, this "beautiful 1850 merchant's townhouse" "elegantly" appointed with Italian white-marble fireplaces, "hand-carved" wood accents and Waterford crystal chandeliers may be an "old warhorse, but it still runs like a winner"; the daily bill of fare showcases "reinvented" Continental-American "classics" (the "tasting menu is a good choice" if you want to go all out) brought to table by an "attentive" staff, making it a "classy" destination for any "special occasion."

Brewer's Alley S
| 20 | 18 | 19 | $23 |

124 N. Market St. (bet. Church & 2nd Sts.), Frederick, 301-631-0089
◪ Set in Frederick's onetime town hall and opera house, this "lively" hangout is a "casual spot" with an American menu that's "a step up from regular pub food", as well as a "variety" of "tasty" "beers brewed on-premise"; insiders advise come with "moderate expectations and you'll be all right", so best "stick to the basics."

Brighton's S
| 25 | 27 | 25 | $44 |

Harbor Court Hotel, 550 Light St. (bet. Conway & Lee Sts.), 410-347-9750
■ A "perfect" "take-your-mother-to-lunch" kind of place, this "bright" and "gorgeous" (it always "feels like a spring day" here) hotel dining room boasts a view of the Inner Harbor that's "too good to be true"; it's located down the hall from well-regarded sibling Hampton's at the Harbor Court, and the link shows – from the "fancy" Chesapeake-inspired breakfast and lunch menus to the "delightful afternoon tea" and "excellent" dinner choices.

Cafe de Paris S
| – | – | – | E |

8808 Centre Park Dr. (Rte. 108), Columbia, 410-997-3560
To the delight of fans who followed him from Citronelle to his own place in Laurel, Erik Rochard recently reopened

his Country French bistro in a Columbia office building; in a pretty space lined with red banquettes and appointed with gleaming light oak (with a piano at the ready), he works the room while his wife presides at the counter of her adjacent French deli; early signs are they're doing it right.

Cafe Hon S   16   16   17 $17
1002 W. 36th St. (bet. Falls Rd. & Roland Ave.), 410-243-1230

◪ Take a "trip back to the '50s" at this tribute to the blue-collar past of Hampden, a "Norman Rockwell painting come to life", where "real Bawlmer hons" sling "mom's kitchen" dishes (think American eats like meatloaf with mashed potatoes and homemade pies) in a "kitschy" "hodgepodge" of a setting; fans who love it "for what it is" beg "please don't change", but foes who think its "camp value" has worn thin lament that it has become "a victim of it's own success."

Café Troia S   23   20   22 $37
28 W. Allegheny Ave. (Washington Ave.), Towson, 410-337-0133

◪ "Gino Troia's back in the kitchen" at this "unassuming" yet "sophisticated" family-run cafe where a "veritable who's who of Towson" congregates for "refined" Tuscan-style specialties prepared "like they are in Italy"; the cooking seems more "seductive" than ever ("better than most in Little Italy"), but "parking is still always a problem."

Cafe Zen S   21   14   19 $18
438 E. Belvedere Ave. (York Rd.), 410-532-0022

◪ "Fast and efficient", this "neighborhood old faithful" near the Senator Theatre is ideal for a bite before or after a movie; in a small, "spare room" with "fluorescent lighting" and "a hint of Berkeley" in the air, sample a "tasty" variety of Chinese-Japanese dishes that are "fresh and healthy" (including sushi and "lots of veggie choices"), but best to check ahead about its "odd closing" hours.

Captain Harvey's S   19   15   17 $31
11510 Reisterstown Rd. (Nicodemus Rd.), Owings Mills, 410-356-7550

◪ Over three generations, this "pleasant" Owings Mills seafood house has cultivated a "longtime following" with its "generous portions" of "good all-around" Chesapeake-style dishes, delivered with "motherly service" in a clubby, "comfortable" room with a "nautical" motif; those looking for a more "laid-back" meal repair to the adjacent "down-home crab shack" for "steamed-to-order" crustaceans; critics, however, who carp "ordinary" choose to "fish elsewhere."

Cerando's Kitchen & Bistro   –   –   –   M
8801 Baltimore Nat'l Pike/Rte. 40 (Rte. 29), Ellicott City, 410-750-3353

Gourmands in Ellicott City are excited that this catering kitchen has branched out to become a real restaurant and a dining destination; in a simply appointed space that keeps the focus on the food, they gather around the open kitchen to sample a weekly changing roster of New American dishes, from BBQ NY strip steaks to vegetarian curries.

Chameleon Café ▽ 26 | 19 | 23 | $27

4341 Harford Rd. (3 blocks south of Cold Spring Ln.), 410-254-2376

■ Appropriately named, this "absolute gem" "looks like a neighborhood coffee joint", which it is by day, but come nightfall it transforms itself into a serious food-lover's haunt with a "creative" New American menu that has quickly made Harford Road an "unlikely" "new culinary destination"; it may be "out of the way", but these "world-class" dishes justifiably "draw patrons from all over town", and "once you discover it, you'll be back" too.

CHARLESTON 27 | 26 | 26 | $53

1000 Lancaster St. (Exeter St.), 410-332-7373

■ Surveyors swoon over chef Cindy Wolf's "sublime" "see-and-be-seen" scene at Inner Harbor East, voted the Most Popular restaurant in Baltimore; it's an "impressive" "special-occasion" treat that's just about "perfect" – from her "inventive" New American menu influenced by the Low Country and the wine cellar overseen by husband Tony Foreman to the "elegant" environs and "impeccable" service, this is a "top-notch" experience "to be relished and lingered over."

Cheesecake Factory ◐ [S] 19 | 17 | 17 | $23

Harborplace Pratt Street Pavilion, 201 E. Pratt St. (South St.), 410-234-3990

See review in Washington, DC Directory.

Chester's Steakhouse [S] 19 | 18 | 20 | $30

1717 Eastern Ave. (bet. Ann St. & Broadway), 410-732-9800

■ "Great food for the price" pulls in practical carnivores to this "upbeat" new "steak 'n' potatoes place" in Fells Point; the menu is "limited", but the dishes are competently executed and they're served in an exposed brick–lined room with a sort of "retro" feel by "friendly" people; early enthusiasts predict it's "a favorite in the making."

City Cafe [S] 19 | 17 | 17 | $20

1001 Cathedral St. (Eager St.), 410-539-4252

■ Once merely a "delightful place for coffee and dessert", this Mt. Vernon "hangout" has grown up to become a "crucial urban-energy center" that's "warm and alive", attracting a "hip, diverse Downtown crowd"; whether you're meeting friends to chat or you come alone to "sit and read", you'll be served "solid" American food by a "friendly" crew, making it a "relaxing" "oasis in the city" and "a must on the weekend-brunch circuit."

Clyde's S | 18 | 20 | 19 | $27

10221 Wincopin Circle (Little Patuxent Pkwy.), Columbia,
410-730-2829
See review in Washington, DC Directory.

Combalou Cafe S | – | – | – | M

818 N. Calvert St. (Read St.), 410-528-1117
Fulfilling a longtime dream to erect a shrine to artisanal
cheeses, Jack Fromberg's wholesale operation has
expanded into a cave-themed dining room whimsically
furnished with "cheesy cow-print couches"; it's a casual
spot where the glory of dairy is evident in every dish, from
the weekly changing International sampler plates to the
"really unusual" salads, soups, sandwiches, quiches and
seasonal specials; it's an "excellent" choice for a "light
lunch" east of the Charles Street corridor.

Corks S | 24 | 20 | 22 | $42

1026 S. Charles St. (bet. Cross & Hamburg Sts.), 410-752-3810
■ With a name like this, the fruit of the vine is naturally the
focus at this oenophile's dream set in an 1849 row house in
historic Federal Hill; the "incredibly well-versed" servers
"know their stuff", and they're happy to "guide" novices
through the "heavenly", "fairly priced" compendium, which
highlights boutique American labels (including "some you'll
never see anywhere else"); in the same user-friendly spirit,
each item on the "arty", "seasonal" New American menu
is paired with a suggested glass of wine.

Costas Crab House ◑ S | 25 | 12 | 19 | $34

4100 N. Point Blvd. (Wise Ave.), Dundalk, 410-477-1975
■ "Super", "huge steamed crabs" (the "best") served in a
"no-nonsense" manner in "plain" linoleum-floored digs
with a "bar-type" atmosphere makes this seafood "joint"
"worth the trip to Dundalk, hon"; if you "want to show
guests the real B-more", bring them to this "blue-collar
fantasy" located not far from the steel mill, but heed the
advice of insiders: concentrate on the crustaceans and
"avoid everything else" on the menu.

Crêpe du Jour S | 20 | 15 | 14 | $17

1609 Sulgrave Ave. (Kelly Ave.), 410-542-9000
◪ Bringing a "little bit of Paris" to Mt. Washington, this "cute
little place" provides a "nice change of pace" with its
"delicious" crêpes, both savory and sweet ("don't miss the
Nutella-banana one for dessert), and other serious bistro
items; good news: the "cramped" digs are now less so after
the addition of an expansive covered deck out back.

Da Mimmo ◑ S | 23 | 20 | 22 | $47

217 S. High St. (Stiles St.), 410-727-6876
◪ "Frequented by Baltimore's big names", the "nouveau
riche and conventioneers on expense accounts" ("less so

by natives"), this "swanky" Italian ristorante in Little Italy with "lovely old-world" decor is famed for its "to-die-for veal chop"; scores of "extremely disappointed" diners, however, complain about the "pretentious", "starstruck" staff and warn about the "astronomical" tabs, particularly the "specials without [announced] prices" (some "wish they could say it's worth the money, but it's not").

Della Notte S   20 | 21 | 21 | $32

801 Eastern Ave. (President St.), 410-837-5500
☑ "Crazy neo-Roman" decor, with a "tree right in the middle" of the "open" room ("we're not ashamed to admit that we like sitting under the big branches"), sets the stage at this "busy" Italian; the "surprisingly" "solid" fare (traditional and "creative") "goes beyond marinara", even if it's "a little overpriced", but rare for Little Italy is the fact that it actually has parking; critics, though, pan the "generic" food, "overdone" appointments and "variable" service.

Duda's Tavern ●   21 | 13 | 18 | $18

1600 Thames St. (Bond St.), 410-276-4555
☑ Family-owned since 1949, this "relaxing" "corner bar" with a "slow tempo" is a "comfortable hangout" "off-the-beaten-path" in Fells Point, keeping locals "happy" with an "outstanding" selection of beers (16 on tap, 150 by the bottle) and "a cut above" American pub grub like "great burgers" and "succulent crab cakes"; "if you can tolerate smoking", this "dive" may be "the perfect Baltimore tavern."

Due S   23 | 23 | 22 | $37

McDonogh Crossroads, 25 Crossroads Dr. (McDonogh & Reisterstown Rds.), Owings Mills, 410-356-4147
☑ Owings Mills' "'in' crowd" patronizes this "more informal", "more affordable" "sister restaurant of Linwood's" next door when it "doesn't feel like getting as dressed up"; it's a "pretty place for a fine-dining experience", featuring "wonderful" Northern Italian dishes prepared in the shared kitchen, but even fans admit it's still "expensive" (though it remains "one of our favorite overpriced restaurants").

Dutch's Daughter S   – | – | – | M

581 Himes Ave. (Rte. 40), Frederick, 301-668-9500
"Relocated to the edge of Frederick", this "old-style family restaurant" now housed in a stadium-size building continues to prepare some of the "best crab cakes and crab imperial around"; the rest of the American seafood menu is pretty "terrific" too, "very fresh" and reasonably priced.

Edo Sushi S   24 | 17 | 22 | $25

53 E. Padonia Rd. (York Rd.), Timonium, 410-667-9200
☑ Though the York Road corridor is home to a number of sushi houses, this small BYO Japanese "hidden in a strip mall" in Timonium is worth seeking out; the "friendly owner"

and "entertaining", "chatty" chefs "remember everything and everyone", which explains why it has become a "nice neighborhood place" with "a large following of regular customers"; the only drawbacks: minimal decor and the "lack of a liquor license."

Elkridge Furnace Inn S   22 | 25 | 23 | $41 |
5745 Furnace Ave. (bet. Main St. & Race Rd.), Elkridge, 410-379-9336
☑ Set on tree-dotted grounds a stone's throw from the Patapsco River, this "beautiful" 18th-century inn in Elkridge may be the "most romantic restaurant in the Baltimore" area; the frequently changing French menu is "generally very good", but the consensus is that the food and the "erratic" service are "no match" for the "appealing" setting.

Ethel & Ramone's S   – | – | – | M |
1615 Sulgrave Ave. (Kelly Ave.), 410-664-2971
"If you like New Orleans gumbo, this is the place" to go in Mt. Washington say boosters of "talented" chef-owner Edward Bloom's "funky" Creole-accented Eclectic set in a patchwork of tiny spaces in an old house; his "innovative" menu "changes seasonally", but those in-the-know urge "get any of the specials" and "don't miss the soup sampler" or "homemade desserts"; the vibe is "so friendly you'll feel like a regular right away (and you'll want to be)" and if you're really "lucky", "you'll get to sit out on the porch."

Eurasian Harbor S   23 | 26 | 21 | $38 |
Pier 5 Hotel, 711 Eastern Ave. (President St.), 410-230-9992
☑ Eliciting "wows" for its "chic" setting, this "great addition to the B-more dining" scene at the Inner Harbor "tries" to offer "something for everyone"; the "inventive" Eurasian "fusion" repertoire presents "delicious combinations" that admirers say are "a treat" ("love the 'tiger eye' sashimi"), while the "hip bar" concocts "splashy drinks"; detractors, however, say that despite the "fabulous menu descriptions", the "food doesn't live up to the fancy decor."

Faidley's Seafood   23 | 11 | 15 | $15 |
Lexington Mkt., 400 W. Lexington St. (bet. Eutaw & Paca Sts.), 410-727-4898
☑ "Full of lump meat", the "perfect crab cakes" prepared at this Lexington Market seafood stall have long been the "standard of comparison" in Charm City; not only are they the "freshest in town", but they're also blessed with chef/co-owner Nancy Devine's "secret seasoning", so even if you "must stand to eat" them in "very, um, rustic" digs, who cares when they're absolutely the "real thing"?

Fleming's S   23 | 23 | 22 | $49 |
720 Aliceanna St. (President St.), 410-332-1666
See review in Washington, DC Directory.

Friendly Farm [S] 21 13 21 $22

17434 Foreston Rd. (Mount Carmel Rd.), Upperco, 410-239-7400

◪ "Eat till you burst" at this "family-style" Traditional American set on a "scenic", "expansive" Upperco farm replete with ducks and geese in the ponds; "don't go when you're counting calories", as the long tables positively groan with "down-home" platters of "yummy fried chicken", "excellent crab cakes" and all the "country" fixings, and better prepare for lots of "children and grandchildren" running around, because this "informal" "throwback to the '50s" puts on "the ultimate family sit-down" supper.

Fuji [S] ▽ 24 16 22 $24

10226 Baltimore Nat'l Pike/Rte. 40 (2 mi. west of Rte. 29), Ellicott City, 410-750-2455

■ "A jewel in an otherwise drab strip mall" in an "out-of-the-way area" west of Ellicott City, this "unassuming" "find" is a "nice family restaurant" that features "sushi like butter", as well as "hot dishes cooked with care" (notably the "superb tempura"); it's "small" yet it "doesn't feel too cramped", and the staff is "charming and friendly", leaving envious sorts "wishing it were in my neighborhood."

G&M [S] 21 8 15 $23

804 N. Hammonds Ferry Rd. (Nursery Rd.), Linthicum, 410-636-1777

◪ "Locals are bemused" by the "never-ending lines" for the "huge, softball-size" crab cakes prepared by this American "dump" "near BWI Airport"; it may be "a one-trick pony", but addicts insist it's "well worth the trip" to Linthicum for this "lump meat", "ghastly" decor notwithstanding (the room "could use a lot of sprucing up"); natives who dismiss it as "very overrated", however, sniff "only a tourist could love" these "disappointing" "boulders."

Gertrude's [S] 21 23 20 $30

Baltimore Museum of Art, 10 Art Museum Dr. (Charles St.), 410-889-3399

◪ The "tranquility" of the "sculpture garden provides a lovely setting" for "Old Baltimore elements" to dine in "gracious" style at this "real restaurant" at the Baltimore Museum of Art; enthusiasts "love" what "TV chef" John Shields' (an avid advocate of Chesapeake Bay cookery) kitchen "does with Maryland seafood", but "disappointed" diners who deem it a "major letdown" lament "if only the food matched the surroundings" and add that the "service could be improved" too.

HAMPTON'S [S] 27 28 27 $59

Harbor Court Hotel, 550 Light St. (bet. Conway & Lee Sts.), 410-347-9744

■ Voted No. 1 for Decor in Baltimore, this "opulent" hotel dining room with an "unbeatable view" "overlooking the

Inner Harbor" virtually guarantees a "stellar" experience, "spoiling" guests with "refined, delectable" New American dishes served by a staff that "treats you like royalty"; when you demand "first-class everything" for a "big-time special occasion", this "classy place" is a sure thing; needless to say, it's "very expensive."

Hard Times Cafe S — 18 | 14 | 16 | $15

8865 Stanford Blvd. (Dobbin Rd.), Columbia, 410-312-0700
See review in Washington, DC Directory.

Harryman House S — 21 | 21 | 21 | $33

340 Main St. (1¼ mi. north of Franklin Blvd.), Reisterstown, 410-833-8850

☑ "Between casual and fancy" describes the tone at this "historic log cabin" set on Reisterstown's old Main Street, which brims with quaint antique shops; folks meet here for "comforting" "country" American vittles served in "warm", "rustic" quarters made even "cozier" by its fireplaces; even if it's "maybe a little pricey for what you get", it seems just about "perfect on a crisp autumn evening."

Helen's Garden S — 22 | 20 | 20 | $27

Canton Sq., 2908 O'Donnell St. (Linwood Ave.), 410-276-2233

■ First-time "customers are greeted as new friends" at this "relaxing oasis" in "bar-infested Canton Square" run by "exceptionally" "nice" owners who are "a trip"; it's a "genuine neighborhood cafe" with "colorful" paintings on display, providing an "arty" backdrop for "innovative" New American dishes with plenty of "pizzazz", along with a "super wine selection"; P.S. "the garden is a bargain on Wednesday nights", when a half-price deal is offered.

HELMAND S — 26 | 22 | 24 | $26

806 N. Charles St. (bet. Madison & Read Sts.), 410-752-0311

■ "Afghanistan's gift to Baltimore" has always maintained a "strong following for good reason", but now it is "enjoying renewed interest" due to world events; "no longer a hidden find in Mt. Vernon", it beckons with "exotic" dishes that "consistently" "hit the mark" (you "must try" the *kaddo* – "it'll forever change how you think about pumpkins" – and the *choppan,* "charcoaled rack of lamb at its absolute zenith"), "graciously" served by an "attentive" staff in an "elegant" room; to boot, it's an "incredible value."

Henninger's Tavern — 24 | 23 | 22 | $30

1812 Bank St. (bet. Ann & Wolfe Sts.), 410-342-2172

■ The "best-kept secret in Fells Point" is this "charming", "off-the-beaten-path" tavern, an "intimate", tin-ceilinged "treasure" set in a former candy store; it's a "wonderful blend of casual neighborhood bar and comfortable dining area with linen cloths and fresh flowers", but don't expect the usual pub grub because from the kitchen emerges "excellent", "imaginative" New American fare (including some of the "best mussels we've ever had").

Henry's, an American Bistro 🆂　– | – | – | M |
Manor Shopping Ctr., 3493 Sweet Air Rd. (Jarrettsville Pike), Phoenix, 410-667-6600
In the horse country of Phoenix, north of Towson, this New American addition features a quiet sunroom up front, a granite-topped bar that buzzes with real estate and tack talk, and a simply appointed main room; wherever you sit, look for a menu that ranges from sandwiches like a grilled salmon BLT to pastas like 'Henry's almost famous' penne with blackened chicken to parmesan-crusted sea bass.

Holy Frijoles 🆂　21 | 14 | 17 | $14 |
908 W. 36th St. (bet. Elm & Roland Aves.), 410-235-2326
◪ "Squeezing" into this "crammed" "hangout for Baltimore's alternative crowd" on Hampden's main drag is "like taking a trip south of the border with a van full of art students"; that doesn't seem to bother the amigos who are "prepared to wait" for a "satisfying", "cheap" Mexican meal by passing the time "in the bar across the street" ("they'll come get you" when a table opens up); critics who find the setup "awkward and uncomfortable", however, sniff "Tex-Mex by a bunch of gringos."

Ikaros 🆂　21 | 14 | 20 | $24 |
4805 Eastern Ave. (Ponca St.), 410-633-3750
■ "Just like being in Greece", this "pleasant" "family place" in Greektown is an "old-fashioned" "Baltimore tradition" for "delicious", "honest cooking" ("you can't go wrong with the grilled lamb or whole fish"); there's "nothing sophisticated" about this "time warp", but the people are "wonderfully friendly" and the portions so "enormous" (the "salad is a meal by itself") that stuffed surveyors quip "save time and ask for half of your order in a doggy bag."

Ixia 🆂　23 | 26 | 21 | $41 |
518 N. Charles St. (Centre St.), 410-727-1800
◪ "Strange and interesting", this "chic new kid on the block" in Mt. Vernon boasts a setting so "dramatically" "stunning" it's "like a stage set"; "almost as special as the fabulous space" is its "newfangled" Asian fusion cuisine, which "artfully" "mixes Eastern and Western flavors" to come up with dishes like black mushroom–encrusted rack of lamb and chocolate-banana spring rolls; skeptics, though, feel it's all "a little too contrived."

Jeannier's　23 | 18 | 22 | $35 |
Broadview Apts., 105 W. 39th St. (University Pkwy.), 410-889-3303
◪ "Not for the fast crowd", this "traditional" French grande dame set in a staid apartment building near Johns Hopkins

is where "baby boomers take mom" on her special day; whether you opt for the "attractive" bar/cafe up front or the more "formal" dining room in the back, you'll be presented with "excellent" "standards", but those who aren't members of the "velvet-headband set" "would like to see a little creativity" on the menu.

Jennings Cafe ◐   18 | 12 | 19 | $18

808 Frederick Rd. (Mellor Ave.), Catonsville, 410-744-3824
☑ Catonsville locals "couldn't do without" this "homey" American "institution", a "neighborhood bar" – "nothing more, nothing less" – staffed by genuine "Baltimore hons" who'll "scold you if you don't clean your plate", which is not hard to do, as "there are no better burgers in town" (the "crab cakes and oyster stew are fine" too); as for the "secondhand smoke", it's just "part of the ambiance."

Jimmy's S   17 | 12 | 17 | $14

801 S. Broadway (Lancaster St.), 410-327-3273
☑ "After you work the overnight shift", "stop in" at this "quintessential Bawlmer" version of "a corner diner" in Fells Point (it opens at 5 AM) and "say hello to Nick", the owner; "it looks like a dive, but breakfast is pretty good" and the "wide assortment of people" (including "celebrities, TV people and politicians") eating here lends it plenty of "local color"; though it's strictly "no frills", the "long lines" attest that it "must be doing something right."

JJ's Everyday Cafe S   19 | 11 | 18 | $21

2141 York Rd. (Timonium Rd.), Timonium, 410-308-2700
☑ Granted, "there's absolutely no atmosphere" at this "stark" little "local walk-in" stuck in a "drab" strip mall across from the Timonium fairgrounds, but "loyal" patrons return often for its "varied menu" of "surprisingly good" American chow ("try the crab cakes") at "good-value" prices; regulars regard it as a "real" BYO "find", but cynics carp "we went in with low expectations and they were met."

John Steven, Ltd. S   20 | 17 | 17 | $24

1800 Thames St. (Ann St.), 410-327-5561
☑ "You might just spot a pirate" at this "local joint" near the waterfront, a "diamond in the rough" with a "great Old Baltimore feel" that "epitomizes" Fells Point; it's a "fun place to hang out" (especially on the "pleasant" patio), down a few cold beers and take in the "people-watching"; the seafood-slanted menu is fairly extensive, but those in-the-know advise sticking with the basics by ordering the "awesome" mussels, clams or shrimp from the steamer bar.

Jordan's S   – | – | – | E

8085 Main St. (Old Columbia Pike), Ellicott City, 410-461-9776
Ellicott City's Main Street gets a fancy new steakhouse with this highly comfortable temple of meat where the

plush dining rooms are quiet and dark, with lots of space between the tables, and most cuts of beef are available in choice or prime; parking can be challenging, but a valet service is in the works.

Josef's Country Inn [S] 22 21 21 $37
2410 Pleasantville Rd. (Fallston Rd.), Fallston, 410-877-7800
◪ "Hearty", "old-fashioned" Continental-German fare "competently" turned out in "lovely" surroundings with a "quaint country feel" makes this stalwart "worth the drive" to Fallston; longtimers say the "dependable" "kitchen knows what it's doing" with the classics and also offers "a number of intriguing specials", but the unimpressed are left "lukewarm" by the experience.

Josephine's ▽ 21 15 20 $26
2112 Fleet St. (Chester St.), 410-327-6261
◪ Situated between Fells Point and Canton, this Southern Italian newcomer housed in a two-century-old former brewery hopes to lure denizens from both neighborhoods with its grand old bar and a "very good" roster of red-sauce pastas and more ambitious specials, all served by a crew that "tries to please"; early enthusiasts appreciate it as an alternative to Little Italy, but dissenters deem it only "fair."

Joy America Cafe [S] 22 24 20 $38
American Visionary Art Museum, 800 Key Hwy. (Covington St.), 410-244-6500
◪ If the "crazy art food gets any taller" at this "definitely different" rooftop dining room at the "zany" American Visionary Art Museum, you "might need a demolition permit to eat" the "inventive" New American dishes; even "cooler" than the culinary concoctions is the "joyful" terrace with its "beautiful view" of the Inner Harbor as well as the nutty three-story-tall whirligig in the courtyard; those who don't get it, though, proclaim it "too snotty" and "strange."

Kali's Court [S] 24 24 21 $43
1606 Thames St. (bet. Bond St. & Broadway), 410-276-4700
◪ "They know their fish" at this "attractive" "see-and-be-seen" Greek-Med scene in Fells Point, and it's so "amazingly fresh" "it's worth the effort to try to find a parking place", especially if you can "hold court out on the lovely patio"; detractors note, though, that "reservations aren't honored on time", "it's noisy in the extreme" and the staff can be "rude" ("do you need a secret code to get decent service here?"); the bottom line: the finny fare is "a treat, but expect to pay for it", in more ways than one.

Kelly's ◐ [S] ▽ 21 12 18 $20
2108 Eastern Ave. (bet. Chester & Duncan Sts.), 410-327-2312
◪ "Everyone's a regular" at this quintessential local spot, an "honest" workingman's bar in East Baltimore where first-

timers become "instant friends" as they bond over a pile of steamed "crabs, crabs, crabs" and other Chesapeake-inspired seafood dishes ("without the touristy prices"); given the "old tunes" playing, as well as karaoke on the weekends, "warm, good times" are just about guaranteed.

Kings Contrivance S   23 24 23 $42
10150 Shaker Dr. (Rtes. 29 & 32), Columbia, 410-995-0500
◪ Set in a "lovely", "historic" "mansion", this "romantic" "special destination" has cultivated a loyal following with its "fancy" "old-world" setting (its "many little quaint rooms" foster a "quiet", "intimate dinner") and "consistently fine" New American menu; it's considered one of the "best that Columbia has to offer", but critics who don't think it's "worth a detour" find it "a little tired" and "haughty."

La Madeleine
French Bakery & Café S   16 16 13 $17
6211 Columbia Crossing Dr. (Dobbin Rd.), Columbia, 410-872-4900
See review in Washington, DC Directory.

La Scala S   22 19 23 $32
1012 Eastern Ave. (Central Ave.), 410-783-9209
◪ Three words you can't refuse: "grilled Caesar salad", the signature dish at this non-touristy Italian contender in Little Italy, where a meal is "like dining in [chef-owner] Nino Germano's home"; "truly one of Baltimore's best-kept secrets", it "comforts" fans with "thoughtfully prepared" dishes served in a "relaxing" ambiance, but "disappointed" detractors gripe "no surprises" here; P.S. "his mama's wonderful cannoli" is "not to be missed."

La Tesso Tana S   19 17 18 $34
58 W. Biddle St. (Cathedral St.), 410-837-3630
◪ "Convenient to the Meyerhoff Symphony Hall" and the Lyric Opera House, this "cozy" "basement" Italian is handy for a "pre-performance dinner" because it knows how to "get you out the door in time" for the show; critics, however, caution about "cramped quarters" and note that it can get "too noisy on concert nights."

Legal Sea Foods S   19 16 18 $32
100 E. Pratt St. (Calvert St.), 410-332-7360
See review in Washington, DC Directory.

Liberatore's S   22 20 21 $33
Freedom Village Shopping Ctr., 6300 Georgetown Blvd. (Liberty Rd.), Eldersburg, 410-781-4114
New Town Village Ctr., 9712 Groffs Mill Dr. (Lakeside Blvd.), Owings Mills, 410-356-3100
Timonium Corporate Ctr., 9515 Deereco Rd. (Padonia Rd.), Timonium, 410-561-3300

(continued)

(continued)
Liberatore's
140 Village Shopping Ctr., 521 Jermor Ln. (Rte. 97), Westminster, 410-876-2121
■ "Always bustling", this growing family-operated mini-chain does "upscale suburban Italian" that admirers swear is "as good as Little Italy"; while set in places like "sterile office parks" and strip malls, the "exteriors belie the intimate interiors", which form "pleasant" backdrops for "solid", if "unremarkable", food; P.S. the Timonium branch boasts perhaps the "best adult bar scene in the county."

LINWOOD'S S   26 25 25 $45
McDonogh Crossroads, 25 Crossroads Dr. (McDonogh & Reisterstown Rds.), Owings Mills, 410-356-3030
■ "Cool elegance and seductive fare" combined with "smooth" service make this "sleek" New American "the place to be seen" in Owings Mills; it's a "popular" gathering spot for "power lunches, business dinners" and "long meals with friends", appealing with dishes that "sparkle" and a "Manhattan night club–like" feel; if the "softly lit" dining room is too formal for your taste, "you can go more casual and sit at the counter around the open kitchen" or out on the new landscaped patio.

Louisiana S   25 26 23 $46
1708 Aliceanna St. (Broadway), 410-327-2610
■ Occupying a "beautifully redone" building in Fells Point, this "opulently" "over-the-top" "beauty" could provide the "setting for an Anne Rice novel"; nearly as "fabulous" as the surroundings are the "spectacular", "rich" French dishes "inventively" spun with a Creole twist and brought to table by an "attentive" crew; the consensus: this is a "special-occasion" "keeper" that'll "impress anyone."

L.P. Steamers S   ▽ 20 10 17 $20
1100 E. Fort Ave. (Woodall St.), 410-576-9294
■ A "salty joint" filled with "neighborhood" characters who are definitely "part of its charm", this seafood bar set in a South Baltimore row house "just down the road from Ft. McHenry" is "worth going off-the-beaten-crab-path" (ask chef-owner Bud about his decadent deep-fried hard crabs); it can get smoky inside, but the new rooftop deck is a fine place to take in the urban skyline.

Manor Tavern S   19 19 18 $32
15819 Old York Rd. (Manor Rd.), Monkton, 410-771-8155
■ Trying to offer "something for everyone", this "pleasant horse-country tavern" in Monkton is a "favorite of the rural set" thanks to its "bucolic setting" amid rolling farmland; though its all-American bill of fare is "not exceptional" in any way, it's fine for a burger and a beer by the fire after a "beautiful ride through the Maryland" countryside.

Marconi's 22 | 18 | 24 | $38

106 W. Saratoga St. (bet. Cathedral St. & Park Ave.), 410-727-9522

◪ "It hasn't changed since my grandfather ate here" marvel surveyors of this "man's restaurant" Downtown, and that's just swell by the stalwarts who feel that this "charming" relic of "Old Baltimore still stands up"; its Continental-Chesapeake preparations are "frozen in tradition", so even if the "old-school" fare "isn't for gourmet diners", veterans "love it."

Martick's 22 | 17 | 17 | $30

214 W. Mulberry St. (bet. Howard St. & Park Ave.), 410-752-5155

◪ "Eccentric owner-waiter-chef" Morris Martick, a "real character", "keeps hanging in there" at his highly "quirky" labor of love west of Downtown; though it's set in a sketchy neighborhood of the commercial district, intrepid types are rewarded with an "eclectic treat" of a "daily menu" that's "advertised as French" but brims with whimsical twists, which always results in an "exciting meal"; you'll either "love it or hate it", but there's "nothing like it."

Matsuri [S] 25 | 15 | 19 | $25

1105 S. Charles St. (Cross St.), 410-752-8561

■ At the crossroads of South Baltimore's restaurant scene is this "casual", "popular" Japanese "hangout" that overflows quickly since it's "smaller than a bento box", but those in-the-know are adamant that it's "worth the wait" for "by far the best sushi in town", "terrific teriyaki" and a "good vegetarian selection"; though on "busy nights there's nowhere to queue up" except outside, the "friendly" service and "great prices" more than compensate.

McCabe's [S] 20 | 13 | 18 | $23

3845 Falls Rd. (41st St.), 410-467-1000

◪ "The burger is worth putting up with the smoke" (as are the "remarkable" crab cakes) wafting through this "cute hole-in-the-wall" in Hampden, a "friendly neighborhood place where everyone knows your name"; the all-American eats "draw locals and folks from across the city", but the "too popular" "joint" is "tiny", so "be prepared for a wait."

McCormick & Schmick's [S] 21 | 21 | 20 | $37

Pier 5 Hotel, 711 Eastern Ave. (President St.), 410-234-1300

See review in Washington, DC Directory.

MILTON INN [S] 26 | 27 | 25 | $50

14833 York Rd. (3 mi. north of Shawan Rd.), Sparks, 410-771-4366

■ "Far away from the city" above Hunt Valley is this "quaint", "romantic country inn" that has "survived" for more than half a century; quartered in a 260-year-old fieldstone house, it serves "excellent" "traditional" American "standards" in a series of formal stone-and-wood rooms replete with fireplaces; "expensive but worth it", "it's a perfect place to take your rich uncle when he visits."

MORTON'S OF CHICAGO 🄢   24 21 23 $53
Sheraton Inner Harbor Hotel, 300 S. Charles St. (Conway St.), 410-547-8255
See review in Washington, DC Directory.

Obrycki's Crab House 🄢   21 15 18 $34
1727 E. Pratt St. (bet. Ann St. & Broadway), 410-732-6399
◪ "Crab in all forms" – "steamed, broiled, fried, made into soup" – is the headliner at this sprawling brick fortress in East Baltimore; it's located near enough to the Downtown hotels that lots of "out-of-town visitors" cab over for a meal, but the natives are decidedly divided: while fans say it's "still the place" for seafood, foes carp that it's "too gentrified", "touristy" and "pricey"; P.S. it's best to "call ahead" to "order the big ones."

Orchard Market Cafe 🄢   25 20 22 $24
Orchard Plaza, 8815 Orchard Tree Ln. (Joppa Rd.), Towson, 410-339-7700
■ A gastronomic "oasis in the desert" east of Towson, this "small, simple", "family-run" place stuck "in a strip mall behind a strip mall" thrills those who "can find it" with "lovingly prepared" Persian food delivered in a "warm" atmosphere; its "exotic fare with a homey touch" makes it a "tasty" "change of pace" in the suburbs, while its BYO policy keeps the tabs even more "moderate."

Oregon Grille 🄢   25 26 24 $50
1201 Shawan Rd. (Beaver Dam Rd.), Hunt Valley, 410-771-0505
◪ "For an elegant night out" west of Hunt Valley, the "who's who" "straps on the money belt" and heads to this "clubby" American steakhouse set in a "picturesque" 19th-century farmhouse; "dripping with horse-country richness", it showcases "superb" dry-aged sirloins in "sleek" surroundings that "make you want to sit up straight"; it's "definitely a player", but foes who gripe "way overpriced" wonder "why would anyone pay for so much attitude?"

Paolo's 🄢   18 18 17 $29
Harborplace Light Street Pavilion, 301 Light St. (Pratt St.), 410-539-7060
1 W. Pennsylvania Ave. (York Rd.), Towson, 410-321-7000
See review in Washington, DC Directory.

Papermoon Diner ◗🄢   ─ ─ ─ I
227 W. 29th St. (Remington Ave.), 410-889-4444
You'll either "love the atmosphere" or frown that it's "somewhat disturbing" say those who know about this "bizarre" but entertaining 24/7 American diner in Remington, where "Barbies fly through the sky" and a "mannequin"

poses in the "psychedelic bathroom"; once the haunt of milkmen and cops, it now feeds a mix of "yuppie food" and "traditional" eats to bohemians and "Hopkins students"; the chow is "decent", though it's the "highly original decor" that makes it a "must-see."

Pazza Luna   23 | 21 | 21 | $38
1401 E. Clement St. (Decatur St.), 410-727-1212

▧ "In Garlic We Trust" is stamped on the menu at this "intimate" homage to Italian-American life set in an old melting pot neighborhood near Ft. McHenry, so you should know what to expect from the celestial Northern Italian menu; it's a "warm and wonderful" refuge, and "they try hard to please", but "don't go if you don't like Frank Sinatra."

Peppermill S   19 | 16 | 20 | $25
Heaver Bldg., 1301 York Rd. (bet. I-695 & Seminary Ave.), Lutherville, 410-583-1107

▧ "Not only the senior set" enjoys the "good" American "home cooking" offered at this "pleasant" fallback tucked away in a Lutherville office tower; "youngsters" ("if you're under 60, you'll feel like a kid") come too for a "something for everyone" menu of "reliable, if unexciting", dishes priced "moderately" and served by "charming" folks.

Peter's Inn ⊬   24 | 17 | 20 | $23
504 S. Ann St. (Eastern Ave.), 410-675-7313

▧ "Where else can you eat scallops with caviar while only three feet from a biker drinking beer from a can?" ask regulars of this "tiny" row house in Fells Point, which looks like a "total dive bar" but actually turns out "gourmet" "comfort food"; though "there aren't many choices" on the Eclectic menu, the lineup changes weekly and most everything that emerges from the kitchen is "delicious"; "if you don't like smoke", however, keep moving.

PETIT LOUIS BISTRO S   24 | 22 | 22 | $35
4800 Roland Ave. (Upland Rd.), 410-366-9393

▧ Like "a trip to Paris for $50, and they like Americans too" marvel devotees of this "perfect re-creation of a French bistro" "in the middle of Roland Park"; the "charming" brainchild of chef Cindy Wolf and wine director (and husband) Tony Foreman (the owners of Charleston), it's an "energetic" gathering place suitable for both "drop-in or special-occasion" dining, pleasing with "hearty" fare prepared with "panache" and paired with an "exciting" wine program; the "tables are close" together and "the din makes conversation difficult", but it "deserves its popularity."

P.F. Chang's China Bistro S   20 | 20 | 18 | $26
Mall in Columbia, 10300 Little Patuxent Pkwy. (Wincopin Circle), Columbia, 410-730-5344
See review in Washington, DC Directory.

Phillips S
15 | 15 | 14 | $28

*Harborplace Light Street Pavilion, 301 Light St. (Pratt St.),
410-685-6600*

◪ Though "not a local favorite", this sprawling "tourist
trap" "centrally located" in the Inner Harbor pulls in plenty of
"visitors" with its "wonderful" outdoor tables ("great view"
of the waterfront) and "abundant" seafood buffet ("be
ready to strap on the feedbag"); it's "not too expensive"
("nothing to write home about" either), but the natives are
"embarrassed" by the "mass-produced" grub (made with
"foreign crabmeat"!) and warn there are "tons of better
places in the area"; N.B. there's an outpost in Annapolis.

Pierpoint S
24 | 16 | 21 | $38

1822 Aliceanna St. (bet. Ann & Wolfe Sts.), 410-675-2080

◪ "Old Maryland recipes get a contemporary makeover"
(think "must-order smoked crab cakes") at this "small",
"festive" (in a low-key way) eatery on the eastern edge of
Fells Point; the consensus is that it's "a little hit-or-miss", but
when the kitchen's "clicking", the results are "superb" (it's
"best when [chef-owner] Nancy Longo's cooking"), though
be warned that the tables are "uncomfortably" tight.

Pisces S
23 | 24 | 23 | $42

*Hyatt Regency, 300 Light St. (bet. Conway & Pratt Sts.),
410-605-2835*

■ "Don't let the hotel setting stop you" from trying this
"beautiful" fish house atop the Hyatt Regency, which
boasts a "spectacular harbor view"; it's an "impressive"
destination for "creative", "surprisingly good seafood", as
well as an extravagant Sunday champagne brunch buffet,
tended to by a "skilled staff" in a "great" atmosphere; the
"adequate wine list is a plus."

Polo Grill S
24 | 24 | 23 | $47

*Inn at The Colonnade, 4 W. University Pkwy.
(bet. Canterbury Rd. & Charles St.), 410-235-8200*

◪ "A swanky place for movers and shakers", this "plush"
hotel dining room near the Hopkins Homewood campus is a
"clubby" "power lunch" "scene" that offers habitués an
"all-around excellent experience"; the "outstanding" New
American menu is fairly extensive, though insiders advise
the "fried lobster tail is all you need to know", while hosts
"Gail and Lenny Kaplan still have that magic touch", but "if
you're not in the clique, you may have to wait forever to get
seated at a table."

PRIME RIB ◗ S
28 | 26 | 27 | $53

Horizon House, 1101 N. Calvert St. (Chase St.), 410-539-1804

■ "Old-time dress-up dining" distinguishes this "opulent"
"'40s Manhattan–style supper club" set in a Downtown
apartment house; voted No. 1 for both Food and Service in
Baltimore, it promises a "special evening out", proffering

"sublime prime rib" and other cuts in "luxurious" environs by "professional", tuxedoed waiters, with live music playing softly in the background; of course the "dollars add up", but this "venerable" "institution" elicits "wows on all fronts"; N.B. jacket required.

Purple Orchid S 24 20 21 $38
729 E. Pratt St. (President St.), 410-837-0080
Easily overlooked at a busy intersection between the Inner Harbor and Little Italy, this "yummy" "find" is "still undeservedly undiscovered" after its move from Charles Street; that's a shame because its "amazing fusion of fine French and Pan-Asian" cuisines is "original" and "exquisitely presented" (there's a sushi bar too); "among the best of its genre", it's worth checking out.

Red Maple ● S – – – E
930 N. Charles St. (Eager St.), 410-547-0149
"Perhaps more of a club" than a restaurant, this "chichi" addition to Charles Street aspires to be "the hippest scene in Baltimore"; "gorgeous" in a "minimalist" way, it's a "cool" haunt with "exotic drinks", "tasty", "creative" Asian tapas (the "portions are very small", so "don't come hungry") and a DJ who ratchets up the music till late at night; it merits a visit if you're looking to be "transported", but better "wear black."

River Watch S 18 19 17 $29
207 Nanticoke Rd. (Middleborough Rd.), Essex, 410-687-1422
Moored on the workingman's "Riviera" in Essex, this colorful, boisterous summertime pleasure affords a "view that's alone worth the trip"; the seafood-slanted menu is only "acceptable", but if you "sit on the deck" "overlooking the marina" and order some steamed crabs and a pitcher of beer while listening to live music, you'll swear that this is the "best place in the world to eat in warm weather."

Roy's S 24 24 23 $45
720B Aliceanna St. (President St.), 410-659-0099
"Way different for Bawlmer", this "glitzy" outpost of Roy Yamaguchi's Hawaiian fusion empire recently surfed into Inner Harbor East, bringing his trademark "exotica" to Maryland (such as iron-seared mahi mahi with macadamia-lobster sauce, along with an "excellent variety of fish not usually found on the East Coast"); groupies cheer that it's "as pleasing to the eye as it is to the taste buds", but detractors who feel it's "too slick" for this town want to know "what's the big deal?"

Ruby Lounge 21 21 18 $31
802 N. Charles St. (Madison St.), 410-539-8051
"Fitting well into the Mt. Vernon scene", this "hip", "sultry" "hangout" attracts a "sophisticated, arty crowd"

with its "urban-chic environs"; it's a "stylish meeting place" that features an "incredible martini list" and a "daring" Eclectic menu (the open kitchen has a "deft hand with seafood", as exemplified by its "perfectly fried oysters"); even if it "can be uneven", fans give it the "prize for most unusual combinations that actually taste good."

Rudys' 2900 S   26 | 20 | 23 | $42
2900 Baltimore Blvd./Rte. 140 (Rte. 91), Finksburg, 410-833-5777

■ "Co-owners Rudy and Rudi", the "gracious proprietors", make it "worth the trip to Finksburg", because a "real pro is at work in the kitchen" (that would be "talented" German-born chef Rudy Speckamp), while the "best maitre d'" (Rudi Paul) tends to all details in the front of the house; expect Continental "classics" so "well-prepared" that enthusiasts who have "always" enjoyed a "perfect meal" here swear that you "can't go wrong with whatever you order", though perhaps the decor could use a little "updating."

RUTH'S CHRIS STEAK HOUSE S   24 | 23 | 23 | $49
600 Water St. (bet. Gay St. & Market Pl.), 410-783-0033
1777 Reisterstown Rd. (Hooks Ln.), Pikesville, 410-837-0033
See review in Washington, DC Directory.

Sabatino's ●S   20 | 16 | 19 | $29
901 Fawn St. (High St.), 410-727-9414

◪ No, this "unpretentious" Little Italy "landmark" is "not a hotbed of chic cuisine", but sometimes at "3 AM" its "old-world" "red-sauce cooking" is just what you need; at any time, expect a crowd of "genuine characters" (some with "really interesting hairdos") chowing down on its famous "Bookmaker salad" ("worth it for the dressing alone") and "dependable pastas" served by "career waitresses."

SAMOS ⊭   27 | 16 | 23 | $16
600 S. Oldham St. (Fleet St.), 410-675-5292

■ "Where Baltimore's Greeks eat", this "bustling" little "neighborhood community center" in Greektown is "nothing fancy", but it exudes "true warmth", with a "welcoming staff that makes even sporadic visitors feel like regulars"; from his open kitchen, hardworking chef-owner Nick Georgalas satisfies his "big following" with "down-to-earth" dishes that are both Hellenic and "heavenly", and ridiculously "cheap" to boot.

San Sushi S   22 | 14 | 18 | $25
9832 York Rd. (Padonia Rd.), Timonium, 410-453-0140
10 W. Pennsylvania Ave. (York Rd.), Towson, 410-825-0908

◪ Though "not much to look at", these Siamese siblings more than compensate with "terrific" food and "friendly" service; both feature "excellent sushi", but the Timonium branch also specializes in "great whole fish" and Thai fusion cuisine, while the Towson venue offers "wonderful", traditional tastes; fence-sitters, however, shrug "above average", but "not worth going out of your way."

Sascha's 527 20 23 18 $26

527 N. Charles St. (Centre St.), 410-539-8880

◪ "At the foot of Baltimore's Washington Monument", this "fancy yet funky" "hangout" housed in a former hair salon has won a following with its "over-the-top" decor and an "inventive" New American roster replete with a "mix-and-match sauce system"; admirers appreciate that the menu "includes both light fare and heavier dishes, to suit whatever appetite you may have", but conservative types counter that its "reach outstrips its grasp", resulting in a "disorganized" effort that "needs more work."

Shula's Steak House [S] 20 18 18 $46

Wyndham Baltimore, 101 W. Fayette St. (bet. Charles & Liberty Sts.), 410-385-6601

See review in Washington, DC Directory.

SoBo Cafe [S] 20 15 17 $18

6 W. Cross St. (Charles St.), 410-752-1518

■ "Comfort food at a comfortable price in a comforting atmosphere" sums up this "small, friendly" "neighborhood dive" in South Baltimore; catering to "Generation X", it's an "unpretentiously" "hip scene" with "good art on the walls" and a frequently "changing menu that offers exciting options and old standbys" (including the "best mac 'n' cheese" and chicken pot pie) at "can't-beat prices."

Soigné – – – E

554 E. Fort Ave. (Jackson St.), 410-659-9898

"Everyone's talking about" this "hot spot" near Ft. McHenry, and justifying the "great buzz" is Edward Kim's (the "accomplished" founding chef of Ixia) Pacific Rim "fusion" menu, which showcases "unbelievable combinations" of ingredients that result in "delicious" "innovations"; "a real plus for Baltimore", it's already "right at the top" of the town's restaurant pyramid according to fans who "would eat here every night if we could afford it."

Sotto Sopra [S] 24 25 23 $40

405 N. Charles St. (Mulberry St.), 410-625-0534

■ "Subdued fun" awaits at this "trendy" "date restaurant" on Charles Street that "lives up to the hype" by turning out "classics" so "outstanding" (the "homemade pastas are unusually good") they'll make "discriminating palates" "forget all about Little Italy"; the "eye-catching" decor forms a "lovely" backdrop for the "chichi crowd", which embraces it as a "tasteful" "place to see and be seen" that's "sure to impress your companion."

Spike & Charlie's [S] 21 | 18 | 18 | $38

1225 Cathedral St. (Preston St.), 410-752-8144

◪ "Cornering the market in the cultural district" of Baltimore, this "pre-concert requirement" "across from the Meyerhoff Symphony Hall" "always offers something unusual" on the "ever-changing" New American menu; a vocal majority, however, bellows "what a disappointment" – given its location, "they should be used to getting people well fed and out the door, but it's a struggle" to make the curtain because the "staff doesn't care", which contributes to the "impersonal" atmosphere.

STONE MANOR [S] 27 | 27 | 25 | $57

5820 Carroll Boyer Rd. (Sumantown Rd.), Middletown, 301-473-5454

■ Promising a "great getaway", this "gorgeous stone manor house" set on 114 acres of formal gardens and working farmland in the Middletown countryside is an "intimate, relaxing" "destination" for "memorable" New American cooking that amounts to "high art"; it's "beautifully presented" in "romantic", "understated" environs furnished with antiques and tended to by a "superb" staff, making it a near-"perfect" "experience" that the enchanted insists should "not to be missed."

Sushi Hana [S] 24 | 18 | 21 | $23

6 E. Pennsylvania Ave. (York Rd.), Towson, 410-823-0372

◪ "Better than most of the other" Japanese options in town, this "reliable sushi" den in Towson pleases the cognoscenti with "consistently fresh and delicious" raw fish, "the most imaginative rolls around" and "excellent, personal" service; though it's often "filled with university students", it manages to pull off a "soothing" atmosphere that's only enhanced by the "pleasant" koi pond.

Suzie's Soba [S] 21 | 18 | 19 | $21

1009 W. 36th St. (Roland Ave.), 410-243-0051

◪ Importing some international spice to old Hampden's restaurant row, this "cozy" Asian alternative offers "tasty" Korean dishes from owner Suzie Hong's native land, along with an "excellent" Japanese "noodle feast" ("packed with flavor") and sushi; boosters regard it as a "delightful" "little" "gem", but those who feel the "mediocre" food is "overpriced for what it is" ask "why bother?"

Szechuan ▽ 21 | 9 | 20 | $18

1125 S. Charles St. (Cross St.), 410-752-8409

◪ Amid the Cross Street market hustle and bustle, this tiny "hole-in-the-wall" in South Baltimore is "often overlooked", but it "never fails to please" regulars with its "consistently" "wonderful" Chinese cooking; though it could use "serious redecorating", it's "family-friendly", the "pleasant" staff is

"welcoming" and the prices "cheap"; besides, "if the
waitress likes you, you might get a naughty fortune."

Szechuan Best 🆂　　　　24　13　19　$18
8625 Liberty Rd. (Old Court Rd.), Randallstown, 410-521-0020
◪ "The Chinese community eats here, so you know it's good"
say fans of this "neighborhood" "gem" that's "worth
traveling" to Randallstown; "going way beyond the typical
Chinese menu", it thrills connoisseurs with "authentic" fare
("great Peking duck") and dim sum that "can stand up
to what you find in NYC"; who cares that "it's not much
to look at"?

Szechuan House 🆂　　　　23　14　22　$19
1427 York Rd. (Seminary Ave.), Lutherville, 410-825-8181
◪ Lutherville's "nice little strip-mall find" is not so little
anymore after finally completing a doubling of its dining
room and kitchen; it's still "not fancy", but the Chinese food
is as "tasty" as before, the service just as "friendly" and
the "value" equally "great"; any surprise that partisans
"dine here at least once a month"?

Tapas Teatro 🆂　　　　23　21　19　$25
1711 N. Charles St. (Lanvale St.), 410-332-0110
■ "How did we ever live without this place?" wonder
regulars of this "frenetic" appendage to the Charles Theatre
just above the train station; it delivers an "adventure" for
the taste buds with its "array" of "wonderfully surprising"
"little Mediterranean plates", presented in a room that's
"upscale" in a "casual" way; "plan on waiting for a table",
but it's "worth it" because this is a "great concept."

Tasting Room　　　　－　－　－　E
101 N. Market St. (Church St.), Frederick, 240-379-7772
Decidedly cutting-edge, this addition to restaurant row in
Frederick, set in a grand old merchant's corner store with
big windows, is cultivating a tony following with its popular
wine bar and creative, up-to-the-minute International
menu (think hoisin grilled pork loin with lobster whipped
potatoes); N.B. closed on Sundays, except for its monthly
wine tasting dinners.

Tersiguel's 🆂　　　　25　24　24　$46
8293 Main St. (Old Columbia Pike), Ellicott City, 410-465-4004
◪ Savor "a slice of the French countryside" at this
"charming old house" in Ellicott City, a "sentimental
favorite" for "robust", "remarkable" fare "beautifully
plated"; devotees laud it as "all-around fabulous", with
a series of "warm, comfortable" rooms and "attentive"
service, adding up to a "special" "treat" that's "worth a
trip" to the "outskirts"; the "underwhelmed", though,
who find it "always good but unexciting", feel it's "living
off its past."

Thai [S] 23 14 20 $21

3316-18 Greenmount Ave. (33rd St.), 410-889-6002

◪ "Don't let the neighborhood turn you off" urge boosters of this "tacky" eatery located in a "questionable" part of Waverly, because the "real" Thai food prepared here is the "best in Baltimore" ("love the spring rolls"); not only are the dishes served "quickly", but they're "decently priced" too and there's a "parking lot in the back."

Thai Landing 22 15 21 $22

1207 N. Charles St. (Biddle St.), 410-727-1234

■ "Worth the parking trouble" in Mt. Vernon, this "small", "minimalist" Thai "near the opera and symphony" is a "so friendly" place to enjoy "flavorful", "lovingly prepared" dishes served by a "great" staff at "reasonable prices"; beware, though: "when they say spicy, they mean it."

That's Amore [S] 16 15 17 $27

Mall in Columbia, 10400 Little Patuxent Pkwy. (Broken Land Pkwy.), Columbia, 410-772-5900

See review in Washington, DC Directory.

Timbuktu [S] 19 11 16 $25

1726 Dorsey Rd. (Rte. 100), Hanover, 410-796-0733

◪ A "perfect meeting point" near BWI Airport (though "somewhat hard to find the first time"), this "nothing fancy" (a "dive", truth be told) Greek-American "roadhouse" is "worth" seeking out for "big, real crab cakes" that are "highly superior to others nearby"; they're so "terrific" that they "defy description" and have become such a "cult phenomenon" that "addicts" have to "make a regular trek" here; "don't even bother" with anything else on the otherwise "ordinary" menu.

TIO PEPE [S] 26 22 23 $44

10 E. Franklin St. (bet. Charles & St. Paul Sts.), 410-539-4675

◪ "We love it" shout aficionados of this "wonderful" Downtown "institution" that's renowned for preparing Spanish food "at its best"; it's a "Baltimore favorite for all celebrations" given its "amazing" fare served by a "well-seasoned" team in a "feel-good" atmosphere; for a "special night out", it's an "enduring tradition", but dissenters feel it's "overrated", citing dishes "adapted for the American palate", a "loud, cramped" setting and a "snobby" staff; P.S. "be prepared to wait, reservation" or not.

Towne Hall [S] 15 17 14 $29

Greenspring Station, 2360 W. Joppa Rd. (Falls Rd.), Brooklandville, 410-339-6300

◪ After a "difficult start-up", this "upscale neighborhood bar" (co-owned by Cal Ripken, Jr.) at the Greenspring Station crossroads is now drawing a leisurely lunch trade as well as an active bar crowd; most "locals" "hoped" it would be able to "work out the kinks", but some still find the New American food as "erratic" as the service.

Trattoria Alberto 27 | 20 | 23 | $49
1660 Crain Hwy. S. (Rte. 100 underpass), Glen Burnie, 410-761-0922
◪ Lurking in an "unlikely", out-of-the-way stretch of Glen Burnie, this "expensive" (for the neighborhood) "strip-center" Northern Italian is "not well frequented", but those who've discovered it rhapsodize about "extraordinary" cooking; definitely "not your typical suburban restaurant", you better be "prepared to spend big bucks before you ask Alberto to take care of you."

Turning Point Inn [S] 24 | 24 | 23 | $47
3406 Urbana Pike (Rte. 80), Frederick, 301-831-8232
■ "Worth driving beyond the Beltway" for a "special evening", this "charming" Colonial Revival–style inn "out-of-the-way" near Frederick appeals with its "artistic approach" to New American cooking; the "flavorful", "contemporary" dishes ("start with the lobster bisque") are accompanied by an "extensive wine list" and turned out in "lovely", "romantic" quarters by an "attentive" staff, making it a "delightful surprise."

Union Hotel [S] ▽ 24 | 25 | 23 | $36
1282 Susquehanna River Rd. (south of Rte. 1), Port Deposit, 410-378-3503
■ Set in a "historic" former hotel tucked away in the woods of Port Deposit by the Susquehanna River, this "unique" country destination feels like an old log cabin, soothing with a "lovely" ambiance and crackling fireplaces; in a dining room filled with cozy nooks, waitresses in "period costumes" haul out "Fred Flintstone–size prime rib", "huge steaks" and other traditional American vittles; it's a "must-try at least once"; P.S. the "adjacent barn, converted to a bar", is a favorite among bikers.

Vespa 21 | 20 | 19 | $31
1117-21 S. Charles St. (Cross St.), 410-385-0355
◪ "All the beautiful people" who "scoot" in attired "only in black" make this "spirited" South Baltimore Italian one "hip" hangout; featuring a "chic" "industrial look" (though the "noise level is a serious problem") and a "good-looking" staff, it's a "cool" place to dine on "excellent" fare (the starters are so "tasty" you could "make a meal out of them"), but expect to eat "elbow to elbow with strangers."

Viccino Bistro [S] 22 | 18 | 21 | $36
1317 N. Charles St. (Mt. Royal Ave.), 410-347-0349
■ Just south of the train station by the UB campus, this onetime college-central pizzeria/deli has grown up to

become a "pleasant" bistro featuring "artful presentations" of "creative", "consistently good" New American dishes; it's "convenient" to the "theater district" (it even offers a free "shuttle"), but it "deserves a visit even when you're not going to a show."

Windows S   20 24 21 $38
Renaissance Harborplace Hotel, 202 E. Pratt St. (bet. Calvert & South Sts.), 410-685-8439
◪ Boasting a "spectacular view of the Inner Harbor" from its fifth-floor perch at the Renaissance, this "lovely" New American dining room pulls in a "Baltimore power crowd" at lunchtime, while live jazz attracts a hotel audience at dinner; proponents say the food is a "pleasant surprise", but the "unimpressed" proclaim it "only ok" and advise "stick with the crab cakes."

Woman's Industrial Exchange   18 18 22 $13
333 N. Charles St. (Pleasant St.), 410-685-4388
■ Quite possibly the "last of the crafts and food shops for gentlewomen's" products around, this "landmark" Downtown is a "relic" of "kinder times"; like a cherished "snapshot", it keeps "memories alive" with its "ancient recipes and ancient waitresses"; this is "wholesome", "down-home" American cooking "like your grandma" used to make, served at prices so "inexpensive" it was voted the No. 1 Bang for the Buck in Baltimore.

Woodfire S   19 18 19 $26
580P Ritchie Hwy. (McKinsey Rd.), Severna Park, 410-315-8100
◪ "Wonderful wood-burning aromas" waft through this "neighborhood" American in Severna Park, which "doesn't disappoint" fans with its "good food for the money" (it "doesn't hurt you with high wine prices" either); doubters, however, who judge it "so-so" think that the "inconsistent" menu and service "need to improve."

Ze Mean Bean Cafe S   20 20 20 $24
1739 Fleet St. (Ann St.), 410-675-5999
■ "Eat your dumplings" and other "stick-to-your-ribs" Eastern European fare at this "cozy spot" set "away from the intensity of Fells Point"; over the years, it has grown to be "more than the coffeehouse that its name implies", becoming a real restaurant with "honest" food, "attractive (if a bit cramped)" digs and "live [jazz and folk] music that lends a bohemian feel."

Zodiac S   – – – M
1724 N. Charles St. (Lanvale St.), 410-727-8815
"A good choice before a show" at the Charles or Everyman Theatres across the street, this funky "scene" with '40s-style banquettes attracts a most interesting clientele, from

pierced to political; Christina Miller's (who trained with Emeril) "varied" Eclectic menu is "frequently changing", so there's "always something new and different to try", and it's "vegan-friendly."

Zorba's Bar & Grill ◐ [S] 21 13 17 $22

4710 Eastern Ave. (Oldham St.), 410-276-4484

■ "If you make the trip down the gauntlet", past all the "men drinking at the bar", you'll be rewarded with "flavorful" Greek food at this late-night "gem of Greektown"; followers would gladly "move in" (even if they "need to work on the decor") to feast every day on the "best lamb chops in the world" and "charcoal-grilled" fish; it may be "intimidating at first", but bets are it'll fast become an oft-"visited favorite."

Annapolis

	F	D	S	C

Aqua Terra 🅂
23 | 20 | 21 | $36

164 Main St. (Conduit St.), 410-263-1985

☑ "Remarkably adventurous for Annapolis", this "stylish" New American storefront introduces an "innovative" menu (seared tuna with lemongrass risotto, anyone?) and a "sophisticated" edge to the Main Street scene; "trendy" types "love" the "interesting formula", but conservative sorts deem the "cutting-edge" dishes "too experimental" (if not downright "weird") and caution that the "tables are too jammed together."

Cafe Normandie 🅂
20 | 19 | 18 | $32

185 Main St. (Church Circle), 410-263-3382

☑ "Crêpes ahoy!" cheer devotees of this "cozy" version of a "French countryside bistro" located up Main Street from Annapolis' City Dock; though the area is tourist central, "most diners here seem like repeat customers" appreciating dishes prepared with "flair", but foes cite "inconsistent" food and service and warn about the too-"small" tables.

Cantler's Riverside Inn 🅂
23 | 16 | 18 | $28

458 Forest Beach Rd. (Browns Woods Rd.), 410-757-1311

☑ Boasting "atmosphere to the max", this "ultimate crab house" outside Annapolis is "nothing fancy", but if you "sit out on the deck" overlooking the creek, order a pile of steamed hard crabs and a frosty pitcher of beer, you'll have the "perfect afternoon"; that's enough to make "lines form in the street just to get into the lot", so consider "playing some summertime hooky" to "go during the week"; note, though, that "getting here is an adventure", so it's essential to "get good directions" or "better yet, arrive by boat."

Carrol's Creek 🅂
21 | 21 | 19 | $34

410 Severn Ave. (4th St.), Eastport, 410-263-8102

☑ "Absolutely, the view of Annapolis'" harbor from the "seriously nice" waterside deck is the prime attraction of this Eastport New American cafe; the seafood-slanted menu is "good but not that different", though if you "go on Wednesday nights around 7, you can watch the sailboat races finish" while you sup; granted, it's "expensive for what you get", but someone has to "pay for that view."

Chick & Ruth's Delly 🅂≠
18 | 14 | 18 | $13

165 Main St. (Conduit St.), 410-269-6737

☑ "Where the locals go for breakfast" (when "they're not dieting"), this Annapolis "fixture" is a "real kick"; it's a "dowdy-chic" diner near the State House, where you can "hobnob with the power people" and "find refuge from the shopping insanity" outside while being greeted with a "bowl of pickles on arrival"; the "pictures on the walls" hasten the "journey into nostalgia", as do the old-fashioned "milkshakes that are nothing short of heaven."

Corinthian S   23 | 23 | 21 | $39

Loews Annapolis Hotel, 126 West St. (Lafayette Ave.), 410-263-1299

◪ Near the State House but "away from the Annapolis action", this "cosmopolitan" dining room is "surprisingly pleasant for a hotel restaurant"; with its "sophisticated" New American menu and "lovely", "comfortable" quarters, it makes for a "quiet", "romantic night", though a handful of skeptics shrug "predictable."

Davis' Pub S   18 | 13 | 15 | $18

400 Chester Ave. (4th St.), Eastport, 410-268-7432

■ Whether "fresh off the water" or direct from a B&B, "locals and visitors" jam themselves into this "very small", "hard-to-find" (though apparently not hard enough) "neighborhood dive", a "true Annapolis pub" in maritime Eastport, for "good grub" ("can't say enough about those crab cakes"), a couple of beers and "friendly" conversation.

Galway Bay S   22 | 19 | 20 | $24

61-63 Maryland Ave. (State Circle), 410-263-8333

■ "If you can't visit the Old Sod", this State House–vicinity watering hole may be the "next best thing"; it makes a gallant "effort at being a real Irish pub" (there's a "separate restaurant" area too), featuring "satisfying" "standards" like fish 'n' chips and corned beef 'n' cabbage in a setting so "warm and welcoming" that regulars "practically live here."

Harry Browne's S   23 | 22 | 22 | $38

66 State Circle (bet. East St. & Maryland Ave.), 410-269-5124

■ "Hang out with politicians" and other "movers and shakers" at this "clubby" Annapolis "institution" with a "smashing view of the grand old State House" across the street; supporters say it "keeps doing it right" with "dependably excellent" Continental and Chesapeake Bay dishes turned out in a "classy" main room by a "smooth" service team; some like the "people-watching" when the "legislature is in session", but others say it's more "wonderful without the lobbyists."

Jalapeño S   24 | 17 | 22 | $27

Forest Plaza, 85 Forest Plaza (Riva Rd.), 410-266-7580

■ "Andalusia meets the Chesapeake" at this "pleasant surprise in a strip mall" west of Annapolis; it's a "terrific little place" – "a bit eccentric, a bit exotic" – for "flavorful" Spanish and Mexican dishes (including "excellent tapas" and the "best paella") and "killer margaritas" delivered by a staff that "tries hard", and it's all "reasonably priced", which explains why it's "popular" and thus "crowded."

Joss Cafe & Sushi Bar S | 27 | 18 | 21 | $28 |
195 Main St. (Church Circle), 410-263-4688

■ "Hearty greetings" welcome sushi connoisseurs of "all ages and types" at this "little nook" near the State House, "one of the top places" of its kind "in the U.S."; the "memorable" raw fish is so "fresh, fresh, fresh" "you'd think they caught it themselves", and the staff is "well-informed" and "entertaining", "impressing even native guests"; it may be "tight on space, but it's worth every bit of overcrowding."

Lebanese Taverna S | 23 | 18 | 20 | $26 |
Annapolis Harbour Ctr., 2478 Solomons Island Rd. (Allen Blvd.), 410-897-1111
See review in Washington, DC Directory.

Les Folies Brasserie S | 25 | 22 | 24 | $39 |
2552 Riva Rd. (Aris Allen Blvd.), 410-573-0970

■ Much "more promising than it looks from the outside", this "terrific" "surprise" is really a "bit of France not far from the bay" in Parole; it's the domain of veteran "French owners who know" how to run a "professional" operation and how to turn out "superb" brasserie "classics" served by a "knowledgeable" staff; this is the Gallic version of a "neighborhood place where everybody knows your name."

Lewnes' Steakhouse S | 26 | 21 | 24 | $48 |
401 Fourth St. (Severn Ave.), Eastport, 410-263-1617

◪ "Local in every way", "Annapolis' own" steakhouse is a "manly kind of place" to celebrate a "special occasion"; it offers a "hard-to-beat" combination of "perfectly prepared prime beef" and a "fabulous wine list", along with "private booths" and "attentive" service; a few critical carnivores are left "disappointed" by the experience – and especially by the bill – but supporters are always ready to "prepare their appetites" for this splurge.

Northwoods S | 24 | 21 | 24 | $39 |
609 Melvin Ave. (Ridgely Ave.), 410-268-2609

■ "Especially nice for special occasions", this "cozy", "romantic" Annapolis "hideaway" has "stayed the same for years" and that's why loyalists "love it"; the "excellent" Continental menu is as "dependable" as ever, as is the "professional" service, while the "prix fixe is a bargain."

O'Learys Seafood S | 25 | 21 | 23 | $40 |
310 Third St. (Severn Ave.), Eastport, 410-263-0884

◪ "Skip the touristy" places in Eastport and "head to this gem" instead advise those in-the-know about this "great seafood-without-a-view" spot that lets you "custom mix-and-match" your finny fare and cooking preparation to have it "your way" (don't miss "one of the best crab cakes ever"); sure, it's a bit "noisy" and it "needs a bigger bar", as "there's no place to wait" for a table, but you'll leave "satisfied."

Phillips S 15 | 15 | 14 | $28
12 Dock St. (Randall St.), 410-990-9888
See review in Baltimore Directory.

Piccola Roma Ristorante S 23 | 19 | 22 | $38
200 Main St. (Church Circle), 410-268-7898
■ "Superb" Italian cooking that "rises above the ordinary" sets apart this "upscale" Annapolis ristorante blessed with a "prime location" where patrons like to "sit by the window" and "watch the passing Main Street parade" while dining on "stellar" pastas; the food is "not fussy, just great", and it's delivered in "inviting" environs by a team that pays "attention to the details."

Red Hot & Blue BBQ S 19 | 14 | 16 | $20
200 Old Mill Bottom Rd. S. (Rte. 50, exit 28), 410-626-7427
See review in Washington, DC Directory.

RUTH'S CHRIS STEAK HOUSE S 24 | 23 | 23 | $49
301 Severn Ave. (3rd St.), Eastport, 410-990-0033
See review in Washington, DC Directory.

Sam's Waterfront Cafe S 22 | 23 | 21 | $34
2020 Chesapeake Harbour Dr. E. (Edgewood Rd.), 410-263-3600
■ "A good port in a storm" is "worth finding", so you should make it your business to get to know this "local secret" "hidden" "out of the way" at the Annapolis harbor; it's an "elegant yet relaxing" place where the "picturesque" setting ("love watching the yachts come and go") only enhances the "excellent" New American seafood dishes; "don't miss" this "best bet."

Sputnik Cafe – | – | – | M
1397 Generals Hwy. (Crownsville Rd.), Crownsville, 410-923-3775
Anticipate a "food adventure" at "Crownsville's best-kept new secret" whose Cold War decor (envision faux corrugated Quonset hut walls, plastic designer chairs and space-age chandeliers) provides an offbeat backdrop for the kitchen's International dishes (like its signature wasabi-and-sesame crusted salmon with a vegetarian sushi roll); N.B. there's live entertainment on Thursdays and Saturdays.

Treaty of Paris S 20 | 23 | 20 | $39
Maryland Inn, 16 Church Circle (Main St.), 410-216-6340
◪ At this "history lesson" of an inn that's as old as this country, bask in the "charming" "colonial" atmosphere;

the Continental seafood menu is "above average", "if not excellent", but critics lament it's a "shame" that the "unremarkable" food can't live up to "one of Annapolis' most historic settings."

Tsunami S　　　24　17　21　$29
51 West St. (Church Circle), 410-990-9868

■ On West Street's emerging restaurant scene, this "cool hangout" is the "'in' place to be", attracting a "young, hip crowd" that descends nightly for the "singles" action at the bar; don't be fooled, though, into thinking that the food is an afterthought, because the sushi is "outstanding" and the "styling" Pacific Rim "fusion" cuisine "original" and "terrific", making for "exotic fun" that's a "refreshing" change of pace for "brass-and-fern Annapolis."

Wild Orchid Cafe S　　　23　19　22　$32
909 Bay Ridge Ave. (Chesapeake Ave.), Eastport, 410-268-8009

■ "Delightful and intimate", this "converted" bungalow tucked away in an "out-of-the-way location" in Eastport presents a daily changing New American menu that "always" features "interesting choices" based on a "complex mix of ingredients that works"; the "beautifully arranged" dishes, "deep in flavor", are brought to table by "cheerful" folks in "charming" quarters, which explains why admirers "love" this "hidden treasure."

Yin Yankee Cafe S　　　23　19　21　$28
105 Main St. (Green St.), 410-268-8703

■ Amid the hustle and bustle of Annapolis' City Dock, this "hip sushi bar" offers a "different" option thanks to its "expansive selection" of "surprisingly" "excellent" Asian fusion dishes; add on "cool", "comfortable" digs, "personal" service and "not too expensive" tabs and the result is a "fun find", leading habitués to exclaim "we never tire of the innovative food or funky atmosphere."

Eastern Shore

	F	D	S	C
Alice's Cafe ⊅	▽ 27	20	23	$13

22 N. Harrison St. (bet. Dover & Goldsborough Sts.), Easton, 410-819-8590

■ Already cherished as a "new" "favorite" in Easton, this teeny "diner cares about ingredients", and it's amply evident after one bite of its "wonderful roast beef"; while "fabulous", "creative" Eclectic sandwiches and "custom-baked cookies" rule at lunchtime, its "delicious", "comforting" breakfast plates lure in many an early-riser in the AM.

	F	D	S	C
Bistro St. Michaels [S]	26	22	23	$38

403 S. Talbot St. (Watkins Ln.), St. Michaels, 410-745-9111

◪ Fashion plates like to "get dressed before they drive out to St. Michaels" to sup at this "jewel" (it's also a favorite among "dressed-down boaters"), which pleases with "innovative", "dependably excellent" French bistro dishes ("don't miss" the "best-ever mussels") served by a "doting", "accommodating" staff; it can get "crowded and noisy" inside the "tastefully" decorated room, but the "lovely back porch" provides a "perfect" escape.

	F	D	S	C
Blue Heron	▽ 22	19	21	$34

236 Cannon St. (Cross St.), Chestertown, 410-778-0188

◪ Enthusiasts "drive out of their way" to this "charming little" house set on a leafy residential street in colonial Chestertown for its "imaginative" menu of updated Eastern Shore fare; "steadily" turning out "good food in an everyday environment", it's a "local favorite", but critics lament that it "doesn't live up to its rave reviews."

	F	D	S	C
Columbia	▽ 27	26	26	$46

28 S. Washington St. (Glenwood Ave.), Easton, 410-770-5172

■ Upstairs at this "understatedly elegant" "townhouse" in Easton is "superb" chef-owner Stephen Mangasarian's private residence, while downstairs is his "very special" labor of love, a "warm and charming" haven for a "quiet, romantic" meal; his "creative" New American menu "changes with the seasons", but highlights always include a rack of lamb that's worth "dreaming about"; there are only nine tables in the "cozy" parlor and drawing room, so you can expect "personal, sincere" service.

	F	D	S	C
Crab Claw [S]⊅	20	16	17	$28

156 Mill St. (Talbot St.), St. Michaels, 410-745-2900

◪ After "a day of sightseeing", "sit by the water and crack crabs" at this seafood "shack" next to the Maritime Museum in St. Michaels; it's a "fun outing" where you dig into a pile of steamed crustaceans dumped on picnic tables covered with "brown paper tablecloths" (for those who "don't want to get their fingers dirty", there's a proper dining room upstairs); of course, "it's packed" on summer weekends with "out-of-towners", so service can be "spotty."

Fisherman's Inn/Crab Deck S   20   19   19 $28
3032 Main St. (Rte. 50), Grasonville, 410-827-8807
☑ Providing "a lovely respite" "on the way to the shore", this rambling Kent Narrows hub has dual personalities – the Fisherman's Inn is an "old established restaurant" (circa 1930) with an "old-fashioned" seafood menu and a "nautical" motif replete with an antique oyster plate collection, while the Crab Deck (open seasonally) is an alfresco alternative with "wooden benches" and live music; if you "don't get too complicated" with your order, they're "good places to meet friends."

Harris Crab House S   21   16   18 $28
433 Kent Narrows Way N. (Rte. 50, exit 42), Grasonville, 410-827-9500
■ "On your way to the Eastern Shore", this "classic crab house" "overlooking the Kent Narrows channel" (the "top deck" affords a "gorgeous" "view" of the "boats coming and going") is a "must stop"; it's all "about crabs and beer" (and homemade "nutty buddy" ice cream cones for dessert) here, so expect a highly "casual" atmosphere.

Holly's S   16   10   16 $15
108 Jackson Creek Rd. (Rte. 50), Grasonville, 410-827-8711
☑ A handy "stopping point" for beach travelers "after clearing the Bay Bridge" in Kent Narrows, this "diner of yesteryear" housed in a motel is the "real deal" for "down-home" Eastern Shore eats that are "plain, like they should be"; "you won't go away hungry" after tucking into "maybe the best fried chicken in Maryland", "scrumptious chicken salad" and other "SOS comfort food", washed down by "real milkshakes", but critics caution only "in a pinch."

Imperial Hotel S   ▽ 24   24   23 $43
208 High St. (Queen St.), Chestertown, 410-778-5000
■ "Off the beaten path" near colonial Chestertown's central square, this intimate "gem" set in a "lovely" restored hotel exemplifies the "elegance of days gone by" and makes a "great getaway for a romantic night" in "high style"; many feel the New American menu – "fine but never too fancy" – actually "exceeds its reputation."

Inn at Easton S   ▽ 25   25   24 $44
28 S. Harrison St. (South Ln.), Easton, 410-822-4910
■ "Civilized dining" in a grand Federal-style mansion is the draw at this Easton inn restored by Liz and Andrew Evans,

a "quiet, elegant" showcase for his "simply superb" Asian and New French treatments of local ingredients, paired with a "limited albeit very good wine list" and served by an "exceptional" staff; it's a "real treasure that hasn't yet been fully discovered", so if you're seeking to find "excellence in everything", this is the place.

INN AT PERRY CABIN S   – – – E

308 Watkins Ln. (Talbot St.), St. Michaels, 410-745-2200
Taking better advantage of its "magnificent" "waterside setting" in St. Michaels, this "class act" "retreat" (newly acquired by Orient-Express Hotels) quartered in a "stately" mansion has just unveiled its multimillion-dollar redesign; the dining room, expanded to be closer to the bay, is now appointed with big windows and a nautical theme that gives it an airier look; still manning the stove, though, is Mark Salter, who has introduced an à la carte Continental menu that features Chesapeake Bay seafood specialties.

Kennedyville Inn S   ▽ 25 22 23 $36

11986 Rte. 213 (5 mi. north of Chestertown), Kennedyville, 410-348-2400
■ "Hard to find, harder to forget" swoon the smitten about this "hidden gem" in the countryside of Kennedyville; "everything is wonderful" here – from chef-owner Kevin McKinney's "quirky" yet "fancy" Chesapeake Bay fare (his signature "oyster fritters and crab steak alone are worth the trip") and BBQ to the "cute" decor to the "excellent" service, adding up to a "treat" that "should not be missed."

Latitude 38° S   ▽ 24 22 24 $30

26342 Oxford Rd. (Bonfield Ave.), Oxford, 410-226-5303
■ "Catch up on area gossip" at this "pride of Oxford", a "local favorite" among tradespeople, landowners and sailors; "bravo to chef" Douglas Kirby for his "delicious", frequently changing New American bistro menu based on local ingredients (the "bar dinners are an outstanding bargain") and to the "friendly" crew; "what a find!"

Mason's   ▽ 26 22 22 $39

22 S. Harrison St. (South Ln.), Easton, 410-822-3204
■ Mary and Matthew Mason's grand old family house on what's becoming Easton's restaurant row is home to an "eclectic" mix of "outstanding" French-Med bistro dishes distinguished by "great depth of flavor"; though the "main dining room" is "wonderfully comfortable", the "enjoyable" garden is a veritable "oasis", but wherever your table, you'll be tended to by an "outgoing" staff.

Michael Rork's Town Dock S   20 18 19 $33

125 Mulberry St. (Talbot St.), St. Michaels, 410-745-5577
◪ "Nifty chef-owner" Michael Rork is back to give his undivided attention to this "casual" American seafood

house "superbly located" on a site in St. Michaels with scenic views of the harbor and the river (naturally, the best tables are out on the "relaxing" "dockside" deck); dissenters, though, crab "disappointing after all the hype."

Narrows S   25 21 22 $33
3023 Kent Narrows Way S. (Rte. 50, exit 41), Grasonville, 410-827-8113

■ "A perfect way to start a vacation" in Kent Narrows is to spend a "lovely summer day on the deck overlooking the water" at this American seafood house, long a "local favorite" for the "best crab cakes on the Shore" and an "equally great cream of crab soup"; "everything is right" again at dusk, when a meal is accompanied by a "gorgeous view of the sunset"; "we wouldn't miss it on the way to or from the beach."

Out of the Fire   ▽ 21 22 23 $34
22 Goldsborough St. (Washington St.), Easton, 410-770-4777

◪ "Attractively" decorated with a "revolving art display", this "neat" hangout in the historic district of Easton centers around a stone hearth in the open Mediterranean kitchen, from which emerge "delicious wood-fired" breads and pizzas and "super" roasted entrees; locals "love this place" because they can dine at the chef's counter or nibble on appetizers at the wine bar in the back.

Robert Morris Inn S   21 23 22 $39
314 N. Morris St. (Tred Avon Rd.), Oxford, 410-226-5111

◪ Near the Oxford ferry dock, this "quaint", "comfy" inn dating back to 1710 hasn't changed its Chesapeake Bay seafood menu in three decades, which is just fine with longtime followers who gladly "make the trip" for the "still divine" crab cakes ("James Michener was right – they really are some of the best on the Eastern Shore"); even some stalwarts, though, concede that "everything else here is irrelevant", while foes find it all too "bland and basic" ("time to update the kitchen").

208 Talbot S   27 23 26 $48
208 N. Talbot St. (North St.), St. Michaels, 410-745-3838

■ "Quite a surprise" for the "little sailing town" of St. Michaels, this "sophisticated" "all-time favorite" is "superb in every way", from chef-owner Paul Milne's (a "magician with sauces") "superior" Continental seafood dishes (the "Saturday prix fixe menu is fabulous") to the "romantic" surroundings to the "outstanding" service; "overall, it's a real winner", "worth a drive from anywhere" for "truly fine dining" that makes a meal a "special occasion."

Baltimore, Annapolis and the Eastern Shore Indexes

CUISINES
LOCATIONS
SPECIAL FEATURES

Indexes list the best of many within each category.

All restaurants are in the Baltimore area unless otherwise noted (A=Annapolis and E=Eastern Shore).

CUISINES

Afghan
Helmand

American (New)
Aqua Terra/A
Atlantic
Baldwin's Station
Carrol's Creek/A
Cerando's Kitchen
Chameleon Café
Charleston
Columbia/E
Corinthian/A
Corks
Hampton's
Helen's Garden
Henninger's Tavern
Henry's
Imperial Hotel/E
Joy America Cafe
Kings Contrivance
Latitude 38°/E
Linwood's
Polo Grill
Sam's Waterfront/A
Sascha's 527
Spike & Charlie's
Stone Manor
Towne Hall
Turning Point Inn
Viccino Bistro
Wild Orchid Cafe/A
Windows

American (Traditional)
Baugher's
Blue Moon Cafe
Brass Elephant
Brewer's Alley
Cafe Hon
Cheesecake Factory

City Cafe
Clyde's
Duda's Tavern
Dutch's Daughter
Friendly Farm
G&M
Hard Times Cafe
Harryman Hse.
Jennings Cafe
JJ's Everyday
Manor Tavern
McCabe's
Michael Rork's Town Dock/E
Milton Inn
Narrows/E
Oregon Grille
Pazza Luna
Peppermill
SoBo Cafe
Timbuktu
Union Hotel
Woman's Ind. Exch.
Woodfire

Asian Fusion
Eurasian Harbor
Ixia
Purple Orchid
Red Maple
Soigné
Yin Yankee Cafe/A

Barbecue
Kennedyville Inn/E
Red Hot & Blue BBQ/A

Cajun/Creole
Ethel & Ramone's
Louisiana

Californian
Paolo's

Chesapeake Bay
Antrim 1844
Blue Heron/E
Brighton's
Captain Harvey's
Gertrude's
Harry Browne's/A
Inn at Perry Cabin/E
Kelly's
Kennedyville Inn/E
Marconi's
Pierpoint
Robert Morris Inn/E

Chinese
Cafe Zen
P.F. Chang's
Szechuan
Szechuan Best
Szechuan Hse.

Coffeehouses/Dessert
Cafe Hon
City Cafe
Crêpe du Jour
Ze Mean Bean

Coffee Shops/Diners
Chick & Ruth's/A
Holly's/E
Jimmy's
Papermoon Diner

Continental
Brass Elephant
Harry Browne's/A
Inn at Perry Cabin/E
Josef's Country Inn
Marconi's
Northwoods/A
Rudys' 2900
Treaty of Paris/A
208 Talbot/E

Crab Houses
Barn
Bill's Terrace Inn
Cantler's Riverside/A
Captain Harvey's
Costas Crab Hse.
Crab Claw/E
Fisherman's/Crab Deck/E
Harris Crab Hse./E
Kelly's
L.P. Steamers
Obrycki's

Delis/Sandwich Shops
Alice's Cafe/E
Attman's Deli
Viccino Bistro

Dim Sum
Szechuan Best

Eastern European
Ze Mean Bean

Eclectic/International
Alice's Cafe/E
Bicycle
Combalou Cafe
Ethel & Ramone's
Out of the Fire/E
Peter's Inn
Ruby Lounge
Sputnik Cafe/A
Tasting Room
Zodiac

French
Antrim 1844
Elkridge Furnace Inn
Jeannier's
Louisiana
Martick's
Purple Orchid
Tersiguel's

French (Bistro)
Bistro St. Michaels/E
Cafe de Paris
Cafe Normandie/A
Crêpe du Jour
La Madeleine
Les Folies/A
Mason's/E
Petit Louis

French (New)
Inn at Easton/E

German
Josef's Country Inn

Greek
Ikaros
Kali's Court
Samos
Timbuktu
Zorba's B&G

Hamburgers
Jennings Cafe
Linwood's

Hawaiian
Roy's

Indian
Ambassador Din. Rm.
Banjara

Irish
Galway Bay/A

Italian
(N=Northern; S=Southern;
N&S=includes both)
Aldo's (S)
Amicci's (N&S)
Angelina's (N&S)
Boccaccio (N)
Café Troia (N)
Da Mimmo (N&S)

Della Notte (N&S)
Due (N)
Josephine's (S)
La Scala (N&S)
La Tesso Tana (N&S)
Liberatore's (N&S)
Paolo's (N&S)
Pazza Luna (N&S)
Piccola Roma/A (N&S)
Sabatino's (N&S)
Sotto Sopra (N&S)
That's Amore (S)
Trattoria Alberto (N)
Vespa (N&S)

Japanese
Cafe Zen
Edo Sushi
Fuji
Joss Cafe/A
Matsuri
Sushi Hana
Suzie's Soba
Tsunami/A
Yin Yankee Cafe/A

Lebanese
Lebanese Taverna/A

Mediterranean
Black Olive
Kali's Court
Mason's/E
Tapas Teatro

Mexican/Tex-Mex
Austin Grill
Blue Agave
Holy Frijoles
Jalapeño/A

Middle Eastern
Lebanese Taverna/A
Orchard Mkt.

LOCATIONS

BALTIMORE

Business District/ Downtown/Convention Center/Camden Yards/ Inner Harbor
Babalu Grill
Brighton's
Cheesecake Factory
Eurasian Harbor
Faidley's Seafood
Hampton's
Joy America Cafe
Legal Sea Foods
Marconi's
Martick's
McCormick & Schmick's
Morton's of Chicago
Paolo's
Phillips
Pisces
Purple Orchid
Ruth's Chris
Shula's Steak Hse.
Tio Pepe
Windows

Canton
Atlantic
Austin Grill
Helen's Garden

Downtown North/ Charles St./Mt. Vernon
Brass Elephant
City Cafe
Combalou Cafe
Helmand
Ixia
La Tesso Tana
Prime Rib

Red Maple
Ruby Lounge
Sascha's 527
Sotto Sopra
Spike & Charlie's
Tapas Teatro
Thai Landing
Viccino Bistro
Woman's Ind. Exch.
Zodiac

East Baltimore
Attman's Deli
Josephine's
Kelly's
Obrycki's

Federal Hill/ South Baltimore
Banjara
Bicycle
Blue Agave
Corks
L.P. Steamers
Matsuri
Pazza Luna
SoBo Cafe
Soigné
Szechuan
Vespa

Fells Point
Bertha's
Black Olive
Blue Moon Cafe
Chester's Steakhse.
Duda's Tavern
Henninger's Tavern
Jimmy's

John Steven
Kali's Court
Louisiana
Peter's Inn
Pierpoint
Ze Mean Bean

Hampden/Roland Park/ Homewood/Charles Village
Ambassador Din. Rm.
Cafe Hon
Gertrude's
Holy Frijoles
Jeannier's
McCabe's
Papermoon Diner
Petit Louis
Polo Grill
Suzie's Soba

Highlandtown/Greektown
Ikaros
Samos
Zorba's B&G

Inner Harbor East/ Little Italy
Aldo's
Amicci's
Boccaccio
Charleston
Da Mimmo
Della Notte
Fleming's
La Scala
Roy's
Sabatino's

Mt. Washington
Crêpe du Jour
Ethel & Ramone's

North Baltimore/ York Road Corridor
Cafe Zen
Thai

OUTER BALTIMORE/CENTRAL MARYLAND

Brooklandville
Towne Hall

BWI/Linthicum/Elkridge
Elkridge Furnace Inn
G&M
Timbuktu

Columbia
Asean Bistro
Cafe de Paris
Clyde's
Hard Times Cafe
Kings Contrivance
La Madeleine
P.F. Chang's
That's Amore

Ellicott City/Catonsville
Cerando's Kitchen
Fuji
Jennings Cafe
Jordan's
Tersiguel's

Essex/Dundalk
Bill's Terrace Inn
Costas Crab Hse.
River Watch

Frederick
Brewer's Alley
Dutch's Daughter
Stone Manor

ANNAPOLIS

SPECIAL FEATURES

(Restaurants followed by a † may not offer
that feature at every location.)

Breakfast
(See also Hotel Dining)
Alice's Cafe/E
Baugher's
Brighton's
Blue Moon Cafe
Cafe Hon
Chick & Ruth's/A
City Cafe
Holly's/E
Jimmy's

Brunch
Ambassador Dining Rm.
Blue Moon Cafe
City Cafe
Helen's Garden
Pisces
Polo Grill
Windows
Ze Mean Bean

Buffet Served
(Check availability)
Ambassador Din. Rm.
Banjara
Pisces
Szechuan Best
Windows

Business Dining
Aldo's
Blue Heron/E
Boccaccio
Brass Elephant
Brighton's
Cafe de Paris
Charleston
Corinthian/A

Dutch's Daughter
Fleming's
Hampton's
Harry Browne's/A
Lewnes' Steakhse./A
Linwood's
Marconi's
Morton's of Chicago
Peppermill
Polo Grill
Prime Rib
Roy's
Rudys' 2900
Ruth's Chris
Trattoria Alberto
Viccino Bistro
Windows

BYO
Cafe Zen
Cerando's Kitchen
Combalou Cafe
JJ's Everyday
Orchard Mkt.
Samos

Catering
Alice's Cafe/E
Attman's Deli
Brass Elephant
Cafe Hon
Cerando's Kitchen
Linwood's
Samos
Sascha's 527
Wild Orchid Cafe/A

Child-Friendly
(Besides the normal fast-food places; * children's menu available)
Baugher's*
Cafe Hon*
Chick & Ruth's/A
Dutch's Daughter
Friendly Farm*
Holly's/E

Delivery/Takeout
(D=delivery, T=takeout)
Alice's Cafe/E (T)
Attman's Deli (D,T)
Cafe de Paris (T)
Faidley's Seafood (T)
Holly's/E (T)
Samos (D,T)
Szechuan Hse. (D,T)

Dessert
Alice's Cafe/E
Baugher's
Blue Moon Cafe
Cafe de Paris
Cafe Hon
Eurasian Harbor
Holly's/E
Tapas Teatro

Entertainment
(Call for days and times of performances)
Asean Bistro (guitar/piano)
Atlantic (jazz/Latin)
Babalu Grill (DJ/Latin)
Baldwin's Station (folk)
Barn (bands)
Bertha's (blues/jazz)
Brighton's (jazz/piano)
Clyde's (varies)
Da Mimmo (piano/vocals)
Della Notte (piano)

Gertrude's (jazz)
Les Folies/A (varies)
Oregon Grille (bass/piano)
Out of the Fire/E (guitar)
Pisces (jazz)
Prime Rib (bass/piano/sax)
Red Maple (DJ)
River Watch (bands)
Ruby Lounge (jazz)
Sputnik Cafe/A (varies)
Treaty of Paris/A (jazz)
Tsunami/A (DJ)
Windows (jazz)
Woodfire (varies)
Ze Mean Bean (folk/jazz)

Fireplaces
Antrim 1844
Elkridge Furnace Inn
Harry Browne's/A
Harryman Hse.
Manor Tavern
Milton Inn
Petit Louis
Robert Morris Inn/E
Rudys' 2900
Treaty of Paris/A
Union Hotel
Ze Mean Bean

Historic Places
(Year opened; *building)
1740 Milton Inn*
1744 Elkridge Furnace Inn*
1772 Treaty of Paris/A*
1790s Bertha's*
1791 Harryman Hse.*
1820 Josephine's*
1850 Brass Elephant*
1850 Martick's*
1860 Woman's Ind. Exch.*
1880 Manor Tavern*
1883 Baldwin's Station*

1890 Tersiguel's*
1890s Petit Louis*
1902 Imperial Hotel/E*
1920 Marconi's

Hotel Dining

Antrim 1844
  Antrim 1844
Harbor Court Hotel
  Brighton's
  Hampton's
Hyatt Regency
  Pisces
Imperial Hotel
  Imperial Hotel/E
Inn at Easton
  Inn at Easton/E
Inn at Perry Cabin
  Inn at Perry Cabin/E
Inn at The Colonnade
  Polo Grill
Loews Annapolis Hotel
  Corinthian/A
Maryland Inn
  Treaty of Paris/A
Pier 5 Hotel
  Eurasian Harbor
  McCormick & Schmick's
Renaissance Harborplace Hotel
  Windows
Robert Morris Inn
  Robert Morris Inn/E
Sheraton Inner Harbor Hotel
  Morton's of Chicago
Stone Manor
  Stone Manor
Turning Point Inn
  Turning Point Inn
Union Hotel
  Union Hotel
Wyndham Baltimore
  Shula's Steak Hse.

Late Dining

(Weekday closing hour)
Duda's Tavern (1 AM)
Sabatino's (3 AM)
Zorba's B&G (2 AM)

Meet for a Drink

Bertha's
Blue Agave
Brass Elephant
Cafe de Paris
Henry's
John Steven
Josephine's
Kelly's
Manor Tavern
Red Maple
Ruby Lounge
Soigné
Sputnik Cafe/A
Tasting Room
Towne Hall

Noteworthy Newcomers

Babalu Grill
Cafe de Paris
Cerando's Kitchen
Chester's Steakhse.
Henry's
Ixia
Jordan's
Red Maple
Roy's
Soigné
Sputnik Cafe/A

Offbeat

Alice's Cafe/E
Bertha's
Cafe Hon
Chick & Ruth's/A
City Cafe
Duda's Tavern

Ethel & Ramone's
Faidley's Seafood
Helen's Garden
Jimmy's
John Steven
Kelly's
Martick's
Papermoon Diner
Peter's Inn
River Watch
Ruby Lounge
SoBo Cafe
Sputnik Cafe/A
Tapas Teatro
Zodiac

Outdoor Dining
(G=garden; P=patio;
S=sidewalk; T=terrace;
W=waterside)
Ambassador Din. Rm. (G)
Antrim 1844 (T)
Babalu Grill (P)
Baldwin's Station (T)
Bicycle (G,P)
Bistro St. Michaels/E (P)
Blue Heron/E (P)
Café Troia (S)
Cantler's Riverside/A (T,W)
Carrol's Creek/A (T,W)
Cheesecake Factory (P)
City Cafe (S)
Clyde's (P)
Corinthian/A (P)
Crab Claw/E (P,W)
Crêpe du Jour (T)
Davis' Pub/A (P)
Duda's Tavern (S)
Ethel & Ramone's (P)
Eurasian Harbor (P)
Fisherman's/Crab Deck/E (P,W)
Gertrude's (G)

Harris Crab Hse./E (P,W)
Harry Browne's/A (P)
Harryman Hse. (P)
Helen's Garden (T)
Imperial Hotel/E (G)
Inn at Easton/E (P)
Inn at Perry Cabin/E (T)
Josef's Country Inn (G,P)
Joy America Cafe (T)
Kali's Court (P)
Les Folies/A (P)
Linwood's (P)
L.P. Steamers (T)
Manor Tavern (P)
Mason's/E (G)
McCormick & Schmick's (P)
Michael Rork's Town Dock/E (T,W)
Narrows/E (W)
Northwoods/A (P)
Oregon Grille (P)
Phillips (P,W)
River Watch (P,T,W)
Sam's Waterfront/A (P,W)
Stone Manor (P)
Tapas Teatro (S)
Towne Hall (P)
Turning Point Inn (P)
Vespa (S)
Wild Orchid Cafe/A (T)
Yin Yankee Cafe/A (S)
Ze Mean Bean (S)

Parking
(V=valet, *=validated)
Aldo's (V)
Ambassador Din. Rm. (V)
Black Olive (V)
Boccaccio (V)
Brighton's (V)
Charleston (V)
Corinthian/A (V)
Da Mimmo (V)

Eurasian Harbor (V)
Fleming's (V)
Hampton's (V)
Ixia (V)
Kali's Court (V)
Louisiana (V)
Marconi's (V)
McCormick & Schmick's*
Morton's of Chicago (V)
Pisces (V)
Polo Grill (V)
Prime Rib (V)
Purple Orchid (V)
Roy's (V)
Ruth's Chris (V)
Shula's Steak Hse.*
Sotto Sopra (V)
Treaty of Paris/A (V)
Viccino Bistro (V)
Windows*

People-Watching
Barn
Baugher's
Bill's Terrace Inn
City Cafe
Faidley's Seafood
Harry Browne's/A
Jimmy's
Papermoon Diner
Red Maple
River Watch
Sabatino's
Zodiac

Power Scenes
Boccaccio
Charleston
Hampton's
Harry Browne's/A
Lewnes' Steakhse./A
Oregon Grille
Polo Grill

Prime Rib
Windows

Private Rooms
(Call for capacity)
Aldo's
Black Olive
Boccaccio
Brass Elephant
Cafe de Paris
Cafe Hon
Café Troia
Charleston
Corinthian/A
Dutch's Daughter
Eurasian Harbor
Fleming's
Harry Browne's/A
Ikaros
Jordan's
Lewnes' Steakhse./A
Manor Tavern
McCormick & Schmick's
Milton Inn
Morton's of Chicago
Oregon Grille
Pisces
Polo Grill
Roy's
Sabatino's
Stone Manor
Tersiguel's
Timbuktu

Prix Fixe Menus
(Call for prices and times)
Antrim 1844
Asean Bistro
Atlantic
Café Troia
Corks

Hampton's
Inn at Easton/E
Joy America Cafe
Kings Contrivance
La Tesso Tana
Milton Inn
Northwoods/A
Stone Manor
Tersiguel's
Treaty of Paris/A
208 Talbot/E
Viccino Bistro

Quiet Conversation
Ambassador Din. Rm.
Cafe de Paris
Columbia/E
Jordan's
208 Talbot/E
Woman's Ind. Exch.
Ze Mean Bean

Reserve Ahead
Aldo's
Ambassador Din. Rm.
Antrim 1844
Babalu Grill
Bicycle
Bistro St. Michaels/E
Black Olive
Blue Agave
Boccaccio
Brighton's
Café Troia
Captain Harvey's
Chameleon Café
Charleston
Columbia/E
Costas Crab Hse.
Da Mimmo
Hampton's

Harry Browne's/A
Harryman Hse.
Helen's Garden
Helmand
Inn at Easton/E
Inn at Perry Cabin/E
Jalapeño/A
Josef's Country Inn
Joy America Cafe
Kali's Court
Kelly's
Les Folies/A
Lewnes' Steakhse./A
Liberatore's
Linwood's
Louisiana
Milton Inn
O'Learys Seafood/A
Oregon Grille
Pierpoint
Pisces
Polo Grill
Prime Rib
Red Maple
Sotto Sopra
Stone Manor
Tersiguel's
Trattoria Alberto
208 Talbot/E
Wild Orchid Cafe/A
Windows

Romantic Places
Ambassador Din. Rm.
Cafe de Paris
Charleston
Columbia/E
Hampton's
Helen's Garden
Jordan's
Milton Inn

208 Talbot/E
Woman's Ind. Exch.
Ze Mean Bean

Senior Appeal
Dutch's Daughter
Peppermill
Woman's Ind. Exch.

Singles Scenes
Henry's
Red Maple
Tasting Room

Sleepers
(Good to excellent food,
but little known)
Cerando's Kitchen
City Cafe
Corinthian/A
Fuji
Henry's
Trattoria Alberto

Tea Service
Bertha's
Brighton's
Inn at Perry Cabin/E
Stone Manor
Wild Orchid Cafe/A

Views
Baldwin's Station
Brighton's
Cantler's Riverside/A
Fisherman's/Crab Deck/E
Friendly Farm
Gertrude's
Hampton's
Harris Crab Hse./E
Inn at Perry Cabin/E
Joy America Cafe
L.P. Steamers
Michael Rork's Town Dock/E
Phillips†

Pisces
River Watch
Windows

Visitors on Expense Account
Black Olive
Boccaccio
Brighton's
Charleston
Corinthian/A
Hampton's
Harry Browne's/A
Inn at Easton/E
Inn at Perry Cabin/E
Lewnes' Steakhse./A
Marconi's
Morton's of Chicago
Oregon Grille
Ruth's Chris
Shula's Steak Hse.
Soigné
Tersiguel's
Trattoria Alberto
208 Talbot/E

Winning Wine Lists
Cafe de Paris
Charleston
Corks
Fleming's
Helen's Garden
Oregon Grille
Petit Louis
Tasting Room
Tersiguel's

Worth a Trip
Annapolis
  Cantler's Riverside/A
  Joss Cafe/A
Columbia
  Cafe de Paris

Wine Vintage Chart 1985–2000

This chart is designed to help you select wine to go with your meal. It is based on the same 0 to 30 scale used throughout this *Survey*. The ratings (prepared by our friend **Howard Stravitz**, a law professor at the University of South Carolina) reflect both the quality of the vintage and the wine's readiness for present consumption. Thus, if a wine is not fully mature or is over the hill, its rating has been reduced. We do not include 1987, 1991–1993 vintages because they are not especially recommended for most areas.

	'85	'86	'88	'89	'90	'94	'95	'96	'97	'98	'99	'00
WHITES												
French:												
Alsace	24	18	22	28	28	26	25	23	23	25	23	25
Burgundy	24	24	18	26	21	22	27	28	25	24	25	–
Loire Valley	–	–	–	26	25	22	24	26	23	22	24	–
Champagne	28	25	24	26	29	–	24	27	24	24	–	–
Sauternes	22	28	29	25	27	–	22	23	24	24	–	20
California:												
Chardonnay	–	–	–	–	–	21	26	22	25	24	25	–
REDS												
French:												
Bordeaux	26	27	25	28	29	24	26	25	23	24	22	25
Burgundy	23	–	22	26	29	20	26	27	25	23	26	–
Rhône	25	19	26	29	28	23	25	22	24	28	26	–
Beaujolais	–	–	–	–	–	–	22	20	24	22	24	–
California:												
Cab./Merlot	26	26	–	21	28	27	26	24	28	23	26	–
Zinfandel	–	–	–	–	–	26	24	25	23	24	25	–
Italian:												
Tuscany	26	–	24	–	26	23	25	19	28	24	25	–
Piedmont	25	–	25	28	28	–	24	26	28	26	25	–